Peace of Mind in Earthquake Country

Peace of Mind in Earthquake Country

HOW TO SAVE YOUR HOME AND LIFE

Peter I. Yanev

CHRONICLE BOOKS · SAN FRANCISCO

To Kay, Alexander and Andrew
and to Frank and Mimi Baron

Printed in the United States of America.

Library of Congress Cataloging in Publication Data.

Yanev, Peter I., 1946–
    Peace of mind in earthquake country: how to save
your home and life / Peter I. Yanev.
        p. cm.
    Includes bibliographical references and index.
    ISBN 0-87701-771-9
    1. Buildings—Earthquake effects. 2. Dwellings—
        West (U.S.)
I. Title
TH1095.Y36   1990
693′ .852′0978—dc20   90–45821
                                            CIP

Editing: Charles Robbins and Paula Tevis
Book design: Seventeenth Street Studios
Composition: Another Point
Cover design: John Miller

Distributed in Canada by Raincoast Books,
112 East Third Avenue, Vancouver, B.C. V5T 1C8

10 9 8 7 6 5 4 3 2 1

Chronicle Books
275 Fifth Street
San Francisco, CA 94103

Photograph, map and illustration credits on page 217

Contents

Preface

IN THE LAST 200 YEARS CALIFORNIANS and Nevadans have experienced an average of 5,000 noticeable earthquakes every year. Another 500 jar the surrounding states of Washington, Oregon, Montana and Utah and Alaska's record of tremors is comparable to that of California and Nevada. Most of these shocks are slight: Trees and bushes shake, window panes rattle, animals are startled, a few people pause in their busy day to be reminded of the ever-present danger of earthquakes.

Approximately every four years, a major, potentially destructive earthquake strikes the region. The San Francisco Bay Area and the adjoining counties have about 12 damaging earthquakes per century. Southern California and coastal Alaska have similar records.

So far, other western states have been fortunate, rarely suffering severe earthquake damage. However, most of the large metropolitan areas in these states are cut by faults and are under the shadow of potential disaster.

As ill-informed and ill-prepared as most Californians are regarding their earthquake problem, they are at least aware that there *is* a problem. The inhabitants of other seismically threatened states in the West seldom even know of the high risks they face. Despite the long history of earthquake damage in these areas, and despite principles of earthquake-resistant construction and property location that have been known to engineers for at least three generations, individual property owners and indeed most governing bodies remain blithely ignorant of the factors that determine earthquake risks and of the simple, relatively inexpensive corrective steps that could make their lives and property safer.

In numerous books and films the grave dangers of earthquakes have been clearly pointed out. Writers of countless articles and television features have criticized officials (and citizens) for their inaction. This book attempts another approach. I address *you*, the *individual property owner* to explain what the engineering profession has long known—that the most dangerous earthquake hazards can be largely avoided and that earthquake deaths or damage can be prevented or minimized with just a little knowledge of geology and some relatively simple and inexpensive construction procedures.

This knowledge and these preventive procedures are available in this book in simple, illustrated lessons. My hope is that you will apply this information to your own property and urge your relatives, friends and neighbors to make similar improvements. Then, when disaster strikes, you can ride out the shocks and survive in a city of stronger buildings and wiser citizens.

I also hope that as you see to your own needs, you will join with others in demanding attention to the evaluation and strengthening of our public and commercial buildings. Through your new knowledge and civic actions, you may also save many lives.

Peter I. Yanev
San Francisco and Costa Mesa, California

How to use this book:

Eight steps for determining and minimizing earthquake hazards to your property

*I*T IS NEWS TO NO ONE WHO LIVES IN the western United States that earthquakes remain the most unpredictable and frightening of the natural disasters. They strike without apparent warning, last only seconds, and, in those brief moments, can cause destruction, damage, death and injury comparable only to the devastation wrought by modern weapons of war. That said, I must quickly add that while earthquakes remain frightfully destructive and unpredictable, the physical *effects* of their sudden tremors are highly predictable; knowledgeable pre-earthquake planning and preparation can dramatically mitigate their danger and destructiveness.

The protection of life and property during earthquakes is largely entrusted to the engineering profession. Present computerized analytical techniques have made it possible to design new buildings to withstand the highest earthquake forces without structural collapse and with little or no structural damage. And such reliable earthquake resistance in newly designed buildings can be provided for a small percentage of the building cost. Similarly, most older small buildings can be strengthened simply and inexpensively—in many cases by the property owner.

This book directs attention to the information and safeguards which every property owner in earthquake country should study and implement to minimize the damage of a future earthquake. The following chapters outline:

♦ the causes and the effects of earthquakes;

♦ the varying risks of different areas in the earthquake-active regions of the West;

♦ the geologic and structural earthquake hazards that every owner and prospective buyer or renter should investigate in a home;

♦ the basic repairs and alterations to upgrade the earthquake resistance and safety of a building;

♦ the considerations that will help the property owner make a decision about the need for earthquake insurance;

♦ the steps to take before, during and after an earthquake to protect your family and property.

In short, this book is intended to help you to survive the inevitable "next" earthquake without serious personal loss.

It is a straightforward job to evaluate how your house will perform in an earthquake. You don't have to be an engineer to uncover and correct some of the most damage-prone house details. A few weak features in the typical house tend to cause most of the damage from earthquakes, particularly in older homes. Several of these details are easy to correct; some may require the attention of an engineer specializing in earthquake hazard reduction.

Here's how to evaluate earthquake risk to your property.

STEP 1: DETERMINE YOUR PROPERTY LOCATION WITH REGARD TO KNOWN ACTIVE FAULTS

The most dangerous geologic hazards are the faults that criss-cross the most populous areas of the western states. You can learn about the sources, formation and hazards of faults in Chapters One and Two, which explain how earthquakes are caused, the terminology of earthquake measurement, and the appearance, effects and hazards of faults. Then you learn to locate the specific property of interest to you and discover its proximity to an active fault. This essential information is contained in Appendix A, which lists and illustrates the better known active faults and provides a historical summary of the major earthquakes along these faults.

STEP 2: EXAMINE YOUR BUILDING SITE AND THE APPROPRIATE GEOLOGIC MAPS TO DETERMINE THE SOIL CONDITIONS UNDER THE BUILDING

Next consider the geologic foundations of the property and the varying earthquake risks associated with bedrock, alluvial, landfill, and sandy and water-saturated soil foundations. Different soil foundations respond to a tremor with varying levels of vibrational intensities and, therefore, different areas of a city, such as San Francisco or Los Angeles, face widely varying degrees of earthquake risk. Chapter Three deals with these risks and how to minimize them.

STEP 3: EXAMINE YOUR BUILDING SITE TO DETERMINE LANDSLIDE POTENTIAL

Aside from active faults or unstable soil foundations near a fault, the most hazardous geological situations in earthquake country are landslide-prone areas. Strong earthquakes always trigger numerous landslides, and any property located in known slide areas carries the additional risk of landslide damage. Chapter Three illustrates the tell-tale signs of landslide-prone soils and discusses the risks and how to minimize them.

STEP 4: LOCATE YOUR PROPERTY WITH REGARD TO THE MAN-MADE HAZARDS OF INADEQUATELY CONSTRUCTED DAMS, RESERVOIRS, NEIGHBORING BUILDINGS, ETC.

Dams present the greatest man-made danger in earthquake country. Several dams in California are located in or near active fault zones, and many dams have collapsed during the recurrent earthquakes of the region. Reservoirs, water tanks, large retaining walls, or poorly designed neighboring buildings can be equally unstable. Such structures present very real dangers to a property and must be considered in seismic regions. Chapter Four offers help and advice in this regard.

One myth in earthquake country is that wood frame houses are naturally earthquake resistant. These are examples of total destruction from the 1989 San Francisco or Loma Prieta earthquake. To be earthquake resistant, any house must be properly designed, sited, and built.

STEP 5: EVALUATE THE STRUCTURAL AND ARCHITECTURAL CHARACTERISTICS AND DETAILING OF YOUR BUILDING

Certain architectural and structural characteristics and detailing of buildings are, after geologic considerations, the other major earthquake hazard. These architectural features are directly related to the amount and the type of damage suffered by a building during an earthquake.

Chapter Five stresses the fact that a few basic and rather simple features govern the earthquake resistance of buildings. The scope of this book is necessarily limited to houses and smaller residential or commercial buildings not exceeding three or four stories. However, the principles encompass all types and sizes of buildings.

Chapter Six outlines the specific types of buildings and structural materials that are either hazardous or recommended for seismic areas. You will learn, for example, that unreinforced masonry buildings are

the least resistant to earthquake damage and are also the most likely to collapse. You will also learn that a properly braced wood-frame building is by far the safest small structure in earthquake country.

Chapter Seven deals with the architectural and structural features that are particularly susceptible to damage or collapse during an earthquake—for example, houses on stilts, inadequately supported split-level homes, buildings with heavy roofs or poor foundation connections, and certain older homes. For older wood-frame houses, the two most important features are (1) anchorage of the wood sill to its concrete foundation and (2) bracing (with plywood) of the cripple studs in the crawl space underneath the ground floor.

In all of these chapters, the point is clearly made that a few relatively simple and moderate-cost repairs and alterations in most buildings can significantly increase their earthquake resistance and decrease the probability of any major damage from a quake and its aftershocks. The principles and the techniques of such improvements are discussed in detail and illustrated so that, in most situations, they can be implemented by a handy do-it-yourselfer. The recommendations include remedies for existing buildings as well as for structures still in the planning stage.

STEP 6: EXAMINE YOUR HOME FOR HAZARDOUS AND DAMAGE-PRONE UTILITIES, APPLIANCES, FURNISHINGS AND EXITS

Chapter Eight suggests the practical and simple measures that can be taken in advance to minimize the risks of falling objects, fire, and broken gas lines.

STEP 7: DETERMINE WHETHER YOU NEED EARTHQUAKE INSURANCE

Chapter Nine introduces the subject of earthquake insurance, discussing the different types of policies available, the varying costs of these policies, and the considerations that will help you determine the coverage advisable for your situation. After strengthening particularly hazardous features, insurance is a good second line of defense. It protects you against a financial disaster and/or unrecognized hazards such as unknown active faults or poor construction.

STEP 8: FOLLOW THE PROPER PRECAUTIONS BEFORE, DURING AND AFTER AN EARTHQUAKE

The subject matter of the final chapter—*How to Behave Before, During and After a Quake to Protect Your Family, Yourself and Your Property*—is obvious but of vital importance. Every member of your family should be well-versed in the information and recommendations of this chapter.

You can control how your home will perform in the next strong earthquake. A few basic principles govern the damage to buildings from earthquakes. The most fundamental of these is the land upon which the building stands, and anyone living and/or investing in the western states should make the effort to determine the geologic conditions below the building site, the proximity of active faults and slide areas and the historic behavior of the land in any previous tremors. The other important factor is the structural and architectural characteristics and detailing of the building. Many structural deficiencies can be resolved readily, and architectural problems can either be avoided on the basis of the information in this book or corrected through the strengthening procedures illustrated here. And, finally, there are the ultimate safeguards—earthquake insurance and intelligent behavior before, during and after an earthquake. Surely, a thorough understanding of these basic principles, facts and remedies is a prerequisite for safety, sound real-estate investments and peace of mind in earthquake country.

PART ONE

A primer on earthquakes

CHAPTER ONE

How earthquakes are caused and measured

UNTIL THIS CENTURY, THE CAUSES OF earthquakes remained a profound mystery. The first milestone in our knowledge of earthquakes dates to November 1, 1755, when a great earthquake struck near Lisbon. The city fell in ruins, and 30,000 people perished. After the quake, Portuguese priests were asked to document their observations. Their records represent the first systematic attempt to investigate an earthquake and its effects.

Before that time and for nearly two centuries afterwards, tremors in the earth were generally relegated to that category of natural misfortunes that insurance companies still call "acts of God." Aristotle proposed that the frequent quakes which shook the ancient Greek temples and cities were caused by gales that became trapped in giant subterranean caves. Anaxagoras reasoned that earthquake motion occurred when large sections of the earth cracked and tumbled into the hollow terrestial core. The Roman scholar Pliny said that earthquakes were simply mother nature's method of protesting the wickedness of men who mined gold, silver and iron ores. Other ancient philosophers placed the blame on an ill-tempered Poseidon, god of the sea and the watery element.

The northern neighbors of these philosophers—the tribes of what is now Bulgaria—believed that earthquakes struck when an enormous water buffalo, which carried the world on its back, readjusted its burden to ease its task. Other peoples throughout the centuries have assigned the phenomenon to monstrous mythic animals—giant hogs, catfish, tortoises, spiders, frogs, whales, serpents—whose occasional restlessness caused the world to tremble. As charmingly preposterous as these notions are, early scientists of later centuries had little better to offer. An Italian scholar in the sixteenth century suggested that the best earthquake protection was to place statues of Mercury and Saturn on a building. Even in the scientific age of the nineteenth century, most observers were, like their ancient predecessors, satisfied that earthquakes were not explainable except as a capricious force of nature or the stern work of an offended god. Man's fate was merely to wait and pray.

THE SOURCE OF EARTHQUAKES—THE THEORY OF CONTINENTAL DRIFT AND PLATE TECTONICS

Even today, the causes of earthquakes are not completely understood. But there is now sufficient geologic evidence to conclude that the tremors are the effect of a rebalancing of forces arising from the collision of continuously moving plates of rock that float upon the earth's molten interior. This is the theory of continental drift and plate tectonics, which holds that the land surface of the crust of the earth was once concentrated in a single continental mass— a supercontinent. In the most recent cycle, perhaps 200 million years ago, the mass began to break apart, gradually forming fragments that largely define today's continents and ocean basins—a mosaic of about 20 thick tectonic plates that drift across the molten mantle of the earth and form the planet's shifting crust.

The tectonic plates with their continents and oceans are still moving apart. As some of these plates collide around the globe—many at the intersections of continents and oceans—they cause islands and mountain ranges to rise, land masses to emerge from or sink beneath the seas, volcanoes to erupt and the adjustments of plate frictions which we know as earthquakes.

The newest and thinnest of these tectonic plates are the ocean floors, which are still being formed from molten materials flowing from the earth's interior. This flow emerges in deep rift valleys which form the inner boundaries of the sub-oceanic tectonic plates and which divide vast and continuous mountain ranges that traverse the length of all the ocean basins. The molten materials from the interior of the earth well up through the rift valleys and solidify to build the edges of the oceanic plates. Then in a process known as "sea-floor spreading," these oceanic plates are pushed slowly but steadily from the rift valleys at a yearly rate of two to five inches, pressing the outer edges of the young tectonic plates against the established and heavier plates that make up the continental land masses. It has been demonstrated, for example, that the Atlantic Ocean is spreading from the Mid-Atlantic rift at about two inches a year, so that within the lifetime of a man, the continents of Europe and North America will have moved further apart by about six feet.

As the oceanic plates meet the continental plates, tremendous pressures buckle the earth's surface (the creation of mountain ranges), plunge the thinner, weaker oceanic plates into deep-sea trenches beyond the continental shelves, and spawn volcanoes and earthquakes. Along the western coast of South America, for example, the thinner oceanic plate is forced downward by the heavier continent. As it is propelled below the continental plate and melts into the earth's core, the Andes mountains are pushed continually upward. At the same time, friction causes a temporary lock between the two plates. The inevitable and frequent failures of this bond cause the deep, powerful earthquakes typical of Chile and Peru. A similar type of collision can occur between two continental plates as well. For example, the sub-continent of India is a separate plate which is moving northward against the Asian mass. The soaring Himalayas and the destructive tremors in India and Pakistan are the result.

Some of the largest faults—breaks in the rock of the earth's upper crust—are formed at the line of collision between tectonic plates. Thus, the San Andreas fault system of California is the result of the ancient and continuing collision of the North Pacific plate and the North American continent. Many millions of years ago, the more massive westward-moving continental plate overrode the opposing Pacific plate, driving the latter downward into the earth's crust, pushing up the Sierra and causing the violent blow-outs of such volcanoes as St. Helens, Shasta, Lassen, Rainier and Hood. At the same time, some of the

How earthquakes are caused and measured

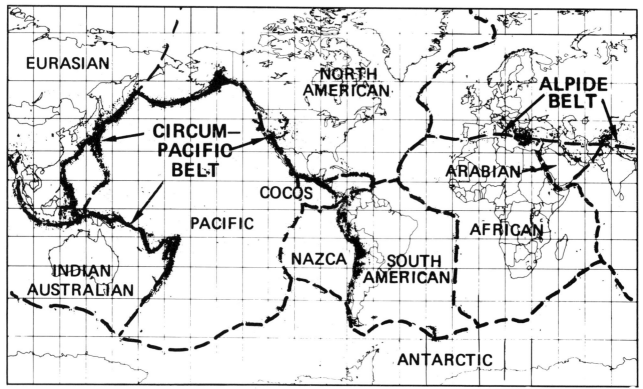

The dark areas on this map indicate the distribution and density of the 42,000 earthquakes recorded throughout the world from 1961 to 1970. These belts of seismic activity mark with dramatic clarity the turbulent boundaries of the drifting, colliding tectonic plates that form the earth's crust. The mid-oceanic lines of activity represent the towering mountain ranges and deep rift valleys where the younger tectonic plates are renewed and pushed outward, altering the sea floors a few inches every year. About 80 percent of the planet's earthquakes occur along the Circum-Pacific seismic belt, which loops completely around the Pacific Basin. The Alpide belt, which extends from Java through the Himalayas and the Mediterranean, is responsible for about 17 percent of the world's seismic activity. The remaining 3 percent of all earthquakes strike along the Mid-Atlantic Ridge and in scattered pockets of seismic activity throughout the world.

plunging Pacific plate was scraped off against the continent at the San Andreas fault zone, so that the coastal surface of western North America grew outward by about 100 miles in a very gradual accretion of new materials forming much of California and its Coastal ranges. Thus, the southwestern third of the state west of the San Andreas fault is made up of relatively new geologic materials riding the Pacific tectonic plate, while the remainder of the state forms the western edge of the North American plate.

Today, these two plates have changed directions, so that they are essentially sliding past one another along the San Andreas fault. The great Pacific plate carries the ocean floor, a part of California and all of the Baja Peninsula northwestward in relation to North America, while the North American plate, pushed by the sea-floor spreading at the mid-Atlantic ridge, moves west at a slower rate. The two plates finally collide directly in the far north, along the Aleutian archipelago, where the Pacific plate is driven downward. It is estimated

California's San Andreas fault is one segment of the line of intersection between the North Pacific and the North American tectonic plates. Both plates are moving slowly north and west at different rates, producing the frictions and temporary locks along the fault that are released in the sudden shifts of earthquakes, the surface distortions of the fault zone and the grad-ual growth of the coastal ranges. The Sierra Nevada ranges were formed when the two plates collided directly, and the thinner Pacific plate was forced downward, buckling the continental plate, lifting the mountain range and forming the westernmost portion of California with an accretion of materials from the oceanic plates.

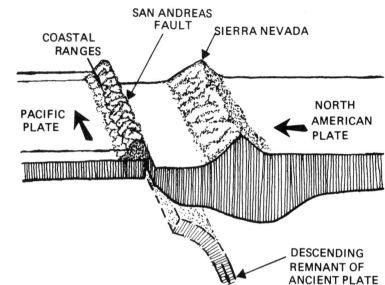

that at the present rate of movement, the Los Angeles area, riding the Pacific plate, will draw abreast of the San Francisco Bay Area in about 10 million years.

THE MECHANISM OF EARTHQUAKES— THE THEORY OF ELASTIC REBOUND

The edges of the plates have a certain amount of elasticity and tend to hold their positions along the fault. Portions of the fault frequently remain locked in this way, under tremendous stress, for several years or even centuries. Finally, when the accumulated sliding force exceeds the frictional force that binds portions of the plates and prevents their natural movement, the distorted rocks along the two sides of the fault suddenly slip past one another in an explosion of movement that allows a new position of equilibrium.

This slippage, termed "elastic rebound," produces powerful vibrations, sometimes ruptures the earth's surface and may shift the positions of the two sides of the fault by several feet both horizontally and vertically. Earthquakes, such as the 1906 and 1989 San Francisco quakes along the San Andreas fault, are the result of these violent adjustments of a temporarily locked fault.

Two types of earthquakes are associated with the different types of plate collisions. Shallow-focus earthquakes, with an average depth of three to ten miles below the surface of the earth, result from the slippage of primarily *laterally* moving plates and are typical of California and most of the seismic regions of the American West. Deep-focus earthquakes usually occur where the plates are directly colliding, and one plate is forced below the other. For example, the great Chile quake of 1960 and the major Peru quake in 1970 were both at a depth of about 25 miles. Many other earthquakes in South America have occurred at depths greater than 75 miles.

The destructiveness of an earthquake is closely related to its depth, for the shock waves of the deeper earthquakes are generally dissipated as they rise to the surface and are therefore less damaging to buildings. On the other hand, the deep-focus tremors usually affect a much wider area. Shallow-focus earthquakes are felt over a smaller area and are therefore sharper and frequently more destructive. For example, earthquakes in the Puget Sound area of Washington have depths typically three to five times greater than equally large earthquakes along the San Andreas fault in California, and historically, these shocks have been considerably less destructive than those in California.

Types of faults and faulting

THE QUIESCENT FAULT

A few faults may move relatively freely and very slowly along the plane of the drifting tectonic plates. This movement is termed fault creep, and it will be damaging to structures above the fault only over a long period of time.

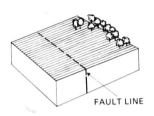

The Calaveras fault and a portion of the San Andreas near Hollister in Northern California have moved in this way in the past several years. Other faults become locked with the friction of the colliding plates and move only when the rocky layers of the plates become strained beyond endurance, then slip apart with the violence of an earthquake.

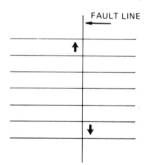

THE STRAINED FAULT BEFORE AN EARTHQUAKE

The gradual movement of the tectonic plates has created a strain in the rock of the fault where the two plates meet. The frictional force of the collision locks the two sides of

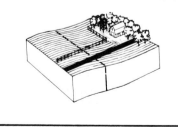

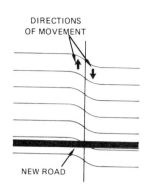

DIRECTIONS OF MOVEMENT

NEW ROAD

the fault and prevents any movement. The limited elasticity of the rock allows the strains of this locked fault to accumulate for decades. Finally, the rocks give way, allowing the two sides of the fault to realign and causing the upheaval of an earthquake and surface displacements.

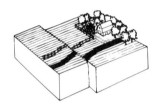

THE ADJUSTED FAULT AFTER AN EARTHQUAKE

The fault has moved into a new, unstrained position, causing surface displacements that have destroyed the continuity of the highway and fence and producing intense shock waves during the quake that have demolished poorly engineered buildings in the fault zone.

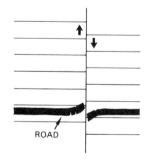

ROAD

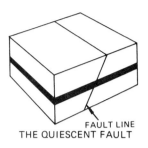

FAULT LINE
THE QUIESCENT FAULT

THE DIRECTION OF FAULTING

Faults typically move either *laterally, vertically* (thrust and/or graben faulting), or in a combination of vertical and lateral shifts. The San Fernando and White Wolf faults in Southern California fit this latter category of movement,

HORIZONTAL FAULTING
(RIGHT LATERAL)

which is quite common. The faults of the San Andreas fault system

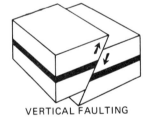

VERTICAL FAULTING

move primarily laterally. The Wasatch fault in Utah and the Kern River and Pleito faults in Southern California are vertically-moving faults.

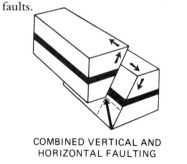

COMBINED VERTICAL AND
HORIZONTAL FAULTING

This drawing of the San Andreas fault system in Central and Southern California illustrates a few of the numerous small crustal blocks and fault divisions created by the stresses of the tectonic plate collision and the frequent upheavals along the San Andreas. These lesser faults generally parallel the lateral *northwesterly movement of the San Andreas and the continental and Pacific plates. However, this parallel movement is interrupted along the intersection with the Garlock fault, where the southern group of blocks encounters the deep crustal roots of the Sierra Nevada and is deflected to the west.*

FAULTS, FAULT ZONES, FAULTING AND CREEP

Fault and *fault system* are the terms used to describe not only the demarcation of opposing tectonic plates, such as the major trace of the San Andreas, but also the related web of numerous crustal breaks that result from the stresses of the plate collisions and the wide-spread subterranean damage of frequent earthquakes along the collision course. California, for example, is made up of a whole network of blocks that move in different directions as a result of the forces of the collision of the North American and Pacific plates and the activity of the San Andreas fault. Each of these blocks is separated by a large fault, most of which are *active* (moving or potentially moving) and therefore capable of the abrupt slippage. In addition, throughout each of these crustal blocks, there are lines of fracture which form lesser faults, also under pressure and capable of slippage and eruption.

Thus, the plane along which the slippage and tremors occur may be a recently active major fault, or it may be a newly created line of fracture in the weakened rock of older and presumably *inactive* ("healed" or unstrained) fault traces. For example, few geologists suspected any earthquake potential along the minor fault

The San Andreas fault through California is often an easily distinguished linear scar across the landscape. The fault is not so easily distinguished once development and building occur in the fault zone.

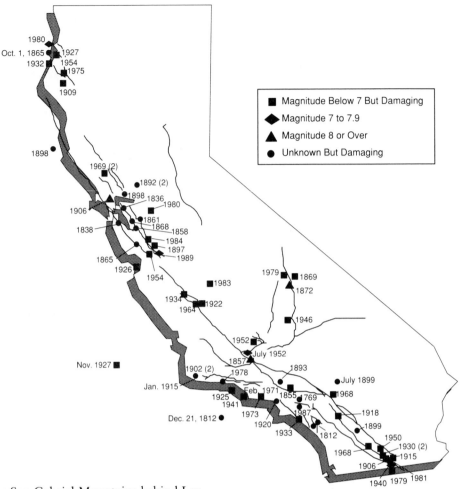

■	Magnitude Below 7 But Damaging
◆	Magnitude 7 to 7.9
▲	Magnitude 8 or Over
●	Unknown But Damaging

in the San Gabriel Mountains behind Los Angeles until it ruptured on February 9, 1971, thrusting some of the mountains six feet higher, killing 64 persons, and demolishing hundreds of buildings in the San Fernando Valley. Similarly, the 1983 Coalinga earthquake in Central California and the Whittier, Los Angeles tremor of 1987 occurred on unmapped faults.

Faults are generally narrow, measuring only a few inches to several feet wide. However, a major fault system, such as the San Andreas, includes not only the most recent active break but also a broad *fault zone* of shattered rock and traces of previous breaks and surface ruptures. The San Andreas fault zone is usually many hundreds of feet wide and is more than 1½ miles wide at numerous locations along its 650-mile length.

When the stresses of a fault are released in an earthquake, the highest-intensity shock waves and vibrations are felt near the fault line and nearest the point of slippage. However, much of the length of a fault may also be affected, so that destructive vibrations can occur for many miles on either side of the earthquake center. In addition, the shock waves disperse from the fault like the rings produced by a pebble dropped into still water, so that significant shocks and damage can affect areas for many miles on either side of the fault. The intensity of shaking always diminishes with distance, of course, but softer, vibration-prone soil many miles from the fault can produce more damage than a strong, rock formation only a few hundred feet away from the source of the quake.

A fence in Olema, north of San Francisco, was split by the 1906 rupture along the San Andreas fault. The foreground moved about 15 feet to the left (north). The area is now part of the Earthquake Trail at the Point Reyes National Seashore.

The large surface displacements of the laterally moving San Andreas fault are vividly illustrated in this photograph of a hillside field near Daly City after the 1906 San Francisco earthquake. The fence crossed the San Andreas in a straight line before the earthquake, and the camera taking this photograph was directed at the original line of the fence at the top of the hill. The massive shift of the earth along the fault during the quake left the abrupt 10-foot crimp in the fence. Naturally, any building straddling the fault during such a large displacement would have been torn apart. This field is now covered by homes.

The energy waves generated by an earthquake are modified by reflection and refraction through the different layers of rock and soil and the various geologic conditions (mountains, hills, plains) that make up the surface of the earth surrounding the fault. The combination of "pushes and pulls," "ups and downs" and reflections and refractions of these waves by the ground itself create the chaotic and violent surface motions.

During a strong tremor, the ground surface along a fault may rupture and shift laterally or vertically by several feet. The 1906 quake on the San Andreas fault resulted in lateral fault shifts of as much as 15 feet. Other earthquakes, such as the tremendously large shock in Owens Valley, California in 1872, or the more moderate Hebgen Lake, Montana earthquake in 1959, have caused vertical displacements of 20 feet or more at the surface. This displacement of ground along a fault during a quake is termed *faulting* and results in the abnormal topographical formations of scarred, crumpled and upthrusted rock and soil that visibly delineate a major and recently active fault. It also results in the certain destruction or severe damage of any structure subjected to the faulting. A small earthquake represents a localized readjustment of fault strain, and usually such shocks are not accompanied by the surface displacements of faulting nor by serious damage to buildings.

Another type of fault movement, *fault creep,* occurs when the two sides of a section

The 1987 Bay of Plenty, New Zealand earthquake, with a magnitude of 6.2, was accompanied by about 6 miles of faulting. The maximum vertical uplift was about 6 feet. Well designed single-story wood-frame houses within a few feet of the fault were usually undamaged. Two-story houses and poorly reinforced masonry buildings were not as fortunate.

A similar situation occurred in the Santa Cruz mountains in front of a house which nearly straddled the ruptured San Andreas fault in the epicentral region of the October 17, 1989 earthquake.

of a fault avoid locking completely and move past one another at an infinitesimally slow and gradual rate of fractions of an inch per year. Occasionally, the creep may halt entirely for a time, or it may drastically increase its speed with spurts of discernible movement within a few days. Whatever the speed of movement, the gradual surface displacements of fault creep can damage buildings in the immediate vicinity of the fault. The fault creep may also be accompanied by barely perceptible micro-tremors.

Some scientists believe that the more or less continuous adjustment of fault stresses through creep reduces the maximum magnitude of a future earthquake along the creeping segment of the fault. Most, however, agree that creeping faults, such as the

Hayward fault or the Calaveras and San Andreas faults near Hollister, are highly susceptible to large surface displacements in the event of a major quake.

FORESHOCKS AND AFTERSHOCKS

A large earthquake is rarely a single shock. A series of *foreshocks* sometimes occur before the main shock, and *aftershocks* may occur over the span of several months and be considered part of one earthquake.

Our present technology cannot adequately distinguish foreshocks from the numerous other small earthquakes that occur frequently in seismically active regions.

The first evidence that some faults are subject to a creeping movement was discovered by earthquake scientists. During a routine investigation in 1956 of some foundation damage in the old Cienega Winery near Hollister, engineers found that the San Andreas fault beneath the winery was moving very slowly without any perceptible earthquake tremors. The photograph shows the offsets and damage caused by the creeping fault beneath a concrete ditch just south of the winery.

Creep, together with some landsliding along the Hayward fault through Berkeley, caused this three-foot deformation in a stone retaining wall. A school was built along the fault only a few hundred feet north of this location. The University of California stadium, as well as several other structures on the campus, also straddle this creeping fault; slowly widening cracks in the stadium indicate that the structure is gradually being split apart by the creep.

Thus, foreshocks cannot yet serve as warnings of impending danger. However, seismologists may someday detect certain characteristics that distinguish foreshocks and allow them to be used as early-warning signals for the size and location of a larger quake.

Aftershocks are caused by the continuing readjustment of stresses at different locations along a ruptured fault and its subterranean fault plane after the main shock. Because of the varied geology along the fault plane, all of the accumulated ener-gy is not released at once by a quake, and the process of localized readjustment continues indefinitely. A very large shock is often followed by hundreds and sometimes thousands of discernible aftershocks for months after the main event.

The San Fernando area, for instance, was disturbed by a minor aftershock on February 9, 1972, exactly one year after the severe earthquake. The main shock in 1971 was typically followed by 33 large aftershocks during the first hour alone. One of the strongest aftershocks of the San Fer-

A large, single-story building was seriously damaged in the strong Coalinga, California earthquake of 1983. The weakened brick structure was then destroyed by aftershocks, as shown in the second photograph.

nando quake struck on March 31, 1971, in the Granada Hills area. It was felt over much of Los Angeles and in eastern Ventura County, but fortunately the shock was slight and caused only minor damage. The October 17, 1989 Loma Prieta (San Francisco) earthquake had a main shock of magnitude 7.1. In the next 20 days, it was followed by 4,760 aftershocks. Two of these were damaging, 20 were strong, and 65 were perceptible to people. Ten months later, aftershocks were still occurring in the area; they will probably continue for several years.

From the standpoint of building damage, some of the larger aftershocks can be quite destructive. For example, a month after the major Kern County earthquake in 1952, an aftershock centered near Bakersfield was strong enough to cause more damage to the shaken and weakened city than the initial quake because it struck much nearer to the city than the main shock.

THE MEASUREMENT OF EARTHQUAKES

Epicenters and hypocenters

All news media reports on an earthquake inevitably give detailed accounts about the *epicenter* of the shock, and the public usually assumes that the epicenter is in the area most seriously shaken by the earthquake. The epicenter *is* very definitely related to the strength of the ground shaking (intensity). However, other factors, such as geologic foundations, length of the fault rupture and the extent of faulting, are much more important to intensity.

The location deep in the crust of the earth where a fault slippage first begins is known as the *hypocenter*, or *focus*, of the earthquake. It is generally 5 miles and no more than about 15 miles deep for typical destructive California shocks. The 1989 Loma Prieta focus was 11 miles deep. The epicenter is the projection of the hypocenter on the ground surface and is always the

This two-story, unrein-forced masonry and wood house was also seriously damaged by the 1983 Coalinga quake. It collapsed two days later from aftershocks.

The drawing on the right shows the relationship between the hypocenter and the epicenter of an earthquake occurring on a vertical fault, such as the San Fernando fault in Southern California. The drawing on the left illustrates a lateral fault, such as the San Andreas, in which the epicenter is projected directly above the hypocenter in the immediate vicinity of the fault zone.

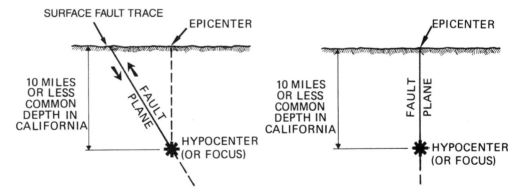

point on the surface closest to the initial slippage. However, the epicenter should not be confused with the point in the affected area which experiences the strongest or the longest shaking; for depending on the angle of the fault through the bedrock,

the surface point nearest the focus of the quake may be several miles away from the fault. And the fault, not the epicenter, is almost always the center of the greatest quake intensity and, therefore, the greatest potential for damage.

How earthquakes are caused and measured

From the standpoint of ground shaking intensity and building damage, the location of the epicenter of an earthquake can be very misleading. The epicenter of the famous 1906 quake was thought to be almost directly on the San Andreas fault near the village of Olema although it may actually have been closer to the Golden Gate. However, the fault ruptured and caused large surface displacements and shock waves that leveled much of Hollister, nearly 100 miles south along the fault from the epicenter. The most severe vibrational intensities were experienced not only in Olema but in San Francisco, 27 miles to the south, and in San Jose, more than 60 miles south of the epicenter. Because of its deep and soft soil foundation, Santa Rosa was also subjected to ruinous vibrational intensities, even though it was 19 miles east of the epicenter and the fault line.

It is important also to consider the response of an entire fault line. For example, in the 1906 earthquake, the epicenter was located near Olema, 27 miles north of San Francisco, but the intensity of the shock was equally strong along the fault in San Francisco and San Jose (more than 60 miles from the epicenter). There were also faulting and intense shock waves as far south as Hollister (100 miles from the epicenter). If you wish to estimate the future earthquake hazard of a specific place, the distance from the active fault becomes the more important criterion than the location of epicenters along that fault.

THE RICHTER MAGNITUDE SCALE

The first question which comes up after an earthquake is "How big was it?" The answer is not as straightforward as the question. Earthquakes are usually measured by two very different scales—the Richter magnitude and the Modified Mercalli intensity scale—and the two are often confusing to the public.

Earthquake *magnitude,* a measure of the total energy released by a quake, was originally defined in 1935 by Professors Beno Gutenberg and Charles F. Richter of the California Institute of Technology in Pasadena. Originally, the magnitude scale was called the Gutenberg-Richter scale. Slowly, however, it came to be known as the Rich-

ter scale. Because there was no way to make a direct measurement of the released energy of an earthquake, Professors Gutenberg and Richter based their scale on the alternations of a sensitive movement-measuring instrument—a seismograph—hypothetically located at a distance of 62 miles (100 kilometers) from the center of surface energy release (epicenter) by the shock. Since the distance from an earthquake epicenter to any one of many seismic recording stations would never be exactly 62 miles, mathematical tables are used to convert the seismograph records into the standard figures of whole numbers and decimals between 1 and 9. Advances in the seismological sciences since the introduction of the Richter scale have allowed for the magnitude of an earthquake anywhere in the world to be reported within minutes of its occurrence.

The Richter magnitude scale is also used for comparing the sizes of earthquakes, but the figures can be misleading without an understanding of the mathematical basis of the scale. The Richter scale is logarithmic, with each whole number representing a magnitude of energy release that is approximately 31.5 *times* the lower number. This means that there is 31.5 times more shaking energy in an earthquake of magnitude 6 than in one of magnitude 5. The graph shown here, which measures earthquake energy in terms of tons of T.N.T., demon-

*The power of earth-
quakes and the severity
of ground shaking were
illustrated graphically by
the magnitude 6.2 Bay of
Plenty, New Zealand
earthquake of 1987. A
stationary 67-ton diesel
train engine was over-
turned and the rails were
twisted. There was no
ground failure beneath
the twisted rails.*

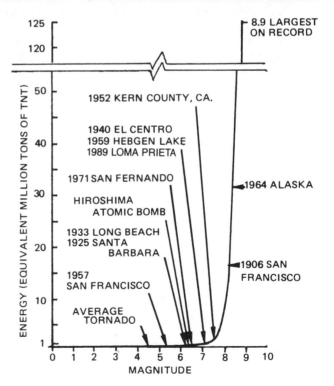

*This graph dramatically
demonstrates the vast differences in force or energy
release between moderate
quakes, such as the San
Fernando, and great
earthquakes, such as San
Francisco in 1906 and
Alaska in 1964. Note
the incredible span be-
tween these latter great
earthquakes and the mag-
nitude 8.9 shocks, which
are the largest on record.*

*How earthquakes are
caused and measured*

strates the vast difference between a small quake, such as that in San Francisco in 1957, and a major earthquake like the 1989 Loma Prieta or the 1906 disaster. It is also very important to note that the effects produced by the detonation of T.N.T. are much less damaging to structures than the equivalent energy release and shock waves of earthquakes.

What may be the greatest quake to strike California in recorded history occurred in 1872 along the Owens Valley fault, east of the Sierra Nevada. The magnitude of that quake is estimated at 8.25 +. The great 1906 San Francisco earthquake is also estimated at 8.25, and the Tejon Pass shock of 1857 reached an estimated magnitude of 8 +. Three recent large and destructive American quakes, in Alaska in 1964, San Fernando Valley in 1971, and Loma Prieta near Santa Cruz in 1989, measured 8.5, 6.5 and 7.1 respectively. A commonly accepted measure for earthquakes that relates magnitude and damage terms a "great earthquake" as one that has a Richter magnitude of 7.75 and above, a "major

Experiencing a strong quake

The October 17, 1989 Loma Prieta earthquake, with a Richter magnitude of 7.1, produced 10 to 15 seconds of strong shaking. All the damage occurred in that very brief period. Normally, an earthquake of that magnitude lasts about 20 to 30 seconds. So, in that respect, the San Francisco Bay Area was lucky.

If the epicenter had been in Oakland or off the Golden Gate nearer San Francisco instead of Santa Cruz, which is about 65 miles away, most people in the Bay Area would have felt a very different and much stronger ground motion—two or three times stronger in the heavily damaged Marina district of San Francisco or downtown Oakland, three to five times stronger in downtown San Francisco, Berkeley or San Jose.

The duration of an earthquake is related to its magnitude, which is a measure of the total amount of energy released by the shock. An earthquake of magnitude 5 or 6 might cause 5 to 10 seconds of strong motion, followed by noticeable but very weak movements. An earthquake of Richter magnitude 6.5, such as the San Fernando shock of 1971, usually lasts 15 or more seconds. A great earthquake,

such as the one in 1906, might last 40 to 60 seconds.

In other words, earthquakes happen very quickly. For those in the middle of the action, however, they seem to last much longer. Typically, people overestimate the duration of a quake. Afterward, they are convinced that it lasted several minutes.

These two recollections are from the 1868 earthquake on the Hayward fault. Estimates for the magnitude vary; it may have been as low as 6.5 or as high as 7 +.

I was then about 15 years of age. My home was near Irvington (today part of Fremont). When the shock came, I was alone in the house with my baby brother. My mother was in the milk house, about 10 steps from the kitchen door. She called to me to get the baby. Though I was thrown the length of the dining room, I managed to get the child over my arm, face down, and a pillow on top. Then, falling and crawling, I worked my way back to the open kitchen door.

My mother was on the ground. Every time she tried to get up, she was thrown again and the milk in the buckets was spilt over her. My two brothers, my stepfather, and the hired man were

also down and were trying to get to the house by crawling and falling.

As I sat there, I could see the ground in waves like the ocean. After the main shock, I think we had 100 shocks during the first 24 hours. The ground opened; we traced a crack through town, and the ground settled several inches in one place. Not a house was left with a chimney on it. Our safe broke through the floor, and the piano was out in the room nearly to the opposite side.

—J. MCD. PRESTON

I was curled up in a big rocking chair, reading, and my two sisters were outside playing, when suddenly there came a swaying of the house. This lasted only a short time; then the house began to shake in earnest. My sisters began to cry and scream. I jumped out of the chair to go to them, and ran from the room, bumping against both sides of two doors.

I finally reached the porch and succeeded in catching hold of a post. I distinctly remember that the pump in the yard was pumping as if someone had a hold of it, and small rocks on the hill in front of the house were rolling down into the creek.

My brother was hauling a load of wheat to San Jose. When the earthquake was at its worst, he thought his ▶

earthquake" at 7 to 7.75, and a "moderate earthquake" at 6 to 7. Thus, the San Fernando quake was in the category of the moderate-sized shock that can be expected approximately every four years somewhere in California. The Loma Prieta earthquake was just a major earthquake and occurs in California on or offshore on the order of every 15 years.

People occasionally believe that the occurrence of many small quakes in one area depletes the fault stresses and therefore reduces the possibility for a large shock. This is a myth and a physical impossibility, for with the Richter logarithmic scale, it would take about 500 shocks of the magnitude of the San Fernando earthquake (magnitude 6.5) or more than 40 Loma Prieta earthquakes (magnitude 7.1) to equal the energy released by the single great San Francisco earthquake of 1906 (magnitude 8.25). On the same basis, it would require about 1,000 San Fernando earthquakes to equal the energy of the 1964 Alaska earthquake (magnitude 8.5).

---

team was choking down and jumped off his wagon to find he could hardly stand.
—MRS. N. AINSWORTH

The following quotation is from Laurence Klauber, a physician and noted herpetologist, who was a student at Stanford when the 1906 earthquake struck. A number of poorly constructed masonry buildings at Stanford collapsed or were severely damaged by the earthquake. Apparently he was in one of those.

The most noticeable part was the noise of the falling buildings. They roared in an astonishing fashion. I remember dimly seeing the new library and the church spire go. They didn't fall exactly, they just settled as if they had been made of sand.

I awoke to find myself standing in the middle of a room filled with sound and falling plaster. The shake was strong enough to throw a person about. However, you couldn't fall, because when you started to, you were jerked in another direction. I felt sort of bruised like a cat shaken by Jack D (Dempsey).

After the plaster quit falling Dug and I got the door open and went into the hall. I remember deliberating on which stairs to take and decided on the main staircase as it was more open . . .

The place was crowded by the skinny student body in an assorted array of pajamas, nighties, and less. A number were hurt by falling plaster and glass, and some from jumping out of windows.

The best summary of the effects of the 1906 earthquake is in "Earthquake of April 18, 1906; Report of the State Earthquake Investigation Commission," which was published by the Carnegie Institution of Washington in three volumes in 1906 and reprinted in 1969. It is available at local libraries.

Here are some excerpts:

REDWOOD CITY: *Many buildings were partially wrecked and the new courthouse was completely ruined. Over 40 houses in the town were moved upon their foundations, and a majority of the houses had plaster badly cracked. Ninety-four percent of the chimneys fell, and dishes and similar objects were universally thrown down.*

MILL VALLEY: *At Mill Valley the visible injury was chiefly to chimneys. From crags on the south slope of Mount Tamalpais, stones were detached and rolled down the slope.*

ROSS TO BOLINAS, MARIN COUNTY: *In the village of Ross, houses were not shifted. The principal injury is to brick chimneys, of which probably more than half fell.*

SAN MATEO: *San Mateo showed the intensity of the earthquake plainly. Almost all brick and cement (concrete) buildings were damaged and several were completely ruined. Many wooden structures suffered by being thrown from their foundations, while others were shifted without material damage. Nearly every brick chimney in town was shaken down, with consequent damage to the houses.*

For San Francisco, the report mentions numerous locations with particularly heavy damage. This concentration of damage often was due to very local effects, such as small, poorly compacted landfills in the midst of good natural ground.

Many of the sites that suffered spectacular damage in 1906 also suffered the worst damage on October 17, 1989.

THE MODIFIED MERCALLI INTENSITY SCALE

Intensity scales measure the *effects* rather than the energy release of an earthquake. There are several intensity scales, all based on reports of ground and building damage and on interviews with people in different locations in the earthquake-affected areas. These scales were developed as a means of evaluating the relative size of an earthquake before earthquake-recording instruments were available. Various categories of earthquake damage, ground effects, and personal sensations, emotions and observations were defined and were assigned numerical designations. Because the categories are mainly related to effects on people and buildings, intensity scales are also known as the "man-scaring, structure-busting" earthquake scales.

The Modified Mercalli intensity (MMI) scale is the one most commonly used in the United States. The MMI scale is denoted with Roman numerals from I to XII, with each number corresponding to descriptions of earthquake damage and other effects. Because the damage and ground effects are influenced by numerous factors, such as distance from the causative fault, the type of soil beneath the observer, the type of building, the accuracy of the personal observations, etc., reported intensities vary considerably from site to site, with large differences sometimes occurring at locations only a few feet apart.

Since earthquake effects vary, an earthquake cannot be assigned a single intensity

---

Modified Mercalli scale of earthquake intensities

Intensity scales were devised before seismographs were invented to give scientific dimension to tremors. The Modified Mercalli Intensity (MMI) scale remains useful in plotting maps which show the general range and severity of ground effects, structural and interior damage, and personal observations and sensations during an earthquake. Because the scale is dependent upon the observations of the victims of an earthquake, these intensity maps are imprecise and approximate.

The MMI scale is based on the following categories of earthquake effects and damage, coded by Roman numerals:

I.   Not felt by people, except under especially favorable circumstances.

II. Felt only by persons at rest on the upper floors of buildings. Some suspended objects may swing.

III. Felt by some people who are indoors, but it may not be recognized as an earthquake. The vibration is similar to that caused by the passing of light trucks. Hanging objects swing.

IV. Felt by many people who are indoors, by a few outdoors. At night some people are awakened. Dishes, windows and doors are disturbed; walls make creaking sounds; stationary cars rock noticeably. The sensation is like a heavy object striking a building; the vibration is similar to that caused by the passing of heavy trucks.

VI. Felt indoors by practically everyone, outdoors by most people. The direction and duration of the shock can be estimated by people outdoors. At night, sleepers are awakened and some run out of buildings. Liquids are disturbed and sometimes spilled. Small, unstable objects and some furnishings are shifted or upset. Doors close or open.

VI. Felt by everyone, and many people are frightened and run outdoors. Walking is difficult. Small church and school bells ring. Windows, dishes and glassware are broken; liquids spill; books and other standing objects fall; pictures are knocked from the walls; furniture is moved or overturned. Poorly built buildings may be damaged, and weak plaster will crack.

VII. Causes general alarm. Standing upright is very difficult. Persons driving cars also notice the shaking. Damage is negligible in buildings of very good design and construction, slight to moderate in well-built ordinary structures, considerable in poorly built ▶

number. Instead, the earthquake intensities observed at various locations are plotted on an intensity, or isoseismal, map. The intensity map illustrated here for the magnitude 7.1 Loma Prieta earthquake of October 17, 1989, is typical. The divisions (*isoseismal lines*) between the intensity zones form an oval pattern about the focal area of the quake. An intensity map of the magnitude 8.25 1906 San Francisco quake covers a much larger area and shows elongated isoseismal lines reflecting the greater magnitude of the earthquake, the effect of the shock waves that emerged along much of the length of the San Andreas fault, and the considerable amount of faulting. The isoseismal lines between intensity zones are always at best a very rough approximation of the boundaries of the different intensities; it would be impossible to include all of the reported variations in damage, observations and sensations for a particular quake.

Intensity maps like the one shown on page 26 are usually published now by the U.S. Geological Survey soon after a major earthquake strikes a populated area. In addition to these large-scale maps of the entire area affected by a quake, very detailed intensity maps of individual cities, and even subdivisions, may be plotted for the quake. The latter, in combination with block-by-block official accounts of earthquake effects, can be very useful to an urban property owner in determining the range of shock wave intensities and damage that can be expected in an area during the next comparably sized earthquake.

or designed structures. Some chimneys are broken; interiors and furnishings experience considerable damage; architectural ornaments fall. Small slides occur along sand or gravel banks of water channels; concrete irrigation ditches are damaged. Waves form in the water and it becomes muddied.

VIII. General fright and near panic. The steering of cars is difficult. Damage is slight in specially designed earthquake-resistant structures, considerable in well-built ordinary buildings. Poorly built or designed buildings experience partial collapses. Numerous chimneys fall; the walls of frame buildings are damaged; interiors experience heavy damage. Frame houses that are not properly bolted down may move on their foundations. Decayed pilings are broken off. Trees are damaged. Cracks appear in wet ground and on steep slopes. Changes in the flow or temperature of springs and wells are noted.

IX. Panic is general. Interior damage is considerable in specially designed earthquake-resistant structures. Well-built ordinary buildings suffer severe damage with partial collapses; frame structures thrown out of plumb or shifted off of their foundations. Unreinforced masonry buildings collapse. The ground cracks conspicuously and some underground pipes are broken. Reservoirs are damaged.

X. Most masonry and many frame structures are destroyed. Specially designed earthquake-resistant structures may suffer serious damage. Some well-built bridges are destroyed, and dams, dikes and embankments are seriously damaged. Large landslides are triggered by the shock. Water is thrown onto the banks of canals, rivers and lakes. Sand and mud are shifted horizontally on beaches and flat land. Rails are bent slightly. Many buried pipes and conduits are broken.

XI. Few, if any masonry structures remain standing. Other structures are severely damaged. Broad fissures, slumps and slides develop in soft or wet soils. Underground pipe line and conduits are put completely out of service. Rails are severely bent.

XII. Damage is total, with practically all works of construction severely damaged or destroyed. Waves are observed on ground surfaces, and all soft or wet soils are greatly disturbed. Heavy objects are thrown into the air, and large rock masses are displaced.

Because the MMI intensity scale and the Richter magnitude scale measure entirely different parameters, it is very difficult to compare the two. The magnitude scale records physical energy with instruments and therefore gives no consideration to the important factor of geologic conditions. The intensity scale, on the other hand, is necessarily less than precise since it is based solely on personal observations.

After a tremor, earthquake scientists gather the public reports of structural damage, ground effects, interior damage and personal observations and sensations and then plot this data on intensity, or isoseismal, maps such as this one from the October 17, 1989 Loma Prieta earthquake. By generalizing all of this information into the Roman numeral code of the Modified Mercalli Intensity scale, the scientists and engineers can compile a useful visual description of the severity and range of a given earthquake. In this case, the serious damage was concentrated in MMI VIII. The damage in MMI VII areas was typically moderate to light except for localized areas. Such areas included the Marina district of San Francisco, where the ground motion was amplified by soft, poor soils.

SOURCE: U.S. GEOLOGICAL SURVEY

PART TWO

The geologic hazards of earthquakes— how to recognize and avoid them

CHAPTER TWO

The hazards of faults and faulting

BUILDINGS LOCATED IN FAULT ZONES are exposed to very high earthquake risk. No measures—whether the most earthquake-resistant bracing and building materials nor the latest and soundest principles of reinforcement—can guarantee that any property astride a fault would survive a moderate quake without severe or total damage. In a study of damaged and undamaged houses on two similar streets in Sylmar after the San Fernando quake, 30 percent of the houses within the fault zone had been posted as unsafe, compared to only 5 percent of the houses adjacent to the fault zone. Similarly, 80 percent of the houses in the fault zone suffered moderate or worse damage, whereas only 30 percent of the buildings immediately beyond the zone suffered such damage.

The greatest hazard to structures in fault zones is ground-surface ruptures during an earthquake, and no reasonable building can normally withstand this faulting beneath it. A ground shift of only a few inches (vertically, horizontally or, most commonly, both) may be sufficient to cause severe structural damage to buildings. A large quake, with its typical displacements in the fault zone of several feet, could demolish the most well-engineered building.

In addition, there is the problem of severe earthquake vibrations in a fault zone. Most structural damage to property during an earthquake is directly related to the intensity of the shock waves in the ground, and the intensity of ground shaking is usually very strong along the fault. Thus, even if there were no faulting, any building located on or within the zone of a fault will be exposed to very strong ground vibrations.

All of these facts about the hazards of building in fault zones have been known to geologists and soils and structural engineers for years. They have also known and mapped the locations of many of the most dangerous fault zones in the western states. Yet, because of pressures from developers and landowners, because of ignorant governmental officials and outmoded zoning laws, and because of the public's ignorance, apathy and short memory, buildings continue to be constructed and bought and sold in fault zones. Many hundreds of homes and large buildings can be found actually straddling obvious evidence of a recent fault rupture.

People are commonly under the misapprehension that contemporary building codes, in notoriously earthquake-prone areas, such as California, take the danger of faults and faulting into consideration. It is true that in California and throughout most of the western states the modern building codes recognize the high risk of earthquakes and set certain *minimal* standards of design and construction. However, in accordance with these building codes, almost all structures must meet the *same* standards. Permits for the construction of residential, commercial and public buildings in areas subject to earthquakes are still issued only on the basis of these minimal earthquake-resistant standards. Except for California, there is not adequate recognition of the existence of the special geologic conditions and hazards of fault zones.

The Hayward fault and the whole East Bay region of the San Francisco Bay Area provide a particularly instructive illustration of our past neglect of the special problem of fault zones in seismic areas. The Hayward fault has experienced significant faulting and continues to display the perceptible activity (including some creep) which indicates the ever-present risk of a large tremor. A *partial* list of the schools, important buildings and places of public assembly which are located directly above or very near to the fault would fill a full page in this book. Presumably, the newer of these structures were carefully designed and built for earthquake resistance. In many cases, however, particularly with these buildings straddling the fault, this care will have been largely futile in a large quake. As for the hundreds of homes, businesses and other buildings which were built with less knowledge and care, an optimistic earthquake scholar would have to predict a broad swathe of damage from San Pablo to Fremont in the event of a long surface rupture along the fault.

This heavy four-story reinforced-concrete building straddled the fault that caused the Managua, Nicaragua earthquake in 1972. The mere eight inches of displacement at the surface of the fault was sufficient to "pancake" the building.

How faulting damages buildings

No building straddling a fault can withstand the abrupt surface ruptures and displacements of earthquake faulting without severe damage.

Unless the faulting is minute (less than a couple of inches), even the most well-built structure of the most flexible materials (wood or steel frame) may sustain difficult-to-repair and costly damage. Foundations are cracked and thrust apart, vertical supports collapse or are knocked askew, floors and roofs sag or fall.

The inescapable conclusion, then, is that anyone holding property or living in an active fault zone with a history of past faulting is gambling the whole investment and perhaps life itself on the slim hope that a large earthquake will not strike again in that area. No earthquake expert will cast the odds favorably.

VERTICAL FAULTING
Vertical faulting thrusts the ground surface upward, destroying the foundation above it—which, in turn, breaks the vertical structural supports of the building. In the photograph at right of faulting damage in the San Fernando earthquake, the thrust of the fault was small. Even so, the structural damage to the house was extensive and very costly to repair. The photograph below is an example of larger faulting during the Hebgen Lake, Montana earthquake in 1959. The damage to this barn was total.

LATERAL FAULTING
Lateral faulting shifts one or the other or both sides of the fault to a new position. The movement splits the foundation and in large displacements can tear an entire building apart. An illustration of what extremely large lateral faulting could do to a foundation slab can be seen in the 1906 photograph of a road which crossed the San ▶

Andreas near Point Reyes Station. The faulting displacement was more than 15 feet in this area near the epicenter of the earthquake. Lateral fault creep along the Calaveras fault in Hollister is gradually damaging not only retaining walls, such as the one in the photograph on the right, but also homes and other buildings straddling the fault.

TENSION CRACKS

A network of tension cracks in the ground surface and a number of small pockets of slight landslide movements are both common earthquake effects in a fault zone passing through deep alluvial soil. The fissures or settlements will crack a foundation, and this damage inevitably results in some fractures in the structural supports of a building. In the lower left photograph of a house in San Fernando, downhill landslide displacements of a few inches opened up the narrow tension crack which passed beneath the house and continued down the slope behind it. The damage to the foundation and the frame of the house is not apparent here, but it was so severe that the house was declared unsafe for occupancy. The right photograph shows typical interior damage from these types of faulting.

The East Bay region of the San Francisco Bay Area includes one of the most densely populated fault zones in the world. The Hayward fault, which bisects the numerous large cities along the bay, has not caused a destructive earthquake since the area became heavily settled, but several destructive quakes occurred on the fault in the nineteenth century. The fault is highly active with frequent, small tremors and creep zones, so that most earthquake experts rank the fault among the top five most dangerous earthquake zones in the United States. Note that the schools, hospitals and other public buildings marked on the map represent only a few of the many important buildings and homes that are in this fault zone.

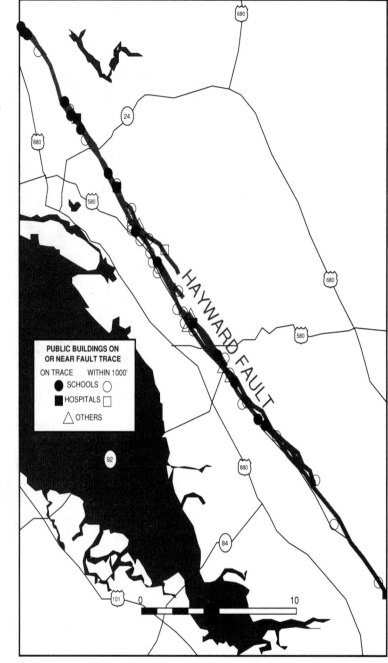

WHERE THE FAULTS ARE—DETERMINING THE FAULT RISK OF YOUR PROPERTY

A look at a geologic map of California will show that few of the major population centers of the state are very far from an active fault. In the greater San Francisco Bay Area, Santa Rosa is only 19 miles from the San Andreas fault. Downtown San Francisco is only 9 miles away. Oakland is about 15 miles from the San Andreas and, worse, is traversed by the Hayward fault as well. San Jose is bounded on the west by the San Andreas and on the east by both the Hayward and Calaveras faults. The Calaveras fault also cuts through some of the heavily populated suburban cities of the East Bay, while the San Andreas crosses residential Daly City and then skirts the suburban cities of the San Francisco Peninsula.

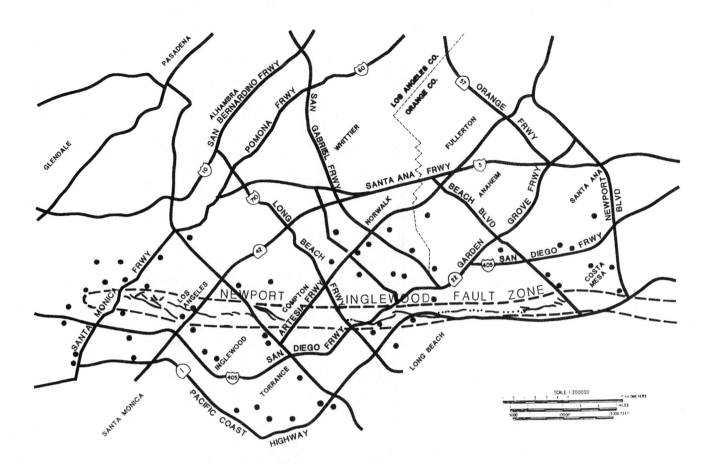

SCALE 1:200000

In terms of overall risk and potential for damage, the Newport-Inglewood fault through the Los Angeles area and Orange County is probably the most dangerous fault in Southern California. It is very similar to the Hayward fault because it bisects heavily populated areas. The dots indicate the locations of hospitals in the vicinity of the fault.

Northeastern Los Angeles is also near the San Andreas fault, San Bernadino is located astride it, and all of metropolitan Los Angeles is criss-crossed by numerous other faults related to the San Andreas. Santa Barbara is near the Santa Ynez fault zone and its subsidiary fault traces. Sections of the Imperial Valley and lower Southern California are bisected by the Imperial fault. In addition, there are numerous other active faults in the state—near Eureka, in the Sacramento Valley, near Bakersfield.

If that were not enough to sober the California resident, there is the problem of determining whether a given fault is active or inactive. The White Wolf fault, a short and relatively insignificant fault in the Arvin-Tehachipi area between Bakersfield and Los Angeles, was considered inactive for many years. Then on July 21, 1952, that theory was dramatically dispelled in a destructive earthquake. Similarly, the San Fernando earthquake occurred on the same type of fault—one which had been dutifully mapped on the more detailed geologic maps and then largely ignored as inactive.

The quake in the Imperial Valley in 1940 took place on a fault which was unknown until it broke the surface of the rich agricultural landscape. More recently, the Coalinga earthquake of 1983 and the Whittier quake of 1987 were both on unmapped faults. Given this record, it is best to assume, for planning purposes, that if your property is not near a known active fault, it may be near an unknown fault which can cause a strong, local earthquake. Therefore, no matter where in California, you should do your best to make your structure earthquake resistant and consider the purchase of earthquake insurance.

Numerous other large and assuredly active faults also exist throughout the other western states. A particularly treacherous fault zone—the East Bench—crosses Salt Lake City. The point is that it is impossible at the present time to predict the future behavior of the known faults, and new faults will continue to appear abruptly as they shake and rupture the ground in an unexpected tremor. Only one thing is certain—earthquakes and the associated faulting will

The San Andreas fault zone on the west side of San Francisco Bay is one of the most famous—and dangerous—in the world. The danger is graphically illustrated in these photographs taken in the western part of Daly City in 1956 and 1966. The sag pond, landslide, and other geologic features of the fault zone in the picture at the top are now obliterated by the landfill and concrete of a surburban tract. Heavy property damage and some loss of life are a certainty when the next big earthquake strikes along this portion of the San Andreas. Fault zones such as this, and many similar areas in the East Bay and in Southern California, provided the ultimate rationale for pleasant and ecologically sound urban "green belts." But the irresponsibility of governmental leaders and the ignorance and apathy of the public allowed the opportunity to pass, and now it is too late in too many cases.

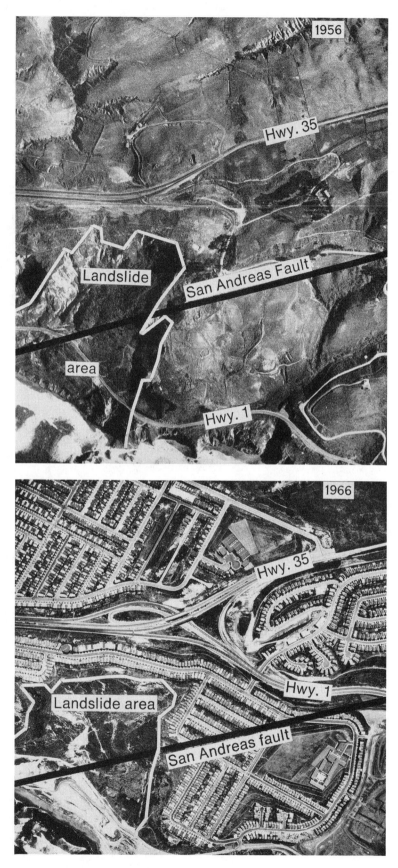

continue to occur in the western states, and there is nowhere, particularly in California and Western Alaska, where one can go to escape the risks of tremors. The other western states are generally less active than California and Alaska, but they are active, and in some ways more dangerous, because we know less about the risks.

Still, the majority of damage from future shocks will occur along the *major* faults, such as the San Andreas, the Newport-Inglewood, the Santa Ynez, the Hayward, which are well-known and well-mapped. Professor Charles F. Richter listed the most likely faults in California to experience *great* earthquakes in the future. They are:

1. A repetition of the 1857 Tejon Pass earthquake along the San Andreas fault in Southern California.
2. A repetition of the 1906 San Francisco earthquake on the San Andreas fault.
3. An earthquake in the Owens Valley, east of the Sierra Nevada, comparable to the great tremor of 1872.
4. An earthquake on some other large fault in California.
5. An earthquake in the central Coastal Range, connecting the sections of the San Andreas which moved in the 1857 and 1906 shocks.

In category 4, most earthquake scientists would include, in no particular order, the Santa Ynez fault near and in Santa Barbara and the Hayward fault. They would also include a few faults outside California, including the East Bench fault in Utah, the offshore fault west of Puget Sound and the highly active fault system along the Pacific coast of Alaska.

The first step in establishing the earthquake risk for a given site is to locate your property on a geologic map which shows the local active and inactive faults. The maps are essential because faults are not always obvious to the eye. The break always occurs initially deep below the surface of the earth, and it may never surface with

ruptures or displacements, even during violent earthquakes like the one in Coalinga in 1983. In addition, surface evidence of faulting can be absorbed and hidden by excavation and landfill, under the natural deposits of deep alluvial soils, or below the ocean or a lake surface.

Certainly, neither individual property owners nor developers are usually anxious to divulge the information that a fault runs under or near their property. In California, legislation in the mid-1970s made it mandatory for the seller of a property in a known active fault zone to divulge that information to the prospective buyer. These zones are called Special Studies Zones and are discussed further in the text. Elsewhere in the West, until regulatory laws and building codes are reformed, the prospective buyer or builder or the present owner can rely only on professional consultants and/or on the information available in the maps of the U.S. Geological Survey and other state and local agencies. The maps are easy to obtain, and are quite simple to read after a little study of the sample materials provided here. The addresses and telephones of the primary agencies are listed in Appendix B.

The second step in establishing earthquake risk for a given site is to determine the history of the nearest fault—the frequency, magnitude, intensity patterns and displacements or surface ruptures of past quakes. All of these considerations are essential in weighing the risks of living or buying or building near (not *in*) a fault zone. You can do at least some of the initial research in Appendix A, which is devoted to a summary of the significant faults and quakes of the West and includes numerous maps of the major faults passing through urban areas of the western states. Appendix A also contains necessarily brief reports and recommendations regarding past faulting, the varying intensities of past earthquakes, and the special geologic conditions and structural/architectural requirements affecting the larger urban areas near each fault zone. Your best resort is to hire a geotechnical engineer or a geologist to advise you.

*The hazards of
faults and faulting*

The Hayward Fault: The odds aren't good

One earthquake risk that's easy to avoid is buying a house on top of the Hayward fault.

The Hayward fault, a branch of the San Andreas fault system through San Francisco's East Bay, is an offspring even more dangerous than its treacherous parent.

Most engineers and seismologists believe that the Hayward fault could produce the most destructive quake in the Bay Area. That's because the fault runs through the most densely populated and oldest cities of the East Bay. It also has the highest probability, based on history, of causing the next 7-plus quake on the Richter scale. The U.S. Geological Survey believes that there is at least a 28 percent chance of such an earthquake on the northern half of the fault and a 23 percent chance on the southern half of the fault in the next 30 years. Further, there is an additional 22 percent chance of a magnitude 7 shock on the Rodgers Creek fault—the northern extension of the Hayward fault. Combined, the odds are greater than 1 in 2 that we'll see a quake there.

Worse, when the San Andreas fault is added, chances are 2 in 3 that a magnitude 7 quake will shake the Bay Area in the next 30 years. Prominent geologists believe that 2 earthquakes will strike the region in the next 30 years.

I live exactly 3.4 miles from the Hayward fault. (Downtown Santa Cruz, by comparison, is more than 12 miles from the part of the San Andreas fault that ruptured on October 17, 1989.) That means that my family and I—and many hundreds of thousands of other people—will feel one or both of the predicted Hayward quakes. If that is not enough reason to evaluate and to strengthen, if necessary, your house or office building, your optimism knows no bounds. I have done both, and I am a born optimist.

The southern end of the Hayward fault lies between Warm Springs and Milpitas, along the Alameda-Santa Clara county lines. Farther south, the fault merges into the Calaveras fault zone, another major branch of the San Andreas system.

The Hayward fault passes through virtually every city on the eastern shores of San Francisco Bay before it enters the bay at Point Pinole near San Pablo. It emerges from the bay in Sonoma County and continues toward Petaluma along the Petaluma Valley. The fault then appears to merge into two other fractures, the Rodgers Creek and Healdsburg faults, which continue north past Santa Rosa to Healdsburg.

The Hayward fault has caused several destructive quakes, including the Hayward earthquake of 1836 (estimated magnitude 6.8 to 7.0), which was one of the largest ever to occur in the Bay Area. According to a recent study of that quake, fissures opened along the fault from San Pablo to Mission San Jose (now part of Fremont), and the tremors caused havoc in the settlements of Monterey and Santa Clara.

In another great quake, in 1868, also with an estimated magnitude of 6.8 to 7.0, the fault ruptured for about 20 miles, from Warm Springs (now part of Fremont) to the vicinity of Mills College in Oakland. ▶

HOW FAR FROM A FAULT ZONE IS FAR ENOUGH?

This is one of those questions that everyone asks, assuming or hoping that it will bring a straightforward answer. It won't. Unless your property is located within an active fault zone, the earthquake hazard varies, and simple distance is not always the most important factor.

Generally speaking, of course, the further you are from a fault, the better off you will be. However, the geologic foundation of your homesite also plays an important role. As you will learn in the next chapter, certain soil foundations intensify the shock waves of a quake. Certain soils are also prone to severe settlement during a quake—an action that can cause serious damage. Thus, in a large earthquake in which the shaking intensity remains strong many miles from the fault, a house on one of these unstable geologic foundations may suffer more damage than a similar house on stable ground very near the fault zone.

In making a decision, then, about the relative risks of different locations, the main considerations should be the geologic

Horizontal displacements were as much as three feet, and every building in the village of Hayward was either severely damaged or completely demolished. Numerous structures in San Francisco, particularly in the filled areas of the bay, were also destroyed or damaged.

Another earthquake, on October 7, 1915, was centered in the vicinity of Piedmont, where most of the damage occurred; the shock was felt as far as Sebastopol and Santa Clara. And on May 16, 1933, the fault erupted again in the vicinity of Niles and Irvington (again, now incorporated into Fremont), where all chimneys were thrown down and numerous dwellings damaged. The most recent damaging earthquake along the Hayward fault occurred on March 8, 1937, in the Berkeley-Albany-El Cerrito area.

The California Division of Mines and Geology has conducted an authoritative study of the effect of a magnitude 7.5 earthquake in the region around the fault. The estimated damages are staggering and widespread.

It's easy to avoid this risk by not buying a house on top of the Hayward fault. It's one of the most studied geologic features in the world and is mapped in great detail. Maps of the entire length of the fault can be seen in your city's engineering office. Most real estate offices should also have these Special Studies Zone maps.

A fault is basically a weakness or crack in the rocky crust of the earth, running deep below the surface for many miles. Earthquakes are generally accompanied by movement along these faults. In 1906, for example, the San Andreas fault moved as much as 18 feet in Marin County.

The greatest hazard to houses in a fault zone is ground-surface rupture which no building can withstand. Since a ground shift of only a few inches is enough to cause severe structural damage, a large quake on the Hayward fault, with its typical fault displacements of several feet, could demolish the best-engineered building.

In addition, vibrations will be severe. Most structural damage is

directly related to the strength of the shaking of the ground, which seems to be strongest along and near the fault. Even if your house isn't precisely on top of the fault, it's exposed to a greater hazard than are houses five or more miles away.

If your house is located on top of an active trace or within the wider fault zone shown on geologic maps, have a geologist or soil engineer check the property, using all available maps. Then ask for a verbal opinion. You do not need a written report.

If your consultant says that the house straddles the fault—or almost certainly straddles the fault—I suggest you find another place to live. The risks for houses on top of an active and potentially explosive fault are simply too high to take.

Several hundred or more homeowners along the Hayward fault will find that out sooner or later. Don't be one of them.

foundations of the sites and the past history and future prospects of the fault. Generally, anyone living in coastal California or Alaska or in Puget Sound or in Utah should presume that they are "too near" a potentially explosive fault zone and should give primary consideration to the geologic foundation of the property, the strength of the building, and the need for insurance coverage.

There is one further consideration. The surface ruptures of faulting are almost always restricted to the relatively narrow area immediately adjacent to the fault line. Some

faults, however, do not follow this linear pattern. Instead, they tend to fracture the ground surface over a broad area sometimes extending for hundreds or thousands of feet. That is why I often recommend the purchase of earthquake insurance.

The problem of soil foundations and the possibilities of reinforcement and insurance are examined in detail in the following chapters. At this point in the book, you are merely reminded that proximity to one of the major active faults is not the sole or even the most important criterion for evaluating earthquake risk to your property.

When and where might the next earthquake hit in California?

To answer this question, let us start by examining the history of earthquakes in the San Francisco Bay Area. Discussions of the 1906 earthquake tend to dominate all conversations about earthquakes. But it has not been the only major earthquake.

The map at right summarizes the history of larger earthquakes in the Bay Area. Except for the 1906 and 1989 earthquakes, these are all shocks with magnitudes that are believed to be in the range of 6.5 to 7 on the Richter scale. Since most occurred before the creation of the Richter scale, we are not certain of their magnitudes.

The 1906 shock had a magnitude of about 8.25. That is believed to be the largest earthquake in California since the state was settled. Note that seven very strong quakes occurred in the 83 years before 1906: among them, 1836 on the Hayward fault, 1838 on the San Andreas fault, 1865 on the San Andreas and almost exactly where the Loma Prieta earthquake was centered, 1868 on the Hayward fault, 1892 near Davis (actually two earthquakes—one near Vacaville and one near Winters) and 1898 near Mendocino. All may have exceeded Richter magnitude 6.5.

Thus, before 1906, a very strong earthquake occurred in or near the Bay Area every 10 to 15 years. Then suddenly, after the great earthquake of 1906 this activity nearly stopped. A few small earthquakes occurred between 1906 and 1979, then, in 1979 activity increased. Damaging shocks occurred near Gilroy in 1979, Livermore in 1980, Morgan Hill in 1984 and finally near Loma Prieta in 1989 with a magnitude of 7.1.

On the basis of our recorded earthquake history, it is reasonable to assume that another cycle of earthquakes will occur before an earthquake like the 1906 occurs. We

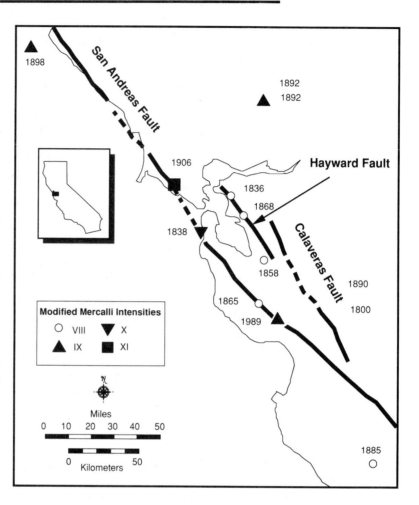

Modified Mercalli Intensities

○	VIII	▼	X
▲	IX	■	XI

should expect a series of destructive, strong earthquakes around magnitude 7 before another earthquake like 1906 happens again. Many scientists now believe that we have entered such a period.

Ten years ago, in an article published in the *Bulletin of the Institute of Governmental Studies* of the University of California at Berkeley (Vol. 20, August 1979, No.4), the history of earthquakes in the Bay Area and in California was discussed in detail. The article was written by Professors Bruce A. Bolt of Berkeley and Richard H. Jahns of Stanford. On the basis of the available historical record and other studies, the two authors wrote:

"What does this evidence tell us about the imminence of damaging earthquakes of magnitude 7 or greater? When all sections of major earthquake-producing faults are considered jointly, a rough estimate of the odds finds them now about even 50-50 that an earthquake with a magnitude greater than 7 will occur in California during the next decade. With every passing year, these odds will steadily increase. In any event, present knowledge supports a working hypothesis that we should anticipate a great earthquake somewhere in California during the next 10 years."

At that time, I wrote the following in the *San Francisco Chronicle*. "I ▶

support the conclusions of the two professors. In addition, I fervently hope that the next strong earthquake is either in an unpopulated area, or at least in Southern California. However, sometime in the next 10 or 20 years we will experience such an earthquake here. I hope that you will be prepared."

The October 17, 1989 earthquake occurred almost exactly 10 years after the professors' prediction. In fact, that earthquake was forecasted in more detail by the U.S. Geological Survey. In 1988, the Working Group on California Earthquake Probabilities, convened by the USGS, determined the recurrence times and probabilities of earthquakes along the San Andreas faults (see the figure below—the probabilities after the 1989 Loma Prieta earthquake). The Loma Prieta earthquake occurred along one of the segments of the fault in

California identified as most likely to experience an earthquake of magnitude 6.5 or greater in the period from 1988 to 2018.

The accompanying figure shows the probabilities of other large earthquakes that are expected in California along a few major faults. The expected big ones in the Bay Area are a repeat of 1906 (less than a 2% chance in the next 30 years) and a 28%, 23%, 23% and 22% chance *each* on the northern half of the Hayward, southern half of the Hayward, the San Andreas fault in the Peninsula south of San Francisco and north of Loma Prieta, and on the Rodgers Creek fault. Effectively, these quakes can all be considered as "big ones" because they will be centered in the middle of the Bay Area. Typically, length of the shaking will be 15 to 30 seconds or up to twice as long as the October 17th event, but the

strength of the shaking will be about 3 or more times stronger than what was felt in October. Overall, chances are more than two out of three that a large earthquake will strike the Bay Area in the next 30 years.

Most estimates indicate that the probability of a large earthquake in Los Angeles and Southern California are higher than in the Bay Area. Worse, the probability of a great earthquake like the 1906 one is much higher for Southern California. Let us assume that a great earthquake occurs in Northern and in Southern California every 150 years. The last great earthquake to shake Southern California was in 1857, 49 years before the 1906 shock, and about 140 years ago. San Francisco's last great shock was in 1906—about 85 years ago. Time is running out faster for Southern California.

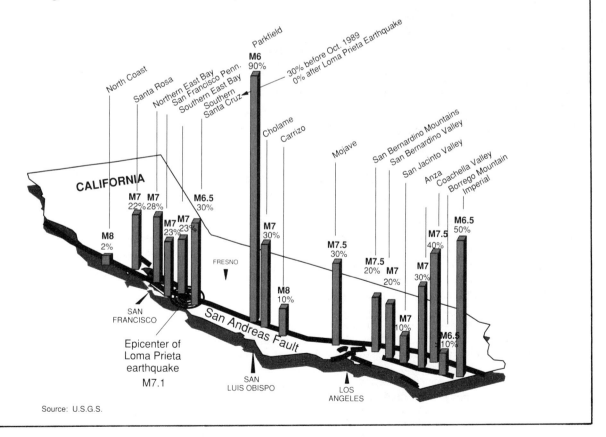

Source: U.S.G.S.

So long as a building is not located *within* the fault zone, it can survive an earthquake *if* (1) it is located on a stable geologic foundation, and (2) it is constructed or reinforced to be sturdily resistant to the forces of the shock.

WHAT TO DO ABOUT A PROPERTY IN A FAULT ZONE

If you are one of the unfortunate people who find their property on or immediately adjacent to an active fault zone, you should

Could the next big San Francisco Bay Area earthquake be on the Hayward fault?

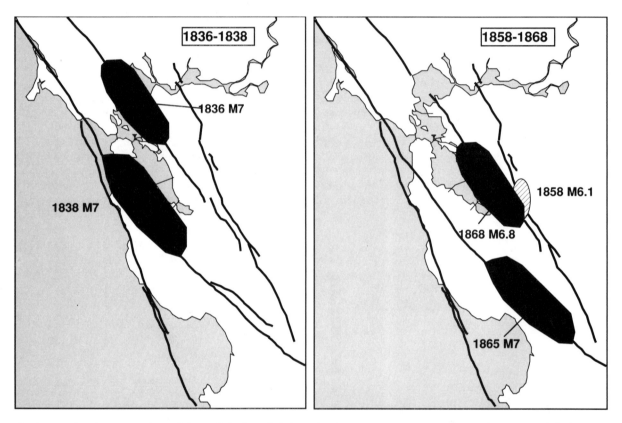

An interesting interpretation of the seismic history of the San Francisco Bay Area proposes that the next big earthquake, with a magnitude of 6.5 to 7, could occur on the Hayward fault. The probability of that happening may be as high as 20% in the five year interval following the Loma Prieta earthquake of 1989. That probability is about twice as high as the publicly published probabilities by the U.S. Geological Survey. The idea of pairing of earthquakes in the Bay Area's history was put forth by Dr. Allan G. Lindh of the USGS. He notes that during the nineteenth century, almost all large earthquakes in the Bay Area occurred in two short time periods in the 1830s and 1860s, as shown. An earthquake with an approximate magnitude of 7 on the Hayward fault in 1836 was quickly followed by a similar magnitude quake across the Bay, in the Peninsula on the San Andreas fault, in 1838 (two years later). Similarly, a magnitude 7 quake in the Santa Cruz area on the San Andreas fault (almost exactly in the same location as the 1989 shock) in 1865 was quickly followed, three years later in 1868, by ►

consult a geologist to determine, first of all, whether the fault has demonstrated surface ruptures, displacements and/or creep in your area in the recent past. If not, there is a chance that the fault beneath or beside you will remain true to its history and that an earthquake on that fault would subject your home only to intense vibrations and not to the foundation-splitting displacements of faulting. In this case, a further contingency is important to the survival of your property: the strength of

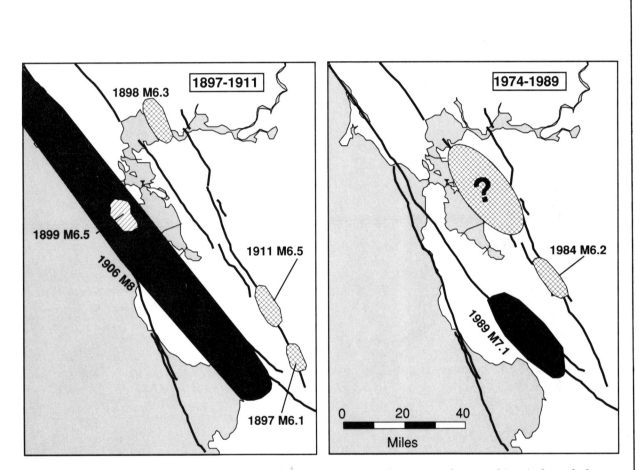

a magnitude of 6.8 to 7 on the Hayward fault. One interpretation is that a quake with a large magnitude on one of the two faults is quickly followed by another similar quake on the other fault. That can be explained more scientifically by assuming that a major shift of one fault causes a stress readjustment of the major faults in the Bay Area which eventually triggers a second earthquake to correct that readjustment. The third figure shows the rupture along the San Andreas fault in 1906. Following 1906, the Bay Area was relatively quiet until about 1974, when a series of small earthquakes began. The 1989 magnitude 7.1 Loma Prieta earthquake may have thoroughly disturbed the stress distribution throughout the Bay Area. If indeed pairs of earthquakes are a historical trend, then the next magnitude 7 (very approximately) earthquake should strike along the Hayward fault. We certainly do not have enough historical data to make a definitive prediction, but the above logic is reasonable. I certainly hope that the hypothesis is wrong, but there is a good chance that it is not.

Finding the nearest earthquake fault in California—your home could be closer to one than you think

The first step in establishing the earthquake risk for a given site is to locate it on a detailed geologic map that shows the local active faults.

The important thing is that your house not be located on top of a fault. Historically, damage close to a fault (say less than an eighth of a

mile away) tends to be more severe and widespread than damage farther away.

▶

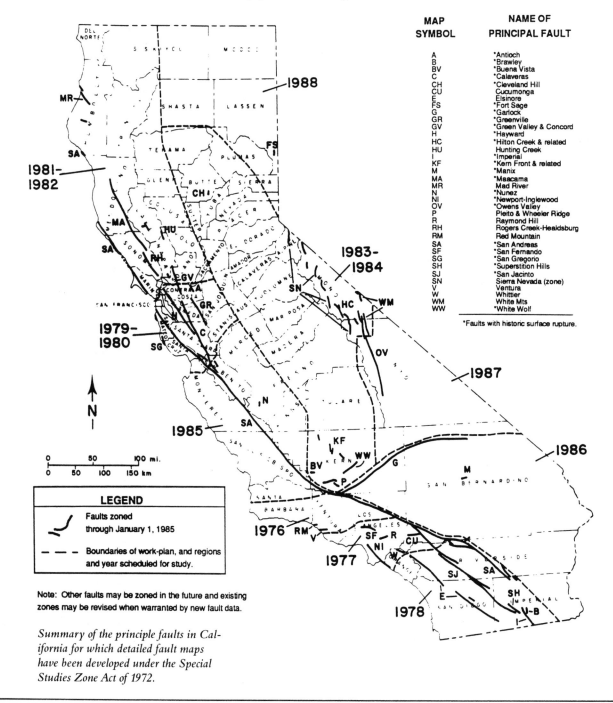

MAP SYMBOL	NAME OF PRINCIPAL FAULT
A	*Antioch
B	*Brawley
BV	*Buena Vista
C	*Calaveras
CH	*Cleveland Hill
CU	Cucumonga
E	Elsinore
FS	*Fort Sage
G	*Garlock
GR	*Greenville
GV	*Green Valley & Concord
H	*Hayward
HC	*Hilton Creek & related
HU	Hunting Creek
I	*Imperial
KF	*Kern Front & related
M	*Manix
MA	*Maacama
MR	Mad River
N	*Nunez
NI	*Newport-Inglewood
OV	*Owens Valley
P	Pleito & Wheeler Ridge
R	Raymond Hill
RH	Rogers Creek-Healdsburg
RM	Red Mountain
SA	*San Andreas
SF	*San Fernando
SG	*San Gregorio
SH	*Superstition Hills
SJ	*San Jacinto
SN	Sierra Nevada (zone)
V	Ventura
W	*Whittier
WM	White Mts
WW	*White Wolf

*Faults with historic surface rupture.

LEGEND

Faults zoned through January 1, 1985

Boundaries of work-plan, and regions and year scheduled for study.

Note: Other faults may be zoned in the future and existing zones may be revised when warranted by new fault data.

Summary of the principle faults in California for which detailed fault maps have been developed under the Special Studies Zone Act of 1972.

The best maps of the active fault zones of California are the Special Studies Zones maps published by the California Division of Mines and Geology, Department of Conservation, State of California. Because available fault data range widely in quality and the locations of some faults are known imprecisely, the fault traces are bounded by zone boundaries positioned at a reasonable distance (about 660 feet, or an eighth of a mile) on both sides of the fault trace.

It is important to realize that there are potentially active faults other than those depicted on the maps, including branches and spurs of the named zones.

If you are thinking of buying a house within one of these zones, you should consult a geologist. If the house is within the zone, the real estate agent will ask you to sign a statement (required by law) that you are aware of potential fault problems. Buying a property and signing such a document without professional help is asking for trouble. ▶

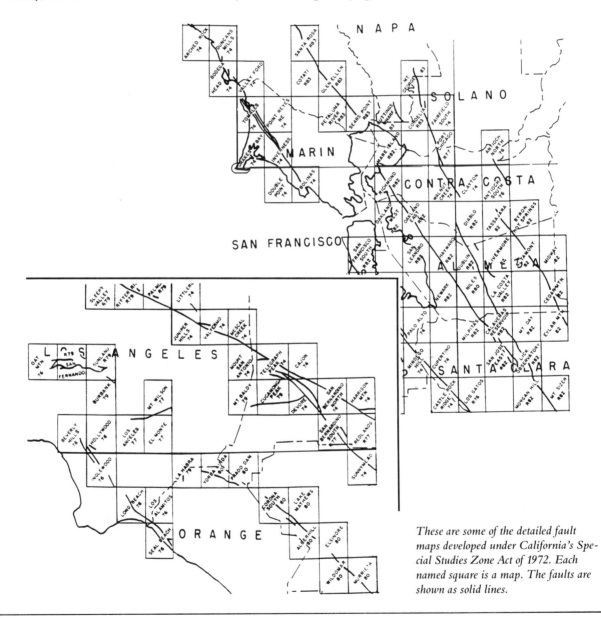

These are some of the detailed fault maps developed under California's Special Studies Zone Act of 1972. Each named square is a map. The faults are shown as solid lines.

The hazards of faults and faulting

In California, your town or county planning department is required by law to make the maps available. Many real estate offices also carry them. You can also consult the maps at the offices of the California Division of Mines and Geology. (For their addresses see Appendix B.)

If you want to purchase the maps, call the Information Desk of the California Division of Mines and Geology or order the maps from: Blue Print Service Co., 149 Second Street, San Francisco, CA 94105. Telephone (415) 495-8700.

An example of a Special Studies Fault Map for the cities of San Lorenzo and Hayward. The solid or dashed lines represent the active Hayward fault. The thin lines connecting the small circles delineate the fault zone. The photo in the lower left typifies the lack of consideration for fault hazards that existed prior to enactment of legislation in 1972. Photo in upper right is an example of development with structures set back from recognized active fault traces.

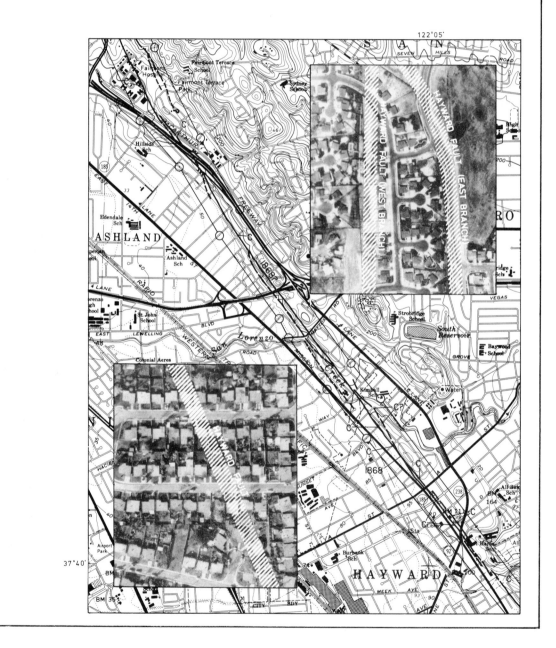

This trace of the East Bench fault in Salt Lake City can be seen in the face of an excavation for an apartment building.

The apartment building in Salt Lake City now straddles one of the most potentially dangerous faults in the United States. Regardless of the strengths of a building, a large earthquake and any faulting will almost certainly destroy a structure straddling the ruptured fault.

The faulting from the 1987 New Zealand earthquake shown in the previous chapter extended within 50 feet of a single story wood-frame house. There was no ground disturbance underneath the well engineered house. It was not damaged.

The line of faulting accompanying the 1971 San Fernando earthquake just caught the right-hand corner of the building, breaking the stairway. The land across the street is now developed and the traces of the fault are covered until the next earthquake on the fault leaves a path of damaged buildings. As a home owner or home buyer in an area crossed by a fault, you cannot rely on the inadequate zoning ordinances of a city or county. You must procure the available detailed fault maps of the area and/or hire a geologist and establish for yourself the proximity of faults and faulting to your property.

the design, structure and materials of your building.

In summary then, these are the rules regarding faults and your property:

1. If you are thinking of purchasing property or a building within an active fault zone, *don't*. If the fault is apparently inactive, hire a geologist for a careful investigation before you take the expensive gamble.

2. If you already own property within an active fault zone, determine from the materials in this book and from a geologic map whether the fault is active. Hire a geologist to assist you in this research.

3. If the answer to 2 is "yes," there are really only three sad and costly alternatives:

How far from a fault zone is far enough?

Buildings located within a fault zone, and most especially those straddling the fault traces, risk severe damage and likely destruction from the ground ruptures and displacements of faulting. For those buildings beyond the fault zone, property damage is directly related to the intensity of the shock waves and ground vibrations, and this intensity level is usually closely related to (1) distance from the surface ruptures of the fault, or if there is no surface faulting, to (2) distance from the epicenter of the earthquake.

In order to understand the importance of the two factors of distance from a fault zone and the history of faulting in that zone, you can look at the typical damage-distance ratios of two very different tremors—the moderate Santa Rosa quake in 1969 and the great, dramatically faulting San Francisco quake in 1906:

Because there were no surface ruptures or displacements in the magnitude 5.7 Santa Rosa shock and the fault beneath the surface ruptured only for a short distance, the intensity map of that earthquake shows the circular pattern of ground effects and building damage arising from the epicenter of the quake.

The approximate distances represented schematically by the intensity map for the Santa Rosa earthquake are shown in this graph. The maximum intensity of VIII affected an area of about five miles around the epicenter. The lowest damaging intensity (V) was experienced about 25 miles away from the epicenter. A stronger shock, with an epicentral intensity of XI, would have generated a damage rating of VII more than about 25 miles away.

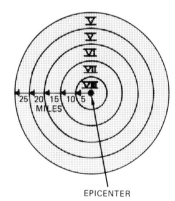

EPICENTER

►

A. Relocate the building to a safer site.

B. Abandon the building or, if possible, lease it for other than a living site. Of course, you could sell or also rent the building as a home, but this would be unconscionable.

C. Hire an engineer to advise you in strengthening the home. Then, try to secure an insurance policy for earthquake damage and hope for the best. Properly reinforced and perhaps restructured, your home can probably be made safer for its occupants. It is very unlikely, however, that such measures could protect the building itself from expensive damage.

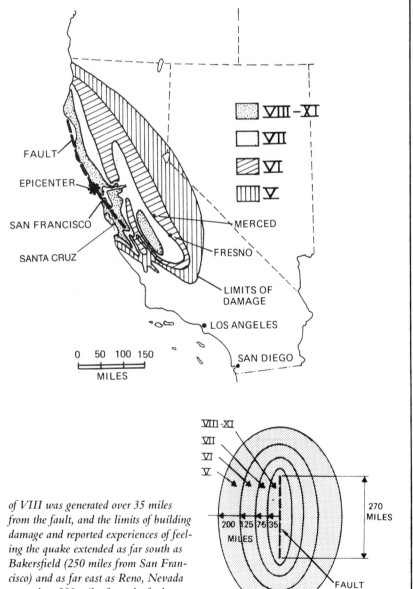

This intensity map of the San Francisco quake shows an elongated rather than circular pattern of ground effects and building damage. This elongated pattern results from the large-scale faulting along some 270 miles of the San Andreas. The violence of the surface ruptures and displacements along the fault generated a 270-mile-long continuous sequence of shock waves that nearly equaled the vibrational intensity surrounding the epicenter of the quake, a few miles north of San Francisco. The lengthy faulting also significantly increased the duration (and therefore the damage) of the vibrations. The strong shaking of the Santa Rosa quake lasted about 10 seconds, whereas the 1906 vibrations exceeded 40 seconds. Note that the 1906 faulting ended roughly with the segment of the fault that ruptured and caused the 1989 Loma Prieta earthquake just east of Santa Cruz.

The distances affected by the great San Francisco earthquake are shown in this graph. The highest intensities (IX or higher) were experienced for 270 miles along the rupturing fault and affected areas as much as 35 miles away from the fault. The very damaging intensity of VIII was generated over 35 miles from the fault, and the limits of building damage and reported experiences of feeling the quake extended as far south as Bakersfield (250 miles from San Francisco) and as far east as Reno, Nevada more than 200 miles from the fault.

CHAPTER THREE

The relative hazards of various geologic foundations

DURING THE EARLY-MORNING 1906 San Francisco quake, some people living on top of the famous hills of the city were not even awakened by the enormous tremor, and numerous unreinforced masonry buildings located on these bedrock hills survived the earthquake without severe damage. On the other hand, in homes atop the landfill along the bay and the alluvial soils between the hills of San Francisco, people were thrown out of bed by the shock and found themselves unable to get on their feet during the 40 to 60 seconds that the motion lasted. Many of the buildings in these flat, deep-soil areas collapsed.

The same thing happened at 5:04 in the afternoon on October 17, 1989 during the Loma Prieta earthquake, which was centered more than 60 miles from downtown San Francisco. Old houses and other buildings on the rock of Pacific Heights suffered no substantial damage, whereas many wood-frame buildings on the old landfill in the Marina, just a few blocks away, collapsed or were severely damaged. The other spectacular damage, in the South of Market Street area and along Interstate 880 in Oakland, where one and a half miles of a two-level freeway structure collapsed, also occurred on very soft soils and old, poorly compacted fills. The strong motion this time lasted less than 15 seconds.

The reason for the sharper effects of the quake in alluvial and landfill foundations is that the intensity of earthquake vibrations increases as the earthquake waves enter a thick layer of soft soil or the less dense mixtures of soil found in some landfills.

These soft, unstable soils act much like jelly in a bowl, responding to and then amplifying the earthquake motions further, so that the shock waves are transformed from rapid, small-amplitude vibrations in the bedrock into slower and more damaging large-amplitude waves. The chaotically undulating motions of these waves can be devastating at the surface, particularly in landfill and water-saturated soils.

An earthquake-hazard map of California, Alaska and much of the West would show that aside from the actual fault zones, the highest earthquake-hazard areas are always the natural alluvial soils and man-made landfills in the valleys and near the coast and bays. The hills and mountains, which are composed mainly of bedrock with a thin soil surface, would appear on the map as the lowest hazard areas.

Even a site on the bedrock of a *steep* hillside is safer than most others, unless the building is located in a landslide area or the contractor has cut into the slope and then used the loose cuttings for landfill lacking the proper grading, compacting and drainage. Post-earthquake studies have consistently shown that structures built on rock near the fault or epicenter of an earthquake fare better than much more distant buildings on soft soils.

A highly detailed soil map would show wide variances in risk from one homesite to another in a city or a neighborhood, since urban areas are inevitably composed of a wide variety of natural and man-made soil foundations, including old and forgotten landfilled water courses, sand dunes, and water-saturated muds disguised by

The violent surface waves of the 1906 quake left their pattern on the badly fractured pavement of Dore Street in San Francisco. The waves and the intense vibrations also threw the buildings off their foundations or caused the ground settlement that left the street deformed and the structures severely raked.

The 1989 earthquake left similar undulations in the soft soils of the Marina district of San Francisco. Again, as in 1906, the damage to buildings on such soil was extensive.

This intensity map of the city of San Francisco during the 1906 earthquake indicates the widely varying effects of the shock in different soil foundations. The most violent areas were the ocean beaches of the city, which are soft soil and are also nearest the San Andreas fault. Other equally violent areas further from the fault are associated with the poorest ground conditions: land-filled swamps, water channels, bayside lands and deep natural soil foundations (alluvium) between the hills. Buildings on the bedrock of the numerous hills of the city were least affected by the powerful earthquake. This pattern was repeated for the much smaller 1989 earthquake. The most affected areas were the black zones in the northeast end of the city.

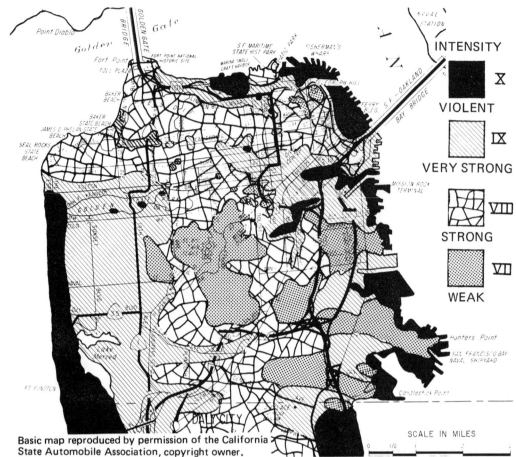

Basic map reproduced by permission of the California State Automobile Association, copyright owner.

INTENSITY

X
VIOLENT

IX
VERY STRONG

VIII
STRONG

VII
WEAK

SCALE IN MILES

housing. During the 1971 San Fernando earthquake, different buildings within the small area of the Caltech campus in Pasadena, many miles from the fault, recorded vibrational levels that varied by a factor of two. This large difference in shock wave intensities is explained by the fact that various geologic foundations beneath the campus responded to the earthquake in considerably different ways. The same condition was observed in San Francisco on October 17, 1989. The ground motions that were recorded in the rock of Pacific Heights, a hill a few hundred yards from the Marina, were one-quarter to one-fifth as strong as the motion in the fill of its less fortunate neighbor.

The importance of the geologic foundation in minimizing earthquake damage can be demonstrated with a profile of the destruction caused by the 1906 quake. The intensity map shown here illustrates the distribution of ground and building damage in the city of San Francisco. The stabil-

ity of rock foundations is clearly shown in the lighter structural damage on the hills of the city—Telegraph Hill, Russian and Nob Hills, Pacific Heights, Twin Peaks, Hunters Point and Potrero Hill. On the other hand, the flat alluvial areas between the hills were hard hit by the quake, with moderate to severe vibrational intensities and structural damage. The parts of the city that suffered the greatest amount of damage were the business district in the vicinity of the Ferry Building and most of the lower Mission district, which were built on landfill atop the already unstable bay mud. The Marina area of San Francisco did not exist then. Although these areas of the city were furthest (some 9 or 10 miles) from the fault, the land heaved and then settled drastically under the force of the shaking, creating havoc among the light wood-frame structures. In addition, numerous fissures several inches wide opened in this unstable ground, allowing the high water table to surge above the surface.

The sandy beach and dune areas along Lake Merced and near Ocean Beach were also severely shaken, partly because of the nearness of the fault and partly because of the unstable water-saturated soils. At the time, this region of San Francisco was sparsely settled and damage was light. Today, an earthquake of the same magnitude would strike a densely settled area with many older homes and buildings lacking the most basic requirements of earthquake-resistant construction and design.

The same lessons were repeated in San Francisco during the 1989 Loma Prieta earthquake. This time, however, sensitive instruments, called accelerometers, recorded the ground motion, so that we can make direct, numerical comparisons. These instruments record acceleration as a fraction of gravity, which is 1.00g.

The strongest acceleration, 0.64g, was recorded at Corralitos near Santa Cruz or about 4 miles from the epicenter. The rock hills of northern San Francisco, at Pacific Heights and Telegraph Hill, recorded 0.06g and 0.08g respectively at about 61 miles from the epicenter. There was no significant damage there. The nearby Presidio, on softer ground, recorded 0.21g. The probable acceleration in the land-filled Marina, which is sandwiched between the above three areas, was about 0.25g to 0.35g or about 4 to 6 times stronger than nearby Pacific Heights. The recorded acceleration in the soft, filled land of San Francisco International Airport recorded 0.33g at about 50 miles from the epicenter. Only 0.14g was recorded in nearby San Bruno on firm ground.

The same comparisons can be made in Oakland, where again, accelerations on soft or filled ground were several times stronger than on rock. This is also the reason why Mexico City suffered so much damage and death in 1985 from an earthquake with a magnitude of 8.1 that was centered more than 200 miles away. The non-damaging accelerations in the rock and firm ground around the old lake bed of Central Mexico City were only about 0.05g. These were amplified as much as 5 times on the soft ground of the central city, to 0.25g. And, of course, this is where the spectacular damage and accompanying huge losses of life occurred in inadequately engineered buildings.

Santa Rosa suffered proportionally even greater damage than San Francisco in 1906 because of its geologic foundations, even though the city is more than 19 miles from the San Andreas fault—twice as far as the farthest point of San Francisco. The central

The central business district of Santa Rosa, at top, was leveled by the 1906 earthquake and the fire which followed it. The town is built over an alluvial plain which intensified the shock waves from the San Andreas fault, about 19 miles away.

Above, the same happened to the old historic central business district of the coastal town of Santa Cruz, south of San Francisco, in October 1989. It also is located on an old river bed which intensified the waves from the nearby epicenter.

The hazards of various geological foundations

A soil map of the Los Angeles basin is a useful indicator of the varying intensities of shock waves that might be expected with an earthquake. The highest intensities (IX and up) would be experienced in and near the fault zones that crisscross the region, but comparable vibrational damage could be expected in the flat, alluvial soil areas if the quake were a large one. The lowest intensities and the least damage (VII or less) would occur in the hills and mountains, which are composed of bedrock with a thin layer of topsoil. A much more detailed soil map would also show pockets of high earthquake hazard in the hills and mountains where developers have used deep landfill in creating homesites.

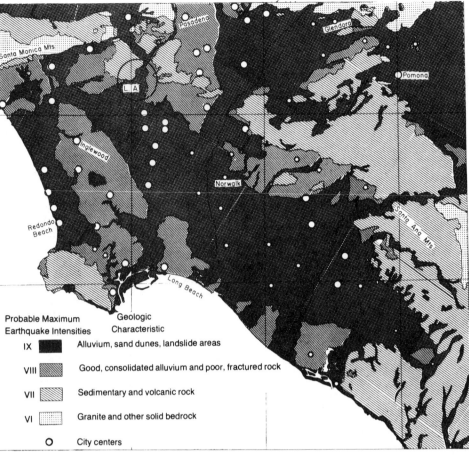

Probable Maximum Earthquake Intensities | Geologic Characteristic

IX — Alluvium, sand dunes, landslide areas

VIII — Good, consolidated alluvium and poor, fractured rock

VII — Sedimentary and volcanic rock

VI — Granite and other solid bedrock

○ — City centers

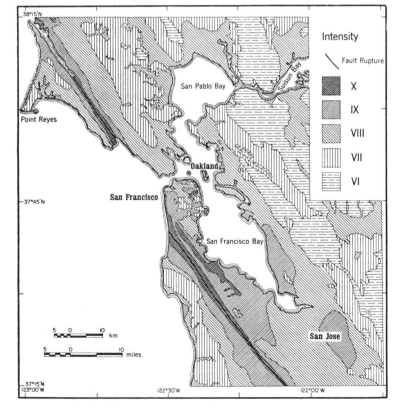

Intensity

Fault Rupture

X
IX
VIII
VII
VI

This intensity map of the Bay Area in the 1906 quake and a similar future earthquake shows the high intensities all along the fault zone, in the alluvial area of San Jose, and on the bayside landfill and mud flats. Note that the lowest intensities are in the range of hills along the east side of the bay—the bedrock foundations furthest from the fault.

business district of the town, which sits atop an alluvial plain, was almost completely destroyed. The same comprehensive damage affected San Jose, which is located on a similar soil foundation nearer the ruptured fault. It is estimated that these and other localities relatively distant from the ruptured fault experienced vibrational intensities equal to or sometimes greater than those in the most affected parts of San Francisco. Residents of the San Fernando Valley, the Los Angeles Basin, Orange and Ventura counties, the valleys and flatlands of the Bay Area, and large sections of Seattle, Anchorage and Salt Lake City should take note of these experiences in 1906 and 1989, for soft soil deposits and a high level of seismic activity are common to these areas.

SOIL LIQUEFACTION

Soil liquefaction is a very common effect of earthquakes in low-lying coastal areas or wherever soft soils and high water tables exist (near bays, lakes, rivers, and deltas and marshlands, for example). The compaction of the soil from earthquake vibrations causes the water to flow upward, and the usually sandy or muddy soils become liquefied into a kind of quicksand. By far the most dramatic example of liquefaction occurred in the coastal city of Niigata, Japan, during a magnitude 7.3 earthquake in June of 1964. Although the epicenter of this major earthquake was about 35 miles from the sea-level city, liquefaction developed over large sections of the city, and numerous buildings, automobiles and oth-

The building failures here are typical of the vibrational and settlement damage in 1906 in the alluvial and "reclaimed" bay lands of San Francisco. Note that some of the buildings, which were either better constructed or located on sounder soil foundations, survived the quake with little apparent damage. The photograph was taken before the fire destroyed the entire block. Note the ominous smoke in the background.

The same scenes occurred in San Francisco in 1989, on the same types of soil and in the areas where engineers had predicted the damage. These scenes are from the Marina. Both of these structures were four-story apartment buildings with garages on the ground floor. Nearby buildings on firm soils suffered no damage.

er heavy objects gradually settled into the "quicksand." Many apartment buildings settled several feet and tilted at such a rakish angle that the occupants made their escape by walking down the walls.

The Marina district of San Francisco suffered extensive liquefaction, as expected, in the 1989 Loma Prieta earthquake. The area was filled for the 1915 Panama Exposition and built-up in the 1920's and 1930's before modern soil compaction techniques were developed. The liquefaction caused extensive damage to hundreds of houses and apartment buildings in the area. Note, however, that the deadly four-story apartment building collapses occurred primarily because of structural weaknesses, as discussed in Chapter 7.

Studies have shown that numerous areas of California, Alaska and Washington are susceptible to equally spectacular effects—in particular the landfill areas in former delta or marsh regions, such as sections of Newport Beach, Santa Barbara, San Diego, Livermore and Pleasanton; the filled or diked lands bordering San Francisco and other bays; ocean beach developments; and the landfill sites near the mouths of rivers in Puget Sound and throughout the Los Angeles area. In owning, purchasing or building a structure in such areas you must seek the advice of a soils or geotechnical engineer regarding the possibility of liquefaction. The problem is expensive to correct.

Most city and county engineers' offices in California and other larger cities such as Anchorage, Seattle and Salt Lake City have prepared maps showing the possible liquefaction areas within their jurisdictions, as required by state law. If you are buying a house, or if you think that you own a house in a fill area, check these maps.

PROBLEMS WITH LANDFILLS

Like any soft soils, landfills—and particularly hydraulic sand fills and other poorly compacted fills typical of construction before the middle 1950s—introduce a much higher risk for earthquake damage than most other soil foundations. Indeed, im-

properly engineered landfill is often significantly more damaging to structures than even some of the poorest alluvial soils; for the fill is often loose and insufficiently cohesive and will shake and settle drastically when the shock waves of an earthquake pass through it. Poor landfills are also frequently full of organic matter which decays and creates voids and weak spots that are prone to settlement. Old filled refuse dumps, for example, are among the most dangerous sites in earthquake country because of the excessive amount of organic matter beneath the surface. Such sites, particularly when they are close to active faults, should be avoided if you are house-hunting. If you already own such property, relocation or extensive reinforcement and full insurance coverage should be the rule.

Modern methods of landfill engineering, which include careful compaction and selection of fill materials, have reduced the earthquake hazards associated with landfill foundations. During the 1957 and 1989 San Francisco earthquakes, for example, the well-compacted fill under the newest subdivisions of Daly City was apparently not a significant factor in the moderate structural damage to homes in the area, even though some of the fill was 35 feet deep. However, the 1957 earthquake was a minor one, and the 1989 was distant and not sufficiently strong so that these landfill sites were not subjected to great vibrational forces. Whether the filled areas are sufficiently well-engineered to protect structures during a large magnitude quake remains to be seen. Further, good engineering does not guarantee good results, primarily because good design is not necessarily followed by good construction. If the contractor decides to save money or take short cuts, and the engineer does not spot the sloppy work, the quality of the fill will be reduced and liquefaction or settlement could occur. As a rule, a house in a fill area runs a much higher risk of damage in an earthquake because the ground beneath may fail even if the house itself is built properly.

Certain hillside and hilltop developments should be approached with great

This dramatic example of the effects of liquefaction in sandy or other water-saturated soils occurred in Niigata, Japan during the large earthquake centered near there in 1964. The apartment buildings suffered moderate structural damage; but the soil liquefaction left some of them tilted at 80 degree angles. The occupants evacuated some of the buildings by walking down their faces. Liquefaction occurs when the intense ground vibrations of an earthquake cause the settlement and compaction of sandy soil and the upward flow of water, creating a quicksand-like effect.

The same effects could be observed throughout the Marina district of San Francisco after October 17, 1989. Liquefaction and the resultant settlement damaged many homes. The weakest collapsed. This was a four-story apartment building. This area was expected to suffer such damage—and it did and it will again and again in future earthquakes.

This is one of many large fissures that split the pavement in the Mission district of San Francisco during the 1906 earthquake. The crack resembles faulting but is only a local land failure due to poorly engineered landfill in a former swamp area. The structures straddling these fissures were badly damaged. Such problems also occurred from the October 17, 1989 earthquake. The photo at far right shows a similar crack in fill among the columns of the condemned Embarcadero freeway in San Francisco.

How to identify ground settlement

It is essential to identify any signs of local ground settlements under buildings, for the foundations of such buildings will be weakened by the settlement and present a serious hazard during earthquakes. Walls or doors out of plumb; substantial cracks in basement slabs, floors, patios or walls; poorly fitting or obviously separating structural connections—all are signs of damage from ground settlement. Many other indications of damage are illustrated in the discussion of landslides later in this chapter. The shaking of an earthquake always seeks out the weakest structural elements and can greatly magnify the existing structural damage. Thus, a cracked foundation can be rended entirely by the quake or the sagging structural supports of a doorway will collapse. The damage can sometimes be corrected, but the assistance of a structural engineer is strongly recommended. The purchase of earthquake insurance is also a wise alternative. When purchasing a property, you should certainly compute the costs of needed repairs of settlement damage in the final price you pay.

The separation between these buildings is caused by differential ground settlements in the poorly filled former swamp area of the Mission district of San Francisco.

Ground settlements have distorted the sidewalk and the building foundation of this San Francisco building, causing the cracking in the masonry walls. Cracks such as these significantly reduce the earthquake resistance of the building.

caution if you are shopping for a home. Steep hillside sites are obviously going to be largely graded and filled; and if the fill is poorly compacted or the grading is careless, these sites can be very risky. A moderate quake (even a heavy rain) may cause such a fill to slip, taking the house down the hill with it or severely damaging the foundation and structural supports of the building. There is also the danger of a poorly graded or supported cut above the house surging down upon the walls and roof.

Any *substantial* cracks in the foundation or in the driveway, sidewalks or patio of a building situated on a graded hillside or an apparently flat hilltop may be indicative of an inherent or man-made weakness in the site. If you notice such cracks around your home or suspect the existence of localized fills in your development, call upon a soils engineer to aid you in investigating the subdivision records and the nature of your soil foundation. If you are shopping for a hillside or hilltop home, look for evidence of geologic instability. And if you find such evidence, it is probably best simply to look elsewhere. It is very costly and therefore seldom worthwhile to try to shore up a weak and unstable soil foundation.

PROBLEMS OF BAYSIDE, RIVERSIDE AND WATER-COURSE SITES

The flat alluvial lands along the shores of San Francisco Bay, the Santa Ana and Sacramento river deltas, Puget Sound and numerous other such bayside and riverside sites present a special earthquake problem. These areas are largely composed of thick deposits of a soft, silty clay which is highly compressible and unstable and has a high water content—all poor characteristics for high-intensity earthquake regions. The ground motions of an earthquake are amplified by this soft, water-saturated soil, and can cause compaction of the clay and settlement of the ground surface. In addition, the high water content of such soils can induce liquefaction.

As we have noted, ground settlement can be as damaging to a building as fault displacement. All comprehensive engineering reports on residential areas along the

Scenes from the 1906 and 1989 San Francisco earthquakes on soft soils and fill south of Market Street. In 1906 the houses burned down. In the 1989 (lower) photographs every house is also leaning and is severely damaged.

San Francisco Bay are agreed that in large earthquakes, the intensities and the damage can be as high in the bayside developments as they are in the fault zone itself. Such developments as Redwood Shores, Bay Farm Island, Foster City and the marina homes and apartments in Berkeley and Alameda face much greater risks because they are largely on new landfill over bay mud. Some of these developments also face the risk of flooding after an earthquake, because the perimeter dikes that protect them from high tidal waters are highly susceptible to earthquake damage and collapse.

In theory, at least, these waterside developments were constructed with this high risk in mind. A soils-engineering report on Redwood Shores, for example, recommends the "provision of adequate clearances between elements of the structure [to allow for maximum horizontal movement during a quake] and the proper connections of structural elements" in order to minimize the extent of earthquake damage. Although the advice in the report was sound, the building codes do not require such special provisions, and it is therefore solely up to the developer to see that the recommendations are followed. Too often, the economics of construction dictate that such additional precautions be disregarded.

Before you buy a home or apartment in these or similar developments, you would be negligent of your own interests if you did not ask for a full report from the developer on the precautions his firm has taken

Houses along waterways, particularly when on filled land, face higher risks in an earthquake. The foundations of one such house in Foster City, south of San Fran- *cisco (lower photograph), settled from the 1989 earthquake and had to be replaced. The photograph was taken during repairs, seven months after the earthquake.*

During the 1906 earthquake, the ground along numerous rivers in Northern California lurched dramatically toward the river channels, destroying or severely damaging any structures in the vicinity. This example of a riverside ground failure was photographed along the Salinas River near the village of *Spreckels, more than 100 miles from the epicenter of the quake and 20 miles from the San Andreas. The riverside settlements along the Russian River, 140 miles to the north, were particularly hard hit. It is imperative to consult a soils (foundations) engineer before building or purchasing a home in such areas.*

to protect the buildings from severe earthquake damage and flooding. If necessary, have an experienced engineer review any written reports on earthquake risk. If you are building in these areas, see that the principles of structural earthquake resistance outlined in Part Three of this book are fully incorporated into the plans for your home. The moderate additional construction costs are very likely to prevent serious damage to your home in an earthquake, and the supplemental reinforcement will always result in a better, stronger, more durable structure. Earthquake insurance is recommended as well in these areas.

Riverside and old water-course sites face essentially the same problems as bay lands. Buildings located near or along present and former rivers, creeks, marshes, etc. usually entail a much higher than average earthquake risk. The strongest shaking in the destructive Long Beach earthquake in 1933 occurred in the vicinity of the coast adjacent to the mouth of the Santa Ana River. An earthquake near Puget Sound in 1965 caused considerable damage to buildings in the low-lying and filled areas along the Duwamish River in the Seattle area. The residential and commercial developments of Harbor Island, at the mouth of the Duwamish River, were also hard hit. Much, if not all, of this island was man-made, perhaps 90 or more years ago, and the soil is not seismically stable by any standards.

The 1906 shock in San Francisco caused some spectacular land failures along several filled creekbeds within the city. During that same quake, much of the ground along the Salinas River in Monterey County lurched and settled severely, completely destroying the small structures located in the area of failure. Numerous buildings along the Russian River, north of San Francisco, suffered similar fates.

Buildings located on old river beds, estuaries and other former water courses are among the worst locations for construction in earthquake country. These soils are usually very unstable, with numerous weak seams and channels. In addition, the landfill that usually accompanies development of such areas can intensify the instability of

these lands. Numerous buildings in San Francisco that were located over and along old creek channels and swamp areas were destroyed or severely damaged by large ground settlements during the 1906 quake. Many were also damaged in the Mission district of San Francisco in the 1989 quake. Another most instructive example of such a localized failure occurred in eastern Turkey in a magnitude 7 earthquake in 1966. A regional school campus had been built across a former river channel there. The majority of buildings actually on the old channel completely collapsed because of the amplified earthquake motions in the soft, unstable soil, whereas similarly constructed buildings on a higher gravel bench above the old river channel survived with only slight or no damage.

PROBLEMS ALONG CLIFFS AND RIDGES

Ocean cliffs in the vicinity of large faults, such as the San Andreas in Northern California, the Santa Ynez near Santa Barbara or the Newport-Inglewood fault zone in the Los Angeles area, present special risks during earthquakes. Because the cliffs are unsupported by ground and rock on one side, they experience more earthquake motion than the ground some distance from the cliff. In addition, as the shock waves emerge from the ground, they are reflected back from the cliff face and cause further amplification of the vibrations. The Westlake Palisades section of Daly City suffered the highest damage of any area during the relatively minor San Francisco earthquake in March 1957. Earthquake experts relate the greater damage in this residential area to the sea cliff that bounds the development on the west. The earthquake waves, rising almost vertically from the nearby San Andreas fault, were reflected and intensified by the steep cliff, resulting in the concentration of damage in that area. The same effect was observed in Aptos just south of Santa Cruz, in the 1989 Loma Prieta shock. In general, houses along the cliffs suffered significantly more damage than their neighbors further in from the beach. Structures along such cliffs should

The heaviest building damage and the highest earthquake intensities were recorded along the ocean cliffs of Daly City during the 1957 San Francisco quake. The cliffs reflected and magnified the shock waves emerging from the San Andreas.

The hazards of various geological foundations

Houses on top of ridges (upper two photographs) appear to experience much stronger shaking due to very localized amplification of the ground motion. On the lower left is one of the several modern houses that suffered damage (cripple stud collapse) in the 1984 Morgan Hill earthquake on a ridge overlooking the ruptured Calaveras fault south of San Jose. These were the only houses that suffered severe damage. One of the highest ground motion accelerations ever recorded (1.3g) was taken nearby. The lower right photograph shows the Madigan Ranch house, near Aptos, a few miles from the epicenter of the 1989 Loma Prieta earthquake. This house, also situated on a ridge, experienced much stronger ground motion than its neighbors on flatter ground, due to its unique location. Its cripple stud lower floor walls collapsed.

be designed for the highest earthquake forces and should be fully insured, particularly if the cliffs are near a major fault zone.

Houses on ridges are also exposed to a higher risk. Much more damage to houses on the edge of cliffs or on ridges has been observed in strong earthquakes including 1971 in San Fernando, 1984 near Morgan Hill in Northern California, 1985 in Chile and the 1989 Loma Prieta. The energy of the earthquake waves appears to be trapped within the peak of the ridge, causing great amplification in a very local area—which leads to much larger forces on the buildings. Therefore, buildings on ridges need to be designed to the highest earthquake standards, comparable to buildings within fault zones, and should be fully insured.

The waterfront and business districts of Kodiak, Alaska were devastated by the tsunami that followed the huge Good Friday earthquake in 1964. Several 20-foot high waves struck the town, hurling the destructive debris of fishing boats, buildings and cars several blocks inland.

TSUNAMIS

Tsunamis, seismic sea waves, are caused by faulting or other abrupt ground movements on the ocean floor or shore during large earthquakes. In the open ocean, the waves are not much above normal height, but they move at very high velocities—sometimes reaching 400 miles per hour—and when they approach a shoreline, the slope can raise them to heights of as much as 50 feet. The most recent destructive *tsunami* to hit the Pacific coast of the United States was generated by the great Alaska earthquake of 1964. It reared more than 30 feet at its highest point and devastated many of the coastal settlements of Alaska—including Kodiak, Seward, Valdez, Whittier and Cordova—causing a large proportion of the deaths associated with the quake. It also damaged settlements along the coasts of Washington and Oregon and inundated a major portion of Crescent City, California, killing several people and causing much property damage. The damage resulted not only from the impact of the wave but from the debris—logs, sections of collapsed buildings, cars, fishing boats—carried by the water.

Tsunamis present a distinct hazard to the coast of Alaska and Hawaii and to the sea-level and beach communities of Washington, Oregon and California. Certainly, the hazard of *tsunamis* should be taken seriously by anyone considering the purchase of property along the Alaskan waterfronts; for the state's record of frequent major shocks makes it especially vulnerable to these destructive sea waves.

LANDSLIDE HAZARDS

Natural landslides and rockslides occur frequently throughout the western states. The reasons for the existence of landslide-prone areas are the hilly terrains, young and weak soil materials, poor geologic foundations and periodic heavy precipitation. The "landslide season" inevitably comes during the wet winter months when the rains saturate the ground, the water table rises dramatically, and the "lubricated" hillside slopes abruptly begin to slide freely along discontinuities in the rock or topsoil.

The landslide problem is particularly acute in the Los Angeles basin of Southern California, where thousands of large landslides have been mapped by the U.S. Geological Survey. This concentration is probably higher than in any other area comparable in size; but the San Francisco Bay Area and the Anchorage area follow closely, and the heavily populated areas of Utah are not far behind. During the winter of 1968-69, the nine counties of the Bay Area suffered a total of $25.4 million in

The hazards of various geological foundations

Thousands of homes throughout the Western states are built in known landslide areas on unstable soil. This house in Lafayette, California slid without the additional inertial forces of an earthquake. A soils engineer should be consulted whenever you buy property on hilly or steep terrain.

landslide damage unrelated to earthquakes.

Earthquakes dramatically increase the landslide potentials. Major shocks will trigger literally thousands of large and small landslides and rockslides throughout a stricken region. In the 1964 Alaska quake, extensive sections of the waterfront areas of Anchorage, Valdez and Seward were carried away and destroyed by the surging rock and mud. And in San Fernando, more than 1,000 landslides, ranging in size from 50 to 1,000 feet, were triggered by faulting and the quake's vibrations. The 1989 Loma Prieta earthquake also triggered numerous landslides—particularly in the mountainous Santa Cruz area and along the coast from Monterey to Bolinas, north of San Francisco. Many homes were severely damaged. Fortunately, both California shocks occurred when the soil was reasonably dry. During a wet winter, many of the residential hillsides that were visibly ruptured by the quakes would have become landslides, and many more moderately shaken and damaged homes would have been totally demolished.

The Turnagain Heights slide in Anchorage during the 1964 quake was the largest and most spectacularly destructive single landslide within a metropolitan area in re-

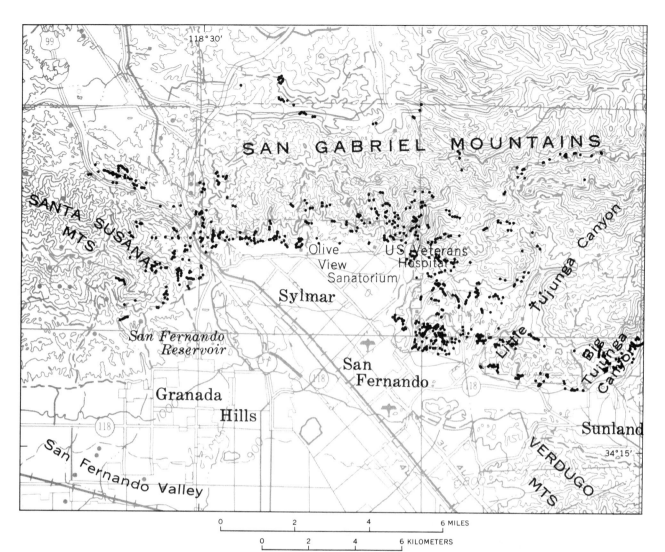

The darkened areas in this map of the San Fernando Valley represent the more than 1,000 landslides and rockslides generated by the 1971 earthquake in the still lightly developed San Gabriel Mountains. The slides, which varied in size from 50 feet to over 1,000 feet, were responsible for a large proportion of the building damage during the quake.

The number of slides was minimal for the size of the earthquake, because the shock occurred during a dry year. A similar earthquake along the heavily settled Newport-Inglewood, Whittier, Wasatch and Hayward faults during a rainy winter could result in a high death toll and millions of dollars of damage to property.

cent memory. During the tremor, a long bluff overlooking the sea broke into thousands of earthen blocks and flowed outward toward the water, sweeping away a land mass nearly two miles long and 800 to 1,200 feet wide. The end of the slide extended far out beyond the previous shoreline, and the head of the slide formed new bluffs as high as 50 feet. More than 70 buildings, among them the finest homes in the city, were carried some 500 to 600 feet by the slide, and all were destroyed. Another slide, which occurred in the middle of the business district along Fourth Avenue, dropped 11 feet almost vertically. All of the buildings in the area had to be removed, and most were complete losses. The city experienced several other smaller slides as well, causing tilting, broken foundations and other heavy structural damage.

The hazards of various geological foundations

The tremendous size and destructiveness of the Turnagain Heights landslide in Anchorage can be seen in these aerial and ground level views of the aftermath of the earthquake. Published studies before the earthquake had indicated that the area was highly susceptible to slide damage, particularly during earthquakes.

For our purposes, there are three interesting and important lessons in this dramatic and tragic ground failure in Alaska. First, the slide hazard in Anchorage was eminently predictable. The geology of the area had been investigated and recorded in great detail by the U.S. Geological Survey in 1959, and a published map indicated that landslides and slumps had occurred in the area in the past. Referring specifically to the Turnagain Heights area, the geologic report stated:

Shocks, such as those associated with earth-

quakes, will start moving material that under most conditions is stable. . . . Stronger shocks may be enough to exceed the shear strength of the dry material and cause it to move.

Had the city government been more conscientious and the home builders and buyers more alert, the destruction might not have occurred.

The second lesson is that much of the area that slid in 1964 is again developed. Expensive homes in the Turnagain area and large buildings downtown have been built right over the unstable terrain. The city's planners and politicians were unable to resist the redevelopment of the area. But the area that slid before will slide again—it is only a matter of time and another strong earthquake.

The third lesson is that the geologic and seismic conditions that resulted in the Anchorage slides are to be found along innumerable bluffs and hillside "view" locations in Washington, California, Utah and other areas of Alaska. As in Alaska, the forewarning maps and reports are readily available for most of these areas. And keep in mind that earthquakes only magnify the possibility of a landslide. In most cases, the danger is already there, and a heavy rain storm could bring the slide down.

Typical causes of localized landsliding

Landslides in hillside subdivisions are not always the result of naturally unstable slopes. Frequently, the slides will occur where a basically stable soil foundation has been disturbed by careless and poorly engineered grading or landfill. Home buyers and builders should consult the available geologic maps or a geologist or soils engineer to be sure that a hillside property has no past history of sliding and no apparent potential for failures. In addition, they should be aware of the characteristics of poor grading or fill and should investigate the stability of the slope above and below the house before committing themselves to the sale.

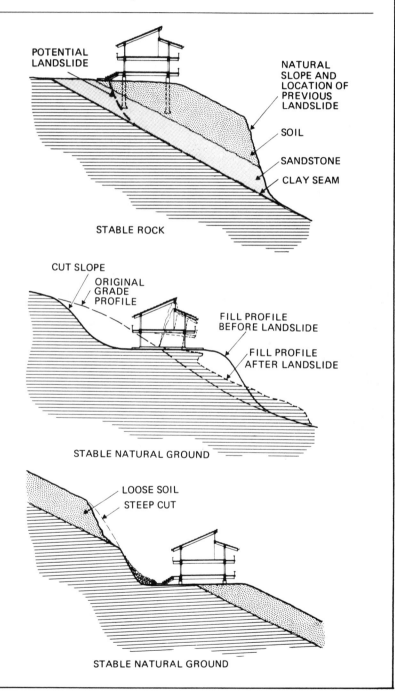

The building site here has the natural ingredients of a landslide area: (1) The gradual rise of the natural slope is abruptly broken by a steep incline—an indication that a slide probably occurred at that point in the past. (2) A thin seam of clay lies between the bedrock and the upper soil levels. Clay is very susceptible to sliding in such circumstances, especially when it becomes water-saturated and "lubricated" by heavy rainfall. Only a careful geologic investigation—usually with drill holes—will reveal these thin clay seams, but many potential slide areas have been recorded and marked on the maps of various agencies and in the files of consulting engineers.

Here, naturally stable ground has been disrupted by improperly graded or compacted landfill. New hillside developments are frequently stacked in a parallel series of cuts into the slope and landfills below the cuts to provide flat building sites. If the fill is not carefully engineered, it will be subject to settlement or sliding during an earthquake.

In this case, there is no problem of landfill. Instead, the cut slope above the house was graded too steeply, and the loose soil along the cut tumbled down during the motions of an earthquake. Such a slide occurs because the poorly graded cut exposes and removes the support from the inclined soil layers or from a weak clay seam.

POTENTIAL LANDSLIDE

NATURAL SLOPE AND LOCATION OF PREVIOUS LANDSLIDE

SOIL

SANDSTONE

CLAY SEAM

STABLE ROCK

CUT SLOPE

ORIGINAL GRADE PROFILE

FILL PROFILE BEFORE LANDSLIDE

FILL PROFILE AFTER LANDSLIDE

STABLE NATURAL GROUND

LOOSE SOIL

STEEP CUT

STABLE NATURAL GROUND

The hazards of various geological foundations

How to read and interpret landslide maps

Anyone owning or purchasing property in known landslide-prone areas, in canyons, on slopes that are not obviously rocky, and on coastal or riverside cliffs or slopes should consult a landslide map to determine the stability of the site. Numerous maps of past landslides and landslide-prone areas are available to the public for a very minimal charge. Appendix B includes a list of the agencies which publish them. The maps can also be examined at many libraries and government offices. The two maps here are typical of those available.

Below left is a detail from Map MF-360, Landslide Susceptibility in San Mateo County, California *(U.S. Geological Survey, 1972). The entire county is zoned for landslide risk. Zone I represents minimal risk; zone IV a serious landslide potential. The "L" notations on the map indicate areas either actively sliding or with a past history of sliding. Note that some of the "L" areas are heavily settled. Maps on a scale such as this are intended primarily for planning subdivision-sized blocks of land in undeveloped areas. The slide locations are indicated approximately, and numerous small slides are not included. Therefore, this type of map is not particularly useful for the siting of single buildings. Still, the maps may be helpful to an individual property owner*

in obtaining a general understanding of the landslide hazard for an area. And if your property or a property you wish to purchase is located within the higher zones—grade III or IV—on the map, it would be essential for you to seek the services of a geologist or soils engineer in investigating the site. The fees of these professionals are minor compared to the total cost of purchasing and developing the property—or salvaging it after a slide.

Below right is a detail from Landslide Susceptibility in San Clemente, California *(California Division of Mines and Geology, 1968). This map of a portion of the San Clemente area is much more detailed and may be used by an individual property owner with* ▶

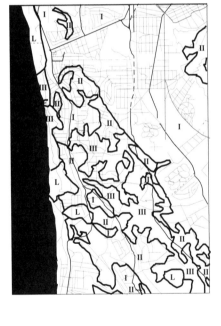

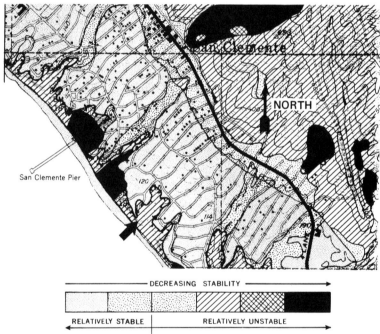

DECREASING STABILITY

RELATIVELY STABLE | RELATIVELY UNSTABLE

greater confidence. A distant but large earthquake along the Newport-Inglewood fault north of San Clemente could easily trigger some of the unstable areas. Many city and county offices have these detailed maps of all landslides which have been recorded and/or have damaged property in the past. Since slide damage is easily and frequently bulldozed and rebuilt by developers, you should always consult a detailed landslide map when purchasing property which shows signs of instability or which is located in the kind of terrain susceptible to sliding.

Even a detailed map such as this is not likely to show the localized pockets of landslide hazard created by faulty landfill and grading. Only the very large landfill subdivisions are generally noted on landslide-susceptibility maps.

The photograph at top shows a view of one of the residential areas plotted on the San Clemente map (see the arrow near the coast). The slope-stability rating for this area was "moderately unstable." Note the house under construction and the old slide debris at the base of the cliff. The picture below it shows the same area after a landslide has damaged several of the expensive homes. In comparing the two photographs, you should note that the first was taken from ground level, well below the houses, whereas the other was taken from above the damaged houses.

The hazards of various geological foundations

The 1989 Loma Prieta earthquake caused failures of sea cliffs from Pacifica, 50 miles north of the quake's epicenter, to Monterey, 30 miles south. The earthquake further undermined the previously exposed and endangered foundations of this apartment building in Capitola, near Santa Cruz. Six units overhanging the cliff had to be removed.

The causes of landslides may be grouped into two general categories: natural geologic deficiencies, and man-made problems. Natural geologic flaws are usually responsible for the large slides, whereas the smaller, localized slides that affect a single or a small cluster of buildings tend to be the result of man-made problems. The danger from earthquakes is equal for both categories.

The most common natural condition for landsliding is a hillside, hilltop or bluff in which the geologic foundation of rock or stable soil is layered by thin clay seams—sometimes so thin as to be virtually indetectable—that give way when they become water-saturated or the lateral forces of an earthquake break the very weak frictional bond holding the clay. The *flow slide* is another common form of natural landsliding, generally occurring in association with earthquakes. Flow slides are triggered by liquefaction under sloping ground. The liquefied soil simply flows away from its base in a muddy morass. The massive landslides in Anchorage were primarily of this type. On a much smaller scale, the slumps that occurred along the shore of Lake Merced in San Francisco during the minor 1957 shock were flow slides.

Man-made slides occur on naturally stable slopes that have been disturbed by poorly engineered grading and landfill for homesites. Typically, a stable slope is cut and filled for a flat lot without the provision of support for the inclined soil layers at the uphill face of the cut. A great deal of rain and/or a moderate earthquake can loosen the freshly exposed inclined soil layers and send them sliding down upon the building below. Similar failures can occur with downhill fills that are graded improperly. With the latter, water saturation or a moderate shock may cause the uncompacted landfill to slide, or the fill may overload the natural soil foundation at the bottom of the cut-slope, causing a failure of the whole hillside.

Many other factors are involved in the incidence of both natural and earthquake-caused landslides: the slope angle of the ground surface, the nature of the bedrock,

How to identify signs of landsliding

Cracks in the street above the house indicate the head of the slide. Note that the asphalt is cracked in parallel fissures and the gutter is fractured.

The weight of the sliding soil and house has buckled the sidewalk below the house.

Although it is not at all obvious to the eye, the house is leaning in the direction of the landslide. The tilt is visible only in the framing of doors and windows which open parallel to the slide. Here the door no longer fits well—a gap of about ½-inch can be seen on the right side in the downhill corner. If several doors, windows or cabinet doors show the same gap in the same direction, a homeowner should assume that the house is leaning and may be slowly sliding.

Typical cracks in the stucco of the same house. Such cracks tend to concentrate around openings (doors, windows, etc.) and in retaining walls.

the slope of the geologic layers, the existence of any surface or underground waterflows, the level of the water table, the type and amount of vegetation that exists or is planted or removed, the proximity of active faults, the amount of rainfall, etc. Some landslide problems are correctable at a reasonable expense, particularly those that are man-made and can be avoided in the first place by good engineering practices. If you are building a home on a bluff or steep slope in earthquake and landslide country, you should, of course, have professional help from a geologist or soils engineer in determining whether the site is basically stable. Then, a structural engineer experienced in the problems of landsliding can aid you and your contractor in designing and building a sound foundation for your structure without harming the basic stability of the natural geology.

If you wish to purchase or already own property on a site that suggests a landslide potential, you should, again, seek the assistance of local professionals in evaluating the site. Local geologists and soils engineers are likely to be familiar with the reliability and building techniques of the contractor who built the home in question. In addition, a professional evaluation is necessary because geologic conditions can vary drastically over surprisingly small distances, and it is therefore often impossible to determine slide hazards from available landslide maps.

Several types of landslide restraints are possible in certain circumstances, but generally the costs would be excessive for most individual property owners. Also, landslide control by modern engineering techniques becomes less and less feasible depending on the size of the potential slide area, the size and instability of any sliding that has already occurred, and the proximity of active faults. Finally, the success of a slide-stabilization program usually depends on constant surveillance and costly maintenance, and there can never be a full guarantee that sliding will not eventually occur anyway.

Thus, in all circumstances, the best advice to follow is that of a local professional. First, investigate an area thoroughly with the help of fault, landslide and other geologic maps and check for any surface signs of landslide potential. Then, if there is any suspicion of instability, especially in the hilly areas in the vicinity of active faults, call in a geologist or a soils engineer. At the same time, it would be wise to purchase adequate earthquake coverage. Keep in mind, also, that if a landslide potential does not exist or can be eliminated, your hillside property represents one of the best possible investments in earthquake country.

CHAPTER FOUR

The man-made hazards to your property—from dams to neighboring buildings

Lake Palmdale and smaller Una Lake are reservoirs created from the natural depressions, sag ponds and scarps of the San Andreas fault zone near Palmdale in the desert of Southern California. The fault can be seen to extend in a line from the dams through Leona Valley. Several smaller sag ponds lie in the distance along the trough of the fault. Sag ponds are formed when the fracturing and tilting of the ground from faulting brings underground water to the surface and then blocks the drainage channels. Since the sag ponds are generally enclosed on all sides, they provide ideal sites for reservoirs but unfortunate and possibly dangerous locations for the dams that create these reservoirs. Lake Temescal in the Oakland hills is another example of a reservoir formed by enlarging and damming a sag pond along a fault zone, in this case the Hayward fault.

CERTAIN STRUCTURES, SUCH AS DAMS, taller neighboring buildings and water tanks, can present a special earthquake hazard. For the purposes of this book, these hazards are categorized in the "geologic" section because they exist as a more or less permanent part of the landscape and generally the individual property owner can do little about them.

DAMS AND RESERVOIRS

Of all structures, dams and reservoirs present the greatest hazard to large, populated areas during an earthquake. The failure of a dam can ravage more buildings and claim far more lives than the shaking of the earthquake itself. Ironically, most major fault zones, such as the Hayward and San Andreas or the Newport-Inglewood and the San Jacinto, provide the narrow canyons and natural sag ponds that are ideal for reservoirs, so that numerous dams serving the cities of the West have been built along or directly over recent scars of earthquake faulting. In addition, heavily populated and highly seismic urban centers like the Los Angeles Basin and the San Francisco Bay Area also contain hundreds of smaller reservoirs within the city

This aerial photo of the Lower Van Norman Dam in San Fernando was taken one day after the earthquake had sheared the sloping concrete facing of the dam into the reservoir. Fortunately, the reservoir was only half full at the time. Even so, the slump of the earthen crest of the dam brought the water to within five feet of spilling. Some 80,000 people were threatened in the spill area of the dam and had to be evacuated. Dam failures such as this present one of the greatest earthquake hazards to property and life, and the purchase of a home in the flood zone of an earthen dam in earthquake country can be a very poor and very dangerous investment.

boundaries. The majority of these dams in the urban areas are old. Many were built well before the principles of earthquake engineering were developed. Since the early 1970's, the State of California has been reviewing the safety of many of these dams. A number have been strengthened and some dismantled.

Several dams have collapsed in past strong earthquakes. Certainly the most frightening earthquake-related dam failure in the recent past was the partial collapse of the Lower Van Norman Dam in the Mission Hills overlooking San Fernando Valley. The massive 142-foot-high earthen dam, constructed in 1915, had been perfunctorily reinforced for earthquake hazard several decades later. However, the intense 15-second San Fernando tremor broke away almost the entire upstream surface, knocking the concrete facing, soil and rock into the reservoir. Fortunately, at the time of the quake, the reservoir was only slightly more than half full, and the slump of the dam still left a slim five-foot margin of earth above the crest of the water. If the water level had been higher, or if the quake had lasted an additional five seconds, or if a large aftershock had struck before the res-

ervoir could be lowered to a safe level, a flood of water would have swept down the hills and through a 12-square-mile area with some 80,000 sleeping residents.

Other areas of California have not been so lucky. A similar failure of the earthen Sheffield Dam during the Santa Barbara earthquake of 1925 resulted in the flooding of the lower area of that city. A breach in the wall of the small Baldwin Hills Reservoir in December of 1963, following several years of creep along the Newport-Inglewood fault zone in Los Angeles, claimed five lives and caused approximately $15 million in property damage. Only the diligence of the reservoir's caretaker and the quick evacuation of the residential area below the reservoir prevented a much greater death toll. The Baldwin Hills reservoir was a modern structure, constructed in 1951 when the dangers of faulting were well-understood. Yet it was built over the very fault zone responsible for the destructive and carefully investigated Long Beach earthquake.

Even a carefully reinforced dam that is well-removed from a fault can present an earthquake hazard to nearby residents. A sudden earthquake-induced landslide into a

Creep along a branch of the Newport-Inglewood fault through Los Angeles caused the failure of the 10-year-old Baldwin Hills Reservoir in 1963. The slow faulting under the dam slightly ruptured the concrete lining, and the water then eroded a wider channel which caused the collapse of a large section of the dam. Several houses in the spill area outlined in the photograph were washed away by the flood, and many others were severely damaged.

SPILL AREA

The houses on the right side of Cloverdale Avenue in the Baldwin Hills area of Los Angeles were completely washed away by the flood from the creep-damaged Baldwin Hills Dam. The remnants of foundations and a swimming pool can be seen in the foreground. Some $15 million in property loss and damage resulted from the decision to build a dam directly over a fault trace.

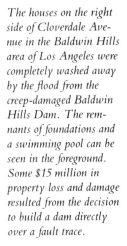

reservoir, for example, can damage the dam or turn the spill over the dam into a destructive flood. Similarly, the sloshing of the contained water can generate waves in a reservoir that overflow the dam. Such waves, called *seiches,* topped the Hebgen Dam near West Yellowstone, Montana during the earthquake there in 1959. This is how the foreman of the dam described the waves:

> . . . *I walked over to the edge of the dam and all we could see was blackness. There was no water. No water above the dam at all. . . and I couldn't imagine what had become of it. By that time the dust had started to clear, and the moon had come out a little. And then here came the water. It had all been up at the other end of the lake. . . . We could hear it before we could see it. When it came over the dam, it was a wall of water about three to four feet high completely across that dam, and it flowed like that for what seemed to be 20 minutes.*

Three distinct waves overflowed the full length of the 720-foot dam and surged down into the unpopulated valley below.

What can you do about the dam hazard in earthquake country? Since many dams, particularly in California, have been

The man-made hazards to your property

strengthened, you should first establish whether the dam has been reinforced recently for earthquake loads. If it has been reinforced, or if it is a new dam meeting recent California standards, the structure is probably safe. Still there is some risk and earthquakes always teach us new lessons. If the dam is old, built pre-1972, and has not been evaluated and/or strengthened, you may be facing a very serious threat. I would never purchase property in the potential inundation area of such a dam.

DIKES AND LEVEES

Typically, dikes and levees are built over and surround some of the worst possible geologic terrain for construction in earthquake country. The previous chapter noted that the water-saturated alluvial or sandy soils along rivers and estuaries, the land-filled areas over the mud of bays and marshlands, and the water-saturated sand dunes along the seashore are subject to especially intense vibrations and to the ground effects of settlement, landsliding and liquefaction during an earthquake. Any of these effects may destroy a dike or levee, so that any buildings which remain standing after the quake may be subjected to the additional damage of flooding.

Until the 1960s, little regulation or engineering analysis went into privately financed dikes and levees. Therefore, anyone living in marina developments or other low-lying waterside sites protected by such structures should find out about their engineering and earthquake resistance. A talk

with the project engineer and with a local civil engineer or the city engineering department may reassure you that all possible measures have been taken to protect the dike or levee from earthquake damage. Even so, both earthquake and flood insurance are a must for a property owner in this type of development.

WATER TANKS

Three types of water tanks present earthquake hazards to residential property: the ground-level tank, the elevated tank, and the rooftop water tanks commonly found on old commercial buildings and old, usually rural homes. The large, ground-level storage tanks of wood or concrete are probably the most hazardous of the three because they may hold a large amount of water and because they are frequently located on hilltops surrounded by residential buildings. Although the quantity of water may not be sufficient to destroy housing, the rapid flow of the water and collected debris can certainly erode the foundations of a home, flood a basement, and cause other substantial property damage. The purchase of property below such a structure is not recommended; for these tanks, and particularly the older ones, are highly subject to earthquake damage. If you already own such a property, be certain to carry adequate insurance for water damage.

Old elevated tanks (as well as new ones) also have a very poor history of survival during earthquakes, since those built before the 1950s are seldom braced properly.

The older, elevated water tanks are seldom reinforced properly for an earthquake. This 100,000-gallon, 100-foot steel tank fell during the Kern County quake in 1952. Similar tanks have collapsed in several other more recent earthquakes.

Residential buildings are usually not located near enough to these old towers to be threatened by their collapse, but if your present home or business is the exception, you should have a structural engineer check the tank and correct any existing problems.

Rooftop water tanks are an earthquake hazard because their position at the highest point of a building subjects them to greater vibrational accelerations than any other part of the structure. And since these tanks are often old, corroded and improperly de-signed for resisting tremors, it is not at all surprising that they frequently collapse during even moderate earthquakes. The rooftop tanks present an additional hazard (and the risk of expensive litigation) if they are also located too near the edge of a roof, so that they fall upon other buildings (or upon people) during a quake. Rooftop water tanks should be inspected for corrosion, properly attached (anchored) to the structure below, and carefully braced to prevent collapse during a shock.

An elevated tank, built a few months before the October 17, 1989 Loma Prieta earthquake, collapsed on the new adjacent industrial building in Hollister, California. The tank fell on the production line equipment inside, which was imported from Denmark, and caused a prolonged business interruption.

The failure was due to a few undersized washers underneath the bolt-heads holding the tank down. A knowledgeable engineer could have spotted the problem before the earthquake, and for a few hundred dollars, could have eliminated the damage and large financial loss.

Thin walled stainless steel tanks are extremely vulnerable to earthquakes, as shown by this damage in New Zealand in the 1987 earthquake. All tanks that were more than half full collapsed. Unfortunately, most of California's premium wines are, at some point, stored in just such weak tanks. A strong earthquake in the Napa Valley, for example, will cause extensive damage to the mostly unprepared wineries.

The man-made hazards to your property

The pounding to these commercial buildings in Oakland after the 1989 Loma Prieta earthquake can be seen in the extensive damage to the facing and windows all along the adjoining walls of the two buildings. Pounding damage occurs because adjoining buildings respond with different movement to the earthquake. The same type of damage can be seen in the lower photo from Santa Cruz after the October 17, 1989 earthquake. The pounding from the lower building severely damaged the adjacent taller building and nearly collapsed it.

SEMI-ATTACHED OR TALLER NEIGHBORING BUILDINGS

Two semi-attached or adjacent buildings with no gaps or only a small gap between their adjoining walls can seriously damage one another during an earthquake. Because the two buildings are structurally independent, they respond to the vibration in two different ways and therefore pound against each other. This pounding can be especially severe at the roof level of the lower of two adjacent buildings.

In addition, a low building next to a taller building is threatened with damage from debris falling from its neighbor. This is particularly true in the larger cities, where a one- or two-story home may be separated by only a few feet from a much taller apartment or commercial building. If the taller building has unreinforced brick or concrete-block walls or veneer, precarious architectural features (such as chimneys, parapets or Spanish tile roofing), the lower building may be very seriously endangered. The worst problem occurs when the shorter building is next to a taller unreinforced masonry building. Components of the brick building often collapse on the adjacent structure, causing severe damage and often going right through the roof. All of the deaths in the town of Santa Cruz on October 17, 1989 were caused by this problem.

A possible solution is illustrated in the photograph on page 80, which was taken shortly after the 1952 Bakersfield aftershock. The engineer who designed the new bank building had the foresight to include in his plans a strong cantilevered wall which very likely prevented a collapse of the fragile, unreinforced masonry parapets of the old neighboring building onto the roof of the bank.

If you have a building adjacent to a taller structure, your best recourse is first to consult an engineer to study the problem, determine if there is danger, and advise you on how you could correct or remove the problem. Alternatively, you should get earthquake insurance and then check with the city engineer's office to see if the dangerous projections or rooftop structures of

A joint of neoprene, stucco, or some other readily crushable material, provides a crumple-section joint which will protect closely adjacent buildings from serious pounding damage. The crumple section must allow some lateral movement of the buildings—about six to eight inches—and must extend to the foundations in order to be effective.

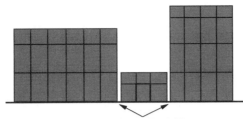

EXPANSION JOINT OR "CRUMPLE SECTION"

An inadequate separation between these two adjacent buildings in Mexico City probably led to the collapse of the taller one in the September 1985 earthquake. Note that the collapse occurred at the roof of the lower building where the maximum impacts were concentrated. Many buildings, including at least one 10-story building in San Francisco experienced similar damage, but did not collapse in the 1989 earthquake.

At left, the collapse of an unreinforced and poorly connected brick wall caused this interior damage to a lower adjoining building in Bakersfield in 1952. A woman in this shop was killed by the falling debris. The same problem occurred in Santa Cruz on October 17, 1989. All of the deaths in the town were due to the collapse of taller brick building parts on adjacent lower buildings (above). Note that the parapet on the adjacent taller building has collapsed.

One possible protective measure against the collapse of the masonry wall or parapet of a taller adjacent building is the construction of a new cantilevered wall—as in this Bank of America building in Bakersfield. The protective wall probably saved the bank from the type of destruction that killed a woman in the dress shop across the street.

your tall neighbor meet current local building safety requirements. If your city codes do not deal with this problem, you are faced with the task of convincing your neighbor that both buildings will benefit from the removal of such hazards and the strengthening of unreinforced masonry or masonry-veneer walls.

Row houses are not subject to this type of damage if they are connected to each other because they move as a unit during a quake. Unattached row houses also are not usually vulnerable, particularly if they have plywood bracing in their ground floor (see Chapter Six for plywood bracing details). An exception are corner houses because they lack support on one side and are, therefore, free to deform and twist. Practically all of the collapsed buildings in the Marina district of San Francisco after the 1989 earthquake were corner buildings. Typically, additional plywood shear-wall reinforcement is needed for older buildings, as discussed further in Chapters Six and Seven. Earthquake insurance is recommended for corner row-house properties, and for the second house from the corner if the roof levels are different heights.

Practically all of the spectacular collapses in the Marina district of San Francisco from the 1989 earthquake were corner buildings which were structurally weak. This was a four-story building. Its neighbors did not collapse.

PART THREE

The structural and architectural hazards of earthquakes— how to correct or avoid them

CHAPTER FIVE

The principles of earthquake resistance in buildings

TWO RECENT EARTHQUAKES—THE strong Soviet Armenia shock in December 1988, and the somewhat larger Loma Prieta quake of October 1989—demonstrated anew that the most practical approach to problems of public safety and the prevention of serious damage during tremors is the earthquake-resistant design and reinforcement of buildings. The Northern California earthquake (magnitude 7.1) resulted in scattered, severe destruction and the death of 62 people, mainly in the collapse of old, unreinforced masonry and concrete frame structures. The magnitude 6.9 shock in Soviet Armenia killed more than 50,000 people and destroyed two towns. The better performance of the buildings in the San Francisco area can be attributed primarily to the more advanced state of earthquake engineering and the public recognition that the risk exists and needs to be controlled.

Knowledge about the effects of earthquakes on buildings has steadily advanced during the years since the Long Beach quake in 1933, and the basic principles of earthquake-resistant design and construction have been well-established since the 1950s. Inevitably, the chief constraint on the incorporation of these principles to an adequate level in new buildings is cost.

Until all building owners and builders and government agencies realize that a very moderate increase in the construction costs of a building will provide a substantially sturdier and more quake-resistant structure, earthquakes will continue to claim lives and to inflict unnecessarily severe and expensive damage to property.

Similarly, a modest outlay of money and effort for structural reinforcement can render most older buildings, and particularly wood-frame structures, far safer both for their occupants and for the investment of their owners.

THE EFFECTS OF EARTHQUAKE FORCES ON A BUILDING

The structural elements of any building are designed chiefly to distribute and then to carry the weight of the building and its furnishings and occupants to the supporting foundation and into the ground. This basic structural system involves some distribution of a building's weight along horizontal planes (beams, roof and flooring, for example), but, obviously, the heaviest load supported by the structure will be along the vertical supports (walls and columns) leading to the foundation. As we have learned, earthquake ground motions generate chaotically irregular horizontal and vertical vibrational forces in the structure. The sudden ground motions push and pull upon a building's foundation, which causes the walls of the building to expand and compress (responding to the vertical shock waves) and to bend and sway from side to side (from the lateral waves). The structure resists these abrupt movements rising from its foundation, and the resistance creates a natural inertia which sharply snaps the building back and forth, up and down. The experience of lateral inertia in a building is precisely the same as the physical response of a person in an abruptly braking and accelerating car, while vertical inertia is comparable to one's sensation in a rapidly rising or descending elevator.

Because buildings are, by their very nature, designed for large vertical loads, the vertical forces of an earthquake are generally resisted effectively by routinely designed and constructed buildings. The horizontal earthquake forces, however, can easily exceed the lateral strength of a conventionally built structure, and these lateral vibrations usually result in damage to the elements of the building and foundation, and the collapse of part or all of a building.

In earthquake country, special techniques of reinforcement—of *lateral bracing* and extraordinarily durable *connections* between all of the structural components— are necessary to enable a building to absorb and distribute the lateral forces of a tremor without severe damage or collapse. In addition, four other factors—the *foundation*, the *building materials*, the *structural and architectural design* and *detailing*, and the *workmanship*—are important to the overall earthquake resistance of a building.

LATERAL BRACING

The most efficient and reliable means of ensuring that the inertial loads generated by an earthquake will be resisted and carried from one component of a building to another and then back to the foundation and the ground is a special system of lateral bracing. Such bracing includes strengthening the connections between the horizontal and vertical components of a structure. That is, lateral bracing has very little to do

The new plywood-sided, and therefore shear-wall braced, home at top survived the San Fernando quake without harm, while a house in the same area (above) suffered very severe damage because of inadequate bracing in the garage walls and along the crawl space beneath the single-story portion of the building. Special lateral bracing is essential for all buildings in earthquake country.

The principles of earthquake resistance

with the actual load strength of a building's walls and columns for normal loads. Rather, it provides the control which allows these vertical supports to remain stable and intact during the onslaught of the lateral vibrational motions of the quake. The walls are then able to support and transfer the additional inertial weight of the building into the foundation. Besides preventing the collapse of a building, lateral bracing also limits the damage because it reduces the building's internal motion.

Lateral bracing for earthquake resistance may follow three basic patterns: *frame-action, shear-wall* and *diagonal*. Frame-action bracing, used most often in large buildings, comprises a series of connected frames of steel or steel-reinforced concrete which resist the lateral earthquake forces by flexing. I do not recommend pure reinforced concrete frames. The bending action in the columns and beams of the frame ab-

sorbs the energy of the earthquake waves. Frame-action bracing is generally very effective in tall buildings. It has only one disadvantage: If the frame is too flexible, the bending action during a quake will cause large lateral deformations in the building leading to shattered or distorted exterior veneers, broken windows and plaster or wallboard, falling ceilings, toppling furnishings and pounding with adjacent buildings.

Shear-wall bracing entails the use of solid, continuous walls of plywood or concrete to tie together, stiffen and strengthen the vertical frame of a building, or to serve as the actual main bearing walls of the structure. This type of bracing adds great strength to the frame. Because the shear-wall bracing is relatively stiff and unbending, it also limits the lateral deformations of the building and thus further reduces the probability of architectural or interior damage.

The basic structural components of any building

♦ The *distributing structural elements* are those that lie in a horizontal plane. These *diaphragms* (roof and floors) and *joists* (beams and trusses) tie the walls together and disperse the static weight of furnishings, occupants and the elements themselves to the walls and foundation.

♦ The *resisting* structural elements are the vertical components of a building (walls, columns, and bracing). These elements support and transfer the load of the distributing elements to the foundation.

♦ The *foundation* supports and ties together the walls and transfers the weight of the building to the ground.

♦ The *connections* (nailing, blocking, joints, etc.) tie all of these components together.

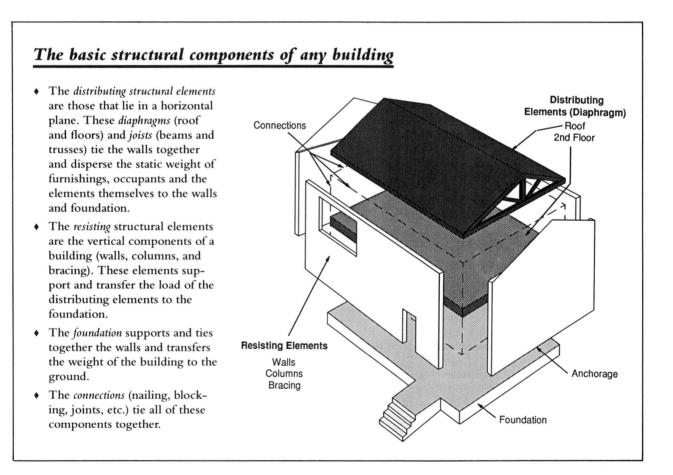

How a building responds to ground shaking

During an earthquake, the ground waves cause lateral and vertical ground movements, or vibrations, which are transferred to a building through its foundation. The vertical earthquake movements cause the walls of the building to expand and compress. This movement is usually not damaging, since buildings are, by their nature, designed to withstand large vertical loads. The lateral earthquake waves, however, are very destructive, since they cause the walls to bend and sway to the point of shattering the wall materials or breaking the connections between the walls and the other components of the building. Both building movements—the swaying and the expansion/compression—are the result of the physical principle of *inertial force,* which causes a naturally stable structure to snap back into its original position when it is deflected by the ground movement. In a typical fifteen second earthquake, a short building may snap between 15 and 75 times (or more), depending on its structural characteristics.

The effect of lateral earthquake movement on a building is clearly shown in this drawing of a three-story structure. The movement emerges from the ground and travels through the foundation to the walls—in effect, one floor at a time. When the waves have reached the roof, they return to the foundation and ground in the same way. All this occurs in a fraction of a second. Of course, the earthquake does not wait for a complete foundation-to-roof-to-foundation cycle to be completed before another ground movement strikes in the opposite direction. Thus, the actual behavior of a building during the several seconds of a strong, nearby earthquake is usually extremely erratic (except for tall buildings).

The earthquake waves inevitably focus on any weak connections or structural members, and once the structural components and connections of a building begin to fail, the behavior of the building changes drastically. It is subjected to a chaotic mixture of new stresses and loads for which it is not designed, and the damage compounds until the building fails.

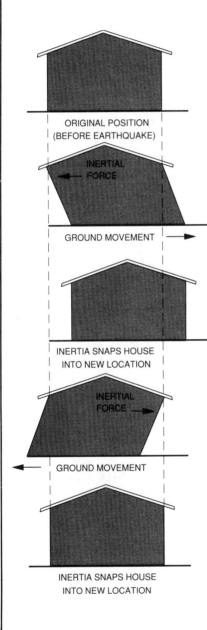

ORIGINAL POSITION (BEFORE EARTHQUAKE)

INERTIAL FORCE

GROUND MOVEMENT

INERTIA SNAPS HOUSE INTO NEW LOCATION

INERTIAL FORCE

GROUND MOVEMENT

INERTIA SNAPS HOUSE INTO NEW LOCATION

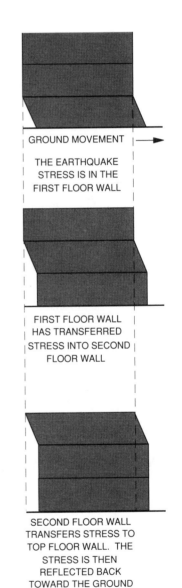

GROUND MOVEMENT

THE EARTHQUAKE STRESS IS IN THE FIRST FLOOR WALL

FIRST FLOOR WALL HAS TRANSFERRED STRESS INTO SECOND FLOOR WALL

SECOND FLOOR WALL TRANSFERS STRESS TO TOP FLOOR WALL. THE STRESS IS THEN REFLECTED BACK TOWARD THE GROUND

Special earthquake bracing

Because of the severe lateral stresses to the walls and columns of a building during an earthquake, a special lateral bracing system is essential. The primary function of the bracing is to assist the frame and other vertical supports, so that their deflection under the force of the lateral earthquake waves will stop short of failing the building. The bracing may also provide an easier, more direct route for the transfer of the earthquake forces to the foundation.

The frame-action bracing of steel or reinforced concrete is common in large buildings. Of the three types of bracing, it allows the most flexibility and movement, which can be a disadvantage—particularly to the occupants and furnishings of the swaying building. Shear-wall bracing is a solid, continuous wall of plywood (over a wood-frame) or reinforced concrete wall attached to the framing of the building. When this type of bracing is added as a supportive wall for the frame, it adds great strength to the vertical super-structure. Most important, shear-wall bracing is very stiff and unbending—thereby reducing the lateral deformations of the walls. This technique of bracing also provides a solid surface for the easy transfer of the earthquake forces back to the foundation.

The use of diagonal bracing is another common bracing technique. Typically, a steel member is attached at an angle across the frame. Very often, two braces are attached in this way to form an x-brace. Both the diagonal and the x-bracing stiffen the framing of the building against deformations and provide a more direct path for the transfer of the earthquake forces to the foundation. Note that wood diagonal bracing for houses is not recommended.

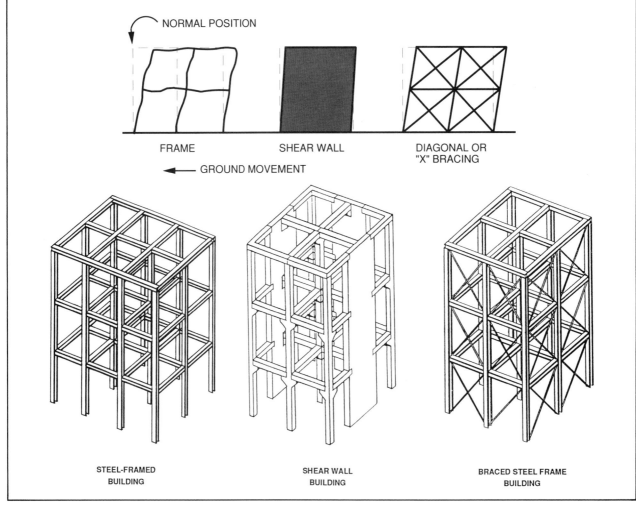

NORMAL POSITION

FRAME   SHEAR WALL   DIAGONAL OR "X" BRACING

◄— GROUND MOVEMENT

STEEL-FRAMED BUILDING   SHEAR WALL BUILDING   BRACED STEEL FRAME BUILDING

Wood-frame buildings can be made especially earthquake resistant by the addition of solid plywood sheathing to brace, tie together and greatly strengthen the stud walls. The shear-wall bracing of large buildings is generally made of steel-reinforced concrete walls.

Diagonal bracing is the type most commonly used in steel framed buildings. It entails braces of steel which are attached typically at some angle across the frame of a building. A single diagonal or two crossed diagonals (called *x-bracing*) or other patterns may be used.

Like the other lateral bracing systems, diagonal bracing stiffens the supporting frame of a structure against damaging deformations during a tremor. This type of bracing also increases the earthquake resistance of a building by providing a more direct, diagonal path for the transfer of the inertial weight of the structure to the foundation.

THE FOUNDATION

Because earthquake movements are transmitted from the ground through the foundation of a building and then into the superstructure, a weak or poorly connected or poorly located foundation may fail even before the shaking reaches the rest of the building. When this occurs, the damage is usually very severe and difficult and expensive to repair. Thus, a strong, well-designed and connected foundation is essential in earthquake country.

THE BUILDING MATERIALS

As noted earlier in this book, certain building materials perform better than others under the duress of earthquake motion. Generally, wood and steel are preferred in earthquake country (1) because these materials are relatively light, which lessens the inertial weight that the walls must support; (2) because the materials are tremendously flexible and can deflect without cracking or breaking. (Of course, too much flexibility can also be a disadvantage, which is one reason that special lateral bracing is required.)

New concrete, concrete-block and other masonry buildings can also be made safe, providing that special reinforcement procedures are carefully followed. Similarly, stucco over wood frame without plywood sheathing requires special reinforcement details to prevent earthquake damage.

THE STRUCTURAL AND ARCHITECTURAL DESIGN AND DETAILING

Engineers go to a great deal of trouble to design a building and to specify detailing which will increase the endurance of a building. It is very important that these details or design recommendations be fulfilled exactly as planned. Esthetic rejection or careless or "penny-wise" execution of these important features is likely to result in expensive and life-threatening damage.

THE WORKMANSHIP

Closely related to the detailing of a building's design and construction is the quality of the construction. Sloppy and careless workmanship leads to weakened buildings; numerous collapses or other severe cases of earthquake damage can be blamed on the poor quality of the work. For example, if a contractor places reinforcing steel in the cavities of a concrete-block wall but neglects to fill the cores of the blocks with concrete to form shear-wall bracing, then his negligence may lead to the collapse of the wall during an earthquake. Anyone building or reinforcing a home must be aware of and attentive to the workmanship.

The preceding, then, are the fundamental and closely related factors that govern the amount of damage which a given structure will or will not experience. A building is earthquake-resistant only when all of the structural components are properly tied together with good connections, when the bracing system is adequate for the type of structure and the seismic conditions, and when all of the features of the design and engineering of a building are properly executed. The following chapters explore all of these factors in detail.

CHAPTER SIX

The best and the worst: types of construction and earthquake resistance

THE BASIC STRUCTURAL MATERIALS OF a building—wood, steel, brick, concrete block, concrete, and the numerous combinations of these materials—are, with the lateral bracing system and other reinforcement measures, the most significant factor in the resistance of the structure to earthquake damage. The same types of buildings that failed in 1906 in San Francisco also failed in 1933 in Long Beach, in 1952 in Bakersfield, in 1964 in Alaska, in 1971 in San Fernando, in 1983 in Coalinga, in 1985 in Mexico City, in 1987 in Whittier, in 1988 in Soviet Armenia, and in 1989 in the San Francisco Bay Area. The same types of buildings will continue to fail until builders and property owners pay adequate heed to history and the principles of physics and earthquake engineering.

WOOD-FRAME BUILDINGS

A carefully designed and constructed modern wood-frame building is the most desirable small-property investment in earthquake country. As noted in the previous chapter, the high earthquake resistance of wood buildings is primarily the result of the lightness and flexibility of the material. The lightness means that the inertial load resulting from the building's resistance to the ground movements will be relatively small; the flexibility enables the supporting components of the building— the walls and columns—to deflect during the ground motion without cracking, breaking or becoming disconnected. Similarly, since wood buildings are not so readily damaged by a tremor, they are better equipped to withstand the aftershocks, which can be more damaging to weakened brick or concrete structures than the main shock.

Wood-frame buildings are not by any means quake-proof, of course. The damage to single-family wood-frame dwellings in the moderate and relatively localized 1971 San Fernando quake, for example, came to a staggering $115 million (1971 dollars), excluding the land and contents. It is notable, however, that much of this damage resulted not from any inherent weakness in the wood but from deficiencies in the building site or from poor design or construction. All engineers would agree that a wood-frame building is most likely to suffer serious earthquake damage when one or more of the following conditions are present:

♦ It is built on unstable ground.

♦ It has a weak or inadequately fastened foundation (sills are not bolted to foundations).

♦ Its crawl space wall, or cripple wall, between the concrete foundation and the ground or first floor of the house is not properly braced with plywood.

♦ It has structurally weak architectural features (all glass and no walls, for example).

♦ It is old or poorly maintained.

♦ It has insufficient lateral bracing or an inadequate number of earthquake resistant shear walls.

- It is improperly braced, or has inadequate connections in the bracing or other poor structural detailing.

- It is built on slender vertical supports, such as the stilts used for some hillside houses.

- It has a heavy roof, such as clay tile.

- It has a "soft" ground story (in a two-or-more-story building) with too many large openings such as a garage and other large windows and doors.

Besides a sound geologic site and a strong, well-connected foundation, the most important condition for a durable and safe wood-frame building is a lateral bracing system. Such special earthquake bracing is now generally required for all new wood-frame construction in most western states. Some lateral bracing is also a common code requirement along the Gulf and Atlantic coasts, which are subject to the strong lateral forces of hurricanes.

Diagonal bracing, which I strongly discourage, is the usual minimal code requirement. This type of lateral bracing entails the mounting of a series of lumber strips or metal straps at an angle across the studs of a building. The diagonal bracing is not nearly as strong as shear-walls of plywood and should not be used.

As stated, shear-wall bracing is the stronger of the two most common lateral bracing systems for wood-frame buildings. It is, therefore, the only recommended bracing for *all* wood-frame houses in earthquake country. Like any other bracing system, shear-wall bracing with plywood

Wood (or metal strap) diagonal bracing, such as this, is not recommended. Instead, plywood sheathing should be used. Diagonal bracing has shown itself to be inadequate in many earthquakes and has led to severe damage.

*These detailed drawings
of the connections of plywood sheathing to the
studs and plates stress the
importance of careful and
frequent nailing.*

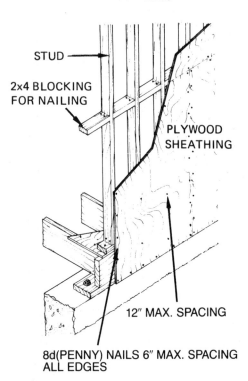

**ALL JOINTS BETWEEN PLYWOOD
PANELS SHOULD HAVE STUDS OR
BLOCKING FOR NAILING**

STUD

2x4 BLOCKING
FOR NAILING

PLYWOOD
SHEATHING

12" MAX. SPACING

8d(PENNY) NAILS 6" MAX. SPACING
ALL EDGES

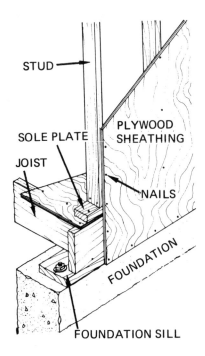

STUD

SOLE PLATE

JOIST

PLYWOOD
SHEATHING

NAILS

FOUNDATION

FOUNDATION SILL

panels will be effective only if the wood is good quality and the nailing is adequate. If you are applying the plywood directly to the studs, it should be at least ⅜-inch thick and, whenever possible, the panels should extend from sole plate to top plate. If the ceilings are taller than the usual 4 x 8-foot plywood panels, use 10-foot panels or two panels of equal height if greater than 10 feet. Never patch the few inches or feet above an eight-foot panel with a small piece of sheathing. This would introduce a break in the continuity, and a weak seam, very near the vital top-plate connection with the studs.

A variety of other products, such as composite or particle boards, exist which can be used in lieu of plywood. I recommend plywood, but if you are thinking of another method, it is best to check with a civil or structural engineer.

The conventional "double wall" construction of sheetrock and stucco very common to the western states is simply not strong enough and such construction should be reinforced with additional shear-walls of plywood. The main loadbearing walls of "double-wall" construction should be faced with plywood siding. That is particularly important for two-or-more-story houses.

The traditional wood clapboard siding of the majority of older houses and many modern structures is much weaker than shear-wall bracing with plywood. For single-story houses, shear-wall bracing is always better, of course, but if the clapboard is a good quality lumber, and if the boards are fitted tightly together and are well-nailed and maintained, the walls should survive even the largest quake. For two-or-more-story older houses, it will be prudent to reinforce the entire ground floor with plywood sheathing. For that, the advice of a structural engineer would be needed. Wood shingle siding (and asbestos siding) does *not* provide the effect of shear-wall bracing, however, so that shingled buildings should be strengthened with plywood sheathing.

Plywood sheathing—shear-wall bracing—when properly and adequately nailed is superior to any other type of bracing for a small wood-frame structure. It provides tremendous strength against damaging deformations of the walls during an earthquake, and it greatly enhances the dispersal of the earthquake forces back to the foundation. Plywood shear-wall bracing is commonly found in earthquake country both as an exterior architectural feature (with battens, for example) and as a backing for stucco or some other exterior facing.

Good plywood bracing details:
New house under construction. Note the plywood panels next to the windows. The photo at far right shows the dense nailing around the periphery of the plywood panels.

Lower floor of this two-story house, below, is completely sheathed with plywood.

A damaged Marina house, lower right, is strengthened with plywood on its entire exterior (the braces are temporary).

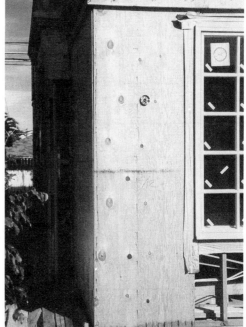

The best and worst
types of construction

The exceptionally strong and durable plywood sheathing kept this building intact despite the blows it suffered both from the huge Alaska earthquake and the landsliding that destroyed its foundation.

Some older, typically pre-1940 houses are sheathed with diagonal boards, called diagonal sheathing, which are usually 1 x 6 boards. This type of sheathing is very strong if it is properly nailed. Each diagonal should be nailed to the foundation sill with two nails and the boards should not be cracked. Any wood rot of the diagonals (particularly near the sill) or of the sill would drastically reduce the effectiveness of the sheathing.

Another valuable reinforcement technique in addition to lateral bracing is the use of steel framing and anchoring devices. These devices greatly strengthen the connections between the different components of a wood-frame building's superstructure. They are also useful in providing continuity between these components, so that the building will move as a unit in responding to the earthquake forces. The framing devices add a little to the cost of the construction, but they also save some money in labor charges, in that they take less time to apply than the conventional techniques of cutting and fitting boards and of mitering structural connections. Most important, these steel devices will add significantly greater strength and continuity to the building.

WOOD-FRAME BUILDINGS WITH STUCCOED WALLS

Although stucco is an easily fractured material, it is not as fragile during earthquakes as one might think. If the stucco is applied to strong wire mesh that has been carefully lapped and securely nailed to plywood sheathing (or to the clapboard of older frame buildings), it will seldom fracture or fall in even a large earthquake, because it is quite flexible and strong. The problem is that many stuccoed buildings are constructed with only diagonal bracing and sheetrock or plasterboard backing, neither of which is strong enough to withstand earthquakes without significant deformations that crack and break the stucco. And if the stucco falls off the walls, not only is it expensive in itself to repair, but it usually indicates that even more serious and expensive structural damage has occurred. Multi-story stucco buildings without shear-wall plywood bracing are especially susceptible to such damage because of the wider deflections of the building caused by the greater inertia of the upper floors.

The newest specifications for *single*-story stucco structures in the Uniform Building Code adopted by many communities call

Numerous special steel framing and anchoring devices add a little to the costs of construction but greatly strengthen the connections of a wood-frame house. They are highly recommended both in construction of a new building and especially in reinforcing an existing building.

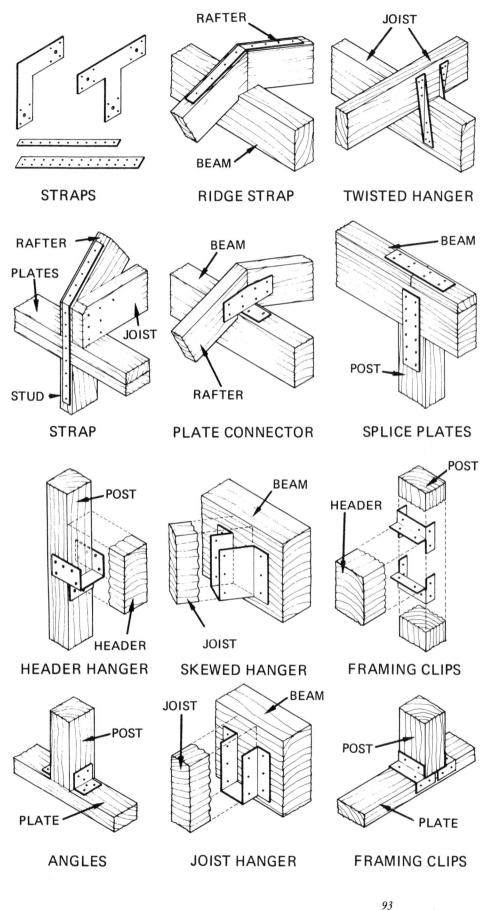

STRAPS

RIDGE STRAP

TWISTED HANGER

STRAP

PLATE CONNECTOR

SPLICE PLATES

HEADER HANGER

SKEWED HANGER

FRAMING CLIPS

ANGLES

JOIST HANGER

FRAMING CLIPS

The best and worst types of construction

The application of stucco directly to conventional wire lath and sheetrock without the additional structural backing of plywood sheathing can be an expensive mistake in areas that can expect high earthquake intensities. The house at right will have no plywood bracing, yet the lower floor is almost entirely windows and doors. Such buildings are collapse hazards. Multi-story stucco buildings in particular are subject to extensive damage. Note the stucco damage to two houses in San Francisco's Marina, below, and an apartment building in San Fernando Valley, at bottom.

for a much heavier and welded wire lath. When this type of mesh is properly overlapped and welded and then mounted directly to the studs (with 16-gauge staples every six inches), a carefully applied one-inch thick stucco covering will have a strength equivalent to ¼-inch plywood sheathing. Thus, single-story stuccoed houses built later than 1973 *and* under these new specifications (check with the city engineer) do not require a plywood backing. If you own a stuccoed wood-frame building without plywood sheathing—and if the building is more than one story or does not meet the above specifications—you should take one or more of the following steps:

♦ At the minimum, carry earthquake insurance.

♦ Hire a structural engineer to advise you on how most effectively to add plywood shear walls on an existing structure.

♦ Stucco damage tends to occur around doors and windows, where the stress paths are interrupted and the earthquake forces tend to concentrate. The damage to these areas can be lessened by the addition of interior or exterior plywood shear walls at selected locations to stiffen and strengthen the house. This measure should not only eliminate the fractures around the windows and doors but also minimize the damage to the rest of the stucco covering of the building,

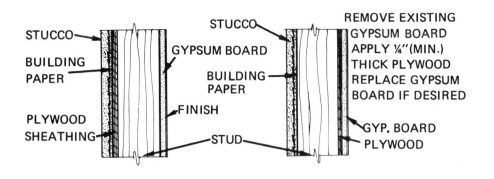

STUCCO
BUILDING PAPER
PLYWOOD SHEATHING

STUCCO
GYPSUM BOARD
BUILDING PAPER
FINISH
STUD

REMOVE EXISTING GYPSUM BOARD
APPLY ¼"(MIN.) THICK PLYWOOD
REPLACE GYPSUM BOARD IF DESIRED
GYP. BOARD
PLYWOOD

The wall cross-section on the left shows a recommended procedure of applying stucco to metal lath backed by plywood sheathing. The detail on the right illustrates a recommended procedure for strengthening existing stucco walls. The wood sheathing stiffens the walls and lessens the deformations that break the stucco. Small buildings constructed after 1973 under the specifications of the Uniform Building Code (1973) may not require plywood sheathing, since the code calls for a heavier and much stronger welded wire lath.

since the window and door fractures frequently extend into a web of cracks and breaks all across the face of a building.

♦ If your building is more than one-story, plywood sheathing is essential at the ground floor of the building and preferably on all floors.

WOOD-FRAME BUILDINGS WITH MASONRY VENEER

Masonry veneer is an appealing architectural feature that is also highly susceptible to earthquake damage. Masonry veneer is any stone, brick, adobe or other such covering—usually on outside walls—that is attached after the main wood framing. The veneer does not support any load from the house.

Unless specifically designed and reinforced for earthquake forces, veneered buildings always suffer far greater damage than clapboard, plywood or stucco-covered wood-frame structures. Multi-story veneered buildings particularly often suffer extensive and expensive damage to their masonry veneers. Most earthquake insurance policies reflect this fact by carrying addendums excluding masonry veneer from the coverage.

You can tell whether brick is veneer by checking if the inside walls are brick. If they sound hollow, as interior walls do, or if you can drive a nail easily through the sheetrock or plaster, you probably have veneer. Most often, looking into the crawl space or basement is sufficient; you should be able to see the wood framing if the exterior is veneer.

The basic structural strengths of veneered and other wood-frame buildings are the same. The problem with the former lies in the additional weight of the masonry facing. During an earthquake, this load generates greater inertial forces which can cause serious structural damage as well as certain damage to the veneer itself. In addition, the anchorages between the brick or stone and the wood frame are often weak or insufficient, so that the veneer will crack or be torn away from the frame during the tremor.

Poor-quality mortar is another factor in the damage to masonry veneers. Lime mortar is particularly notorious for having no resistance when subjected to earthquake forces. There is little that a home builder or homeowner can do to be assured that a consistently strong mortar mixture is being or has been used. If you own or wish to purchase a veneered building, examine the hardness of the mortar. Weak mortar can be readily recognized by its tendency to scrape away easily and to crumble between the fingers. Scrape a coin across the mortar, and if it falls away easily, it is very likely to fail during an earthquake. For the home buyer, the message here should be obvious. For the homeowner, the advice of a professional—a structural engineer—is essential.

The quality of the anchorage system for the veneer is a factor that is easily controlled by the home builder. Title 21 of the California building code for schools includes some very specific and sound requirements for all brick and stone veneer construction:

♦ All veneer, except for ceramic facing, should be anchored to its backing by means of non-corrodable metal ties de-

Reinforcement for masonry veneer

These views of masonry-veneer construction show the proper placement of anchors at least every one and a half square feet over the facing.

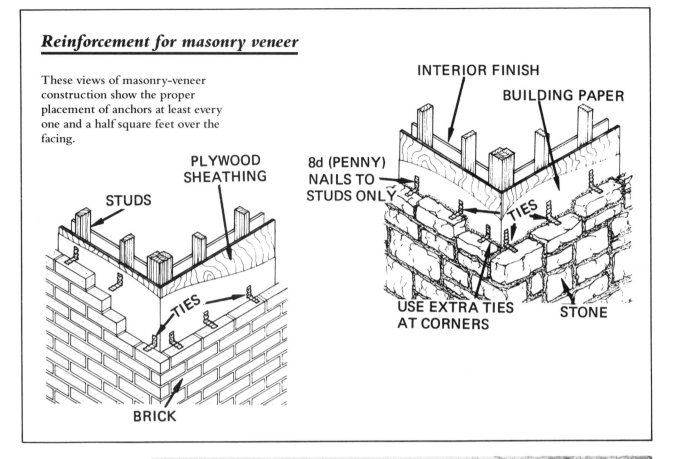

STUDS

PLYWOOD SHEATHING

TIES

BRICK

INTERIOR FINISH

BUILDING PAPER

8d (PENNY) NAILS TO STUDS ONLY

TIES

USE EXTRA TIES AT CORNERS

STONE

These older wood-frame houses in San Fernando were stripped of their stone veneer by the tremor. It is probably fortunate that the heavy veneers were not anchored to the frames, for the collapse of the stones might have taken large portions of the structures with them. Note that the glass is not broken. The shock occurred at 6:04 in the morning. Imagine the surprise of the occupants when they left the building and saw the result of the shaking. Fortunately, they did not exit the house during the tremor, while the veneer was collapsing.

An apartment building in the Marina district of San Francisco lost much of its poorly attached brick veneer. The photo- *graph on the right shows the same building, six months later, after the brick veneer was removed.*

This Coalinga, Central California house was reinforced by plywood shear walls, which prevented any serious structural damage, but the concrete slump block veneer was not adequately tied to the plywood. Several brand new houses suffered similar damage *in an earthquake with a magnitude less than 5.0 in May of 1990 in the town of Alamo along Northern California's Concord and Calaveras faults. Contractors still neglect to attach such veneers even in the most earthquake prone zones of California.*

signed to withstand a horizontal force equal to twice the weight of the veneer.

♦ There should be a tie anchor for each 200 square inches of wall area.

♦ Anchorage should be by 14-gauge anchors in 22-gauge anchor slots secured to the studs with 10d [10 penny] duplex nails at 12-inch maximum spacing.

♦ Veneers on wood-frame walls should not be permitted more than 15 feet above ground level.

Because stone veneer is usually heavier than brick and is placed in irregular patterns, the anchors must be even more carefully placed. As a general rule, it is recommended that one anchor be placed at least every one and a half square feet for veneer less than three inches thick. For veneer exceeding three to four inches in thickness, one anchor should be used every square foot. It is not advisable to cover large areas, such as entire walls, with stone veneer—particularly when the building is in an area which may experience high earthquake intensities. The very probable failure of the heavy veneer can seriously damage the frame of the building and may be a hazard to nearby property, to passers-by and to the occupants. Small and low stone (or brick) veneered areas, such as

The best and worst types of construction

Long Beach and Compton had many unreinforced brick buildings before the magnitude 6.3 1933 earthquake, and virtually all were severely damaged or demolished by the moderate shock. Generally, the failure of the brick walls led to the disconnections of the diaphragms that brought the whole building down. Most of the fatalities in American earthquakes are attributed to the collapse of unreinforced brick structures.

partial walls and foundation coverings, do not present such hazards, of course.

UNREINFORCED BRICK BUILDINGS

Those buildings constructed of brick which has not been reinforced by steel and poured-concrete framing have consistently suffered the most severe damage during earthquakes. So far, these buildings have caused the majority of deaths in California earthquakes. The major weakness in these structures is that an unreinforced brick wall is easily damaged by the lateral thrusts of an earthquake. The brick is heavy and inflexible, so that the lateral motions create an overwhelming inertial load that cracks the usually weak mortar connections and can cause the bricks to separate. Once damage starts to occur, the entire building can collapse progressively. Only the presence of numerous wood-frame interior bearing walls and partitions—typical of

older brick residences, offices and apartment buildings—has often prevented total collapse of the structure in such circumstances.

The quality of the mortar between the bricks is particularly important to the performance of unreinforced brick buildings during an earthquake. When the mortar is poor or old (usually both), the lateral earthquake stresses cause cracks to form in a zig-zag course through the mortar and around the bricks. During large shocks of long duration, such cracks tend to propagate diagonally across the walls, gradually spreading from foundation to roof and rapidly reducing the strength of the walls. In California, mortar in old buildings has been so bad that it has earned a nickname, "buttermilk mortar." After many of the large earthquakes in California, it has been possible to collect the fallen bricks from damaged buildings, wash off the remaining mortar with a hose, and re-sell the bricks.

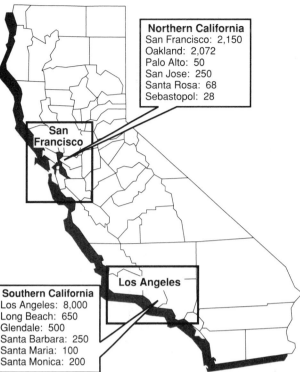

Northern California
San Francisco: 2,150
Oakland: 2,072
Palo Alto: 50
San Jose: 250
Santa Rosa: 68
Sebastopol: 28

San Francisco

Los Angeles

Southern California
Los Angeles: 8,000
Long Beach: 650
Glendale: 500
Santa Barbara: 250
Santa Maria: 100
Santa Monica: 200

Thirty-eight years after the lesson of the Long Beach disaster, the moderate San Fernando earthquake brought down the walls of many unreinforced brick buildings. The wood-frame partition walls of the apartment building at top prevented the total collapse of the structure, but the falling bricks destroyed the interiors of the adjacent lower buildings and presented a terrible hazard to people on the street. The service building of the Olive View Hospital Complex in San Fernando was not as fortunate—it collapsed completely.

In 1989, the California Seismic Safety Commission estimated that there were between 30,000 and 50,000 unreinforced masonry buildings throughout California. The map lists estimates of such buildings for a few cities. Meanwhile, downtown Santa Cruz, Whittier and Coalinga have inadvertently corrected their problem— most of the unreinforced masonry buildings were destroyed in their respective quakes of 1989, 1987 and 1983. In Salt Lake City, Utah about 60 percent of all buildings are of unreinforced masonry. A strong earth-

quake there could cause a disaster comparable to the Soviet Armenia earthquake of 1988, when more than 50,000 died and two cities were practically destroyed.

Old brick buildings have by far the worst earthquake record. A study after the Bakersfield quake of 1952 found that only one of the 71 older brick buildings in the city survived the tremor undamaged, and more than 30 of the buildings had to be either torn down or substantially revamped by removing one or more of the damaged upper stories. After the 1983 Coalinga earthquake most of the 90 brick buildings downtown were removed. Aging brick buildings are the structures that usually kill people in California quakes (although aging concrete frame structures are probably more dangerous because they house more people and can be structurally just as weak). For example, most of the 64 or so killed in the San Fernando earthquake of 1971 (Richter magnitude 6.5) died in the collapse of a single brick hospital in the Sylmar area. Most of those who died on October 17, 1989 in the San Francisco Bay Area earthquake, apart from the collapsed Cypress I-880 structure, were killed by falling bricks, including five in one old unreinforced building.

The best and worst types of construction

Fifty years after the Long Beach earthquake, Coalinga's mostly brick downtown was nearly destroyed in 1983 (upper photos). The 1987 magnitude 5.9 Whittier earthquake in the Los Angeles area destroyed much of downtown Whittier and caused severe damage to brick buildings in Pasadena (above left), Pico Rivera, Alhambra, Rosemead, Vernon and many other towns. The 1989, magnitude 7.1 Loma Prieta earthquake destroyed the beautiful Pacific Garden Mall and downtown Santa Cruz (above right) and severely damaged many brick buildings in Watsonville, Oakland, San Francisco, Berkeley and many other towns.

A major cause for the damage to older brick (and older concrete-block) buildings is the lack of sufficient lateral ties between the unreinforced walls and the diaphragms (roof and floors). The failures of these connections result in the collapse of the masonry walls, particularly in the upper floors and along high architectural facades, such as parapets and gables. The problem of diaphragm connections will be discussed in detail in the next chapter.

Old, unreinforced or faulty masonry buildings are difficult and expensive to repair or reinforce. The cost of such work often exceeds 25 to 50 percent of the value of the buildings. When a new Long Beach, California earthquake code in 1959 required reinforcement of all existing brick buildings, more than half of the owners chose demolition because of the high costs involved. On the other hand, when local codes have been less stringent, brick structures that have survived previous earthquakes with what appears to be only light

damage to the brick walls have been "reinforced" by the "plaster and paint" method—the cracks are plastered over and the walls are then painted to cover the patching and the inherent weaknesses of the building. The idea that "older buildings are substantial because they have stood the test of time" can be a very dangerous fallacy for earthquake country.

In general, little can be offered in the way of encouraging advice to the owner of an unreinforced brick building. It is worthwhile, in my opinion, to save as many of these buildings from demolition as possible. Unfortunately, the costs will be high. But the buildings must be fixed or they will disappear anyway in the next strong earthquake—as did so many in downtown Santa Cruz, California in 1989 or in downtown Coalinga, California in 1983, or in downtown Whittier, California in 1987. It is best for everyone concerned to phase out these buildings as soon as possible. However, if you own such a building and are

One method of strengthening unreinforced brick walls is the removal of the outer layer of brick and its replacement with four-inch thick gunite in which new diaphragm and joist anchors have been carefully embedded. Such repairs are expensive, and generally it is better to phase out such structures in earthquake country.

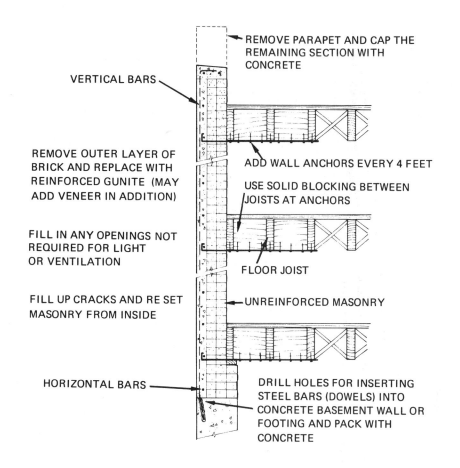

VERTICAL BARS →

← REMOVE PARAPET AND CAP THE REMAINING SECTION WITH CONCRETE

REMOVE OUTER LAYER OF BRICK AND REPLACE WITH REINFORCED GUNITE (MAY ADD VENEER IN ADDITION)

ADD WALL ANCHORS EVERY 4 FEET

USE SOLID BLOCKING BETWEEN JOISTS AT ANCHORS

FILL IN ANY OPENINGS NOT REQUIRED FOR LIGHT OR VENTILATION

FLOOR JOIST

FILL UP CRACKS AND RE SET MASONRY FROM INSIDE

UNREINFORCED MASONRY

HORIZONTAL BARS →

DRILL HOLES FOR INSERTING STEEL BARS (DOWELS) INTO CONCRETE BASEMENT WALL OR FOOTING AND PACK WITH CONCRETE

willing to invest a substantial amount to protect the occupants and minimize earthquake damage, there are methods which will strengthen the building to a degree. One of the more common repair techniques entails the removal of the outer layer of bricks and their replacement with a four-inch thickness of gunite (spray-on concrete) reinforced with steel bars. The gunite is certainly not as attractive as brick, but it can strengthen the walls adequately against collapse. At the same time, the connections between brick walls and the floor and roof joists are strengthened with steel anchors that are driven through the brick and embedded in the gunite. Often, it is also necessary to remove parapets and even the upper floors so that the repaired building can meet new earthquake code requirements.

Another common method for strengthening old brick buildings is through the construction of a braced steel frame within the existing building. The intent here is to provide an earthquake resistant system which would keep the floors from collapsing even if the brick is severely damaged. The basic problem, however, remains. It is very difficult to tie all of the brick to the steel, and much of it can come off, leaving a damaged and seriously disfigured building.

Brick buildings present a serious dilemma for historical conservation or the preservation of older buildings for housing of the poor. For example, much of the charm of Chinatown in San Francisco is due to its old buildings—most of which are of unreinforced brick—and many of which are densely populated by elderly people and others who can not afford newer and safer housing. However, a large percentage of these buildings will collapse in a future strong earthquake. Such a large scale disaster is only a matter of time. It will occur unless these buildings are strengthened or eliminated. San Francisco, in particular, has been very slow in fixing its dangerous buildings. It lags far behind Los Angeles,

The collapse on October 17, 1989 of the parapet and upper floor walls of this building in San Francisco's South of Market Street area killed five people who were waiting in parked cars. The parapet was going to be strengthened under the city's ordinance.

which since 1981 has required owners of unreinforced masonry buildings to strengthen them. By 1990 about 40 percent of the residential buildings have been strengthened, at a cost of $4,000 to $7,000 per residential unit. Meanwhile, San Francisco keeps planning and talking. Berkeley, another city that has been in the forefront of social legislation, has done nothing to protect its citizens. Most of the downtown buildings of Berkeley are constructed of unreinforced brick—and are therefore collapse hazards. If the Hayward fault lets go, there will be no downtown Berkeley. It is too bad that more planners and city officials did not visit Soviet Armenia after the 1988 earthquake—there similar negligence led to an indescribable disaster.

If you are contemplating the purchase of an unreinforced brick building, don't buy until you have consulted a structural engineer who specializes in building renovation and earthquake hazard abatement. The engineer will be able to advise you about the feasibility and costs of making the structure safer and will also likely advise you that the public and governmental agencies are becoming more and more aware of the high risks involved with such buildings and may well invoke a policy of large-scale condemnations of these buildings at any time in the near future. Certainly, it is more desirable to pay the moderate fee for an engineer's consultative services than to risk lawsuits, your entire investment and your life in a future earthquake.

CAVITY-WALL BRICK BUILDINGS

Cavity-wall brick buildings, as the name indicates, are constructed with a double wall of brick separated by a small gap. There are many examples in the older West Coast cities and throughout the Midwest, but the largest number of cavity-wall structures are found in Salt Lake City, St. Louis and other midwestern cities. Even when the double walls of such buildings are tied together with anchors (which is not usually the case), they have practically no resistance to the lateral forces of a quake and are readily damaged. The cavity and double wall of these buildings make the

The earthquake damage to this unreinforced cavity-wall brick building in Newcastle, Australia from the magnitude 5.5 earthquake of December 28, 1989 is expensive to repair. Many examples of this type of building are found in the American West, particularly in Salt Lake City. Unless such buildings are reinforced, they present a very serious earthquake hazard.

In both of these Alaskan structures, the concrete-block walls were unreinforced and therefore highly subject to collapse. The results of such inadequate design and construction are evident here. Neither the Anchorage apartment house nor the Valdez hotel were salvageable after the 1964 quake, and it was a miracle that none of the occupants was killed by the falling concrete blocks. Note the undamaged wood-frame structures on both sides of the hotel.

difficult and expensive reinforcement procedures even more complex and costly. Consult an engineer specializing in earthquake reinforcement if you wish to tackle the formidable and expensive task of renovating such a structure.

CONCRETE-BLOCK BUILDINGS

When the hollows of concrete blocks are properly reinforced with vertical and horizontal steel rods and then carefully grouted with poured concrete, the walls of concrete-block buildings form solid and continuous shear-wall units. Thus, reinforced concrete-block buildings can exhibit great strength and resistance under the stress of earthquake forces. Attention to detailing and workmanship is critical however. Because the walls are an assemblage of separate block units joined by poured concrete and mortar, they can share many of the weak points of brick construction if the mortar is faulty or poorly executed, if the poured concrete does not completely fill the cavities, if the steel reinforcing is inadequate, if the connections with the diaphragms of the building are weak or insufficient, or if the engineering design is poor.

Any of these mistakes in structural design or workmanship can cancel the advantages of this type of construction. For example, a large percentage of the damage, injuries and more than 5,000 fatalities in the Managua, Nicaragua earthquake in

The importance of good workmanship and careful supervision in all construction in earthquake country cannot be overemphasized. This photograph of severe quake damage to a concrete-block structure illustrates what happens when the blocks contain no grouting, which makes the reinforcing steel completely ineffective in strengthening the wall.

The best and worst types of construction

1972 were caused by the partial or complete collapse of poorly designed and constructed concrete-block buildings. All *unreinforced* concrete-block structures are, of course, totally unacceptable—and dangerous—even in areas subject only to moderate earthquakes.

The following design and construction features enhance the strength of reinforced concrete-block buildings:

Reinforcement for concrete-block construction

♦ The quantity of vertical and horizontal steel reinforcements should meet the requirements of the 1988 (or newer) Uniform Building Code. Special attention should be given to the corners of the exterior bearing walls and the intersection of the bearing walls with other interior walls.

♦ The vertical steel reinforcements should be continuous from the floor slab or foundation footing to the beams of the roof or the next floor. The bars should also be bent at their anchorages at each end.

♦ The horizontal and vertical reinforcements should not be more than two feet apart and should be tied together with wire.

♦ Carefully compacted concrete should fill every cavity, and the horizontal reinforcements should be embedded in continuous beams of poured concrete.

♦ The blocks around window and door openings should be reinforced more heavily with steel bars.

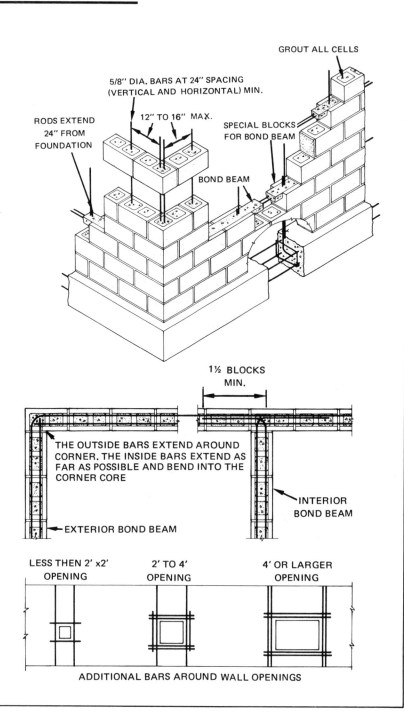

GROUT ALL CELLS

5/8" DIA. BARS AT 24" SPACING (VERTICAL AND HORIZONTAL) MIN.

12" TO 16" MAX.

RODS EXTEND 24" FROM FOUNDATION

SPECIAL BLOCKS FOR BOND BEAM

BOND BEAM

1½ BLOCKS MIN.

THE OUTSIDE BARS EXTEND AROUND CORNER. THE INSIDE BARS EXTEND AS FAR AS POSSIBLE AND BEND INTO THE CORNER CORE

INTERIOR BOND BEAM

EXTERIOR BOND BEAM

LESS THEN 2' x2' OPENING

2' TO 4' OPENING

4' OR LARGER OPENING

ADDITIONAL BARS AROUND WALL OPENINGS

The two most common patterns for concrete-block construction are the staggered common bond and the vertically aligned stack bond. The former is recommended for earthquake country because of its greater strength and resistance to lateral earthquake forces.

COMMON BOND

STACK BOND

The stack-bond, concrete-block walls of the steam plant for the San Fernando juvenile facility were reinforced with vertical steel bars but lacked sufficient horizontal bars and concrete grouting. A staggered common-bond pattern might have lessened this damage from the 1971 quake.

STEAM PLANT

- The vertical reinforcing steel bars or rods should be continuous from the floor slab or foundation footing, through the wall, and into the collar beams of the roof or the next floor. The ends of the bars should be bent so that they can not slip or be pulled from their anchorage.

- The vertical reinforcements should be inserted in the hollow of every other concrete block, or at least every two feet.

- The horizontal and vertical bars or rods should not be more than two feet apart, which means that approximately every third or fourth layer of concrete block should be topped with the horizontal reinforcements. The horizontal and vertical bars should then be connected with wire ties, so that there is a continuous mesh of reinforcing steel.

- Every hollow of the concrete blocks should be filled with carefully compacted concrete. In order to obtain a strong bond between the blocks and the grouting, be sure that the blocks are thoroughly pre-wetted according to the specifications of the supplier.

- Every layer of horizontal steel should be carefully embedded in a continuous beam (bond beam) of poured concrete.

- Additional horizontal and vertical reinforcements should be used at corners and at the intersections of all other walls, so that the walls are well-tied together and will act as one continuous unit during an earthquake.

- The walls should also be reinforced more heavily around any door or window openings. Historically, some of the most severe damage to this type of construction has been concentrated around improperly and insufficiently reinforced windows and doors.

- The two most common patterns for laying concrete block are the staggered *common-bond* arrangement and the parallel *stack-bond* pattern. Of the two, the common bond is more desirable, since the staggered joints enhance the resistance of the walls to lateral earthquake forces.

- The mortar used for the blocks should be very good quality.

♦ Any exterior veneers over the concrete block must be anchored well. A variety of new anchoring systems are available, and their use is strongly recommended.

The purchase of a reinforced concrete-block building in an area subject to high earthquake intensities is somewhat of a gamble; for unless you are present at the construction site, you can not be certain of the adequacy of the reinforcement or the workmanship. Have a structural engineer check the plans to the requirements of the 1988, or newer, Uniform Building Code. If he finds that the reinforcing steel and concrete grouting are ample and well-placed, you can assume that the building represents a fairly safe investment. Even so, earthquake insurance should be considered.

The same rules apply for the present owner of a concrete-block structure. If the engineer informs you that your building is not adequately reinforced, you should investigate possible measures for strengthening the structure. For the protection of those living or working in or near the building, you should precisely follow the recommendations of the consulting engineer.

REINFORCED BRICK BUILDINGS

Reinforced brick buildings are very similar in construction to concrete-block buildings. Two separate layers of brick are laid with connecting steel ties embedded in the mortar, and horizontal and vertical steel reinforcements are then inserted in the space between the two layers. The steel rods are tied together, and the space is then filled with poured concrete. Properly constructed buildings of this type have proven effective in resisting at least moderate earthquake forces and are acceptable for earthquake country provided that there is full-time inspection throughout the construction period by an engineer with considerable experience in earthquake reinforcement.

Brick buildings constructed with superior mortar and thoroughly reinforced with steel rods and ties carefully embedded in poured-concrete have proved effective in enduring moderate quakes. Nevertheless, as a general rule, it is wiser not to buy or build a brick structure in earthquake country. The quality of the workmanship and the materials is always difficult to control in brick construction, and the heavy, brittle walls make even reinforced brick buildings riskier to occupants and investors.

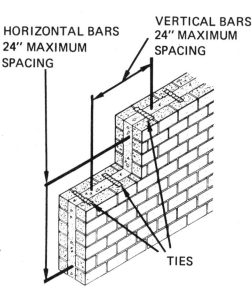

HORIZONTAL BARS 24" MAXIMUM SPACING

VERTICAL BARS 24" MAXIMUM SPACING

TIES

Because of their extreme brittleness and inflexibility, hollow tile structures, such as this guest house of the Veteran's Hospital complex in San Fernando, inevitably suffer proportionally greater earthquake damage than most other masonry buildings. Tile is not an acceptable construction material for earthquake country.

The magnitude 6.9 Soviet Armenia earthquake of December 1988 destroyed the center of Spitak, top right, which had clusters of stone and concrete buildings like that at top left. Essentially, 100 percent of these types of buildings were destroyed. The lower photographs show close-ups of destroyed apartment buildings in Spitak. Many of the existing older buildings in Salt Lake City, which are as weak as these buildings, could collapse in a strong earthquake on the Wasatch fault zone, which crosses the city.

CLAY-TILE BUILDINGS

Hollow clay-tile is similar to concrete blocks save for one important difference—the clay tiles are very brittle and easily shattered. Therefore, clay tile is simply not a sound building material for earthquake areas. Walls of tile have suffered severely during all past earthquakes, and the best course is to avoid such buildings or, if you own one, to carry insurance for the full value of the structure and its furnishings.

UNREINFORCED STONE AND ADOBE BUILDINGS

Stone and adobe buildings, and particularly those without any reinforcement or bracing, are designed to carry only vertical loads and have practically no strength for resisting the lateral forces of earthquakes. The high casualty figures for earthquakes in South and Central America and Southern Europe and Asia are due primarily to

this type of construction. Such structures are still built in the earthquake-prone areas of the United States away from the West Coast, where many old examples remain standing. A small earthquake may be sufficient to destroy such a building. Major alterations are required to improve the resistance of these buildings; and except in the case of historical monuments, such alterations are neither economically feasible nor warranted.

COMMERCIAL BUILDINGS

Although most of us worry about earthquake risk to our houses, some of the highest risks in the earthquake country are in our places of work. Here is a brief summary of the expected performance of various types of commercial buildings. Some keep risk to a reasonable level; some can be extremely dangerous.

The best and worst types of construction

The 19th century cathedral of Leninakan, Soviet Armenia, before and after the 1988 earthquake. The stone structure and others like it collapsed. Numerous older stone and brick churches in California, Utah and elsewhere will, one day, collapse unless they are strengthened to more modern earthquake resistant building codes.

The steel buildings, like this one in Spitak, Soviet Armenia, were practically the only structures still standing in the destroyed city of 40,000 people. This industrial building lost its poorly attached stone and precast concrete facade, but remained standing, practically undamaged. All surrounding unreinforced masonry and other concrete buildings collapsed. Steel framed buildings have outperformed all other types of large commercial buildings in recent large earthquakes.

Steel-frame buildings

Steel-framed buildings have the best record in strong earthquakes; typically, they are the safest commercial buildings.

Most high-rise buildings in California are built around a steel frame. They tend to be earthquake-resistant, due to the relatively light weight of the steel frame and its ability to absorb a great amount of energy and deformation before collapsing. Modern steel structures built since 1973 should generally have adequately designed structural systems and good seismic detailing (particularly at connections), and are built under quality-control guidelines.

With few exceptions, damage to steel-frame structures in major earthquakes has been limited to localized yielding or buckling, connection damage and the cracking and distortion of such nonstructural elements as plaster walls, partitions, ceilings and facades. Most of that damage occurs because the buildings are *too* flexible—the engineers minimized the amount of steel in order to cut down the cost.

The October 1989 San Francisco Bay Area earthquake taught us an interesting lesson: Many old steel-frame buildings with heavy, ornate exterior facades (mostly unreinforced brick, stone and terra cotta) suffered expensive facade damage. Unreinforced interior partition walls often cracked and sometimes shattered. These structures generally were built before the 1940s. They will suffer much more damage in a stronger earthquake or one centered closer to downtown areas.

Old steel framed buildings with facades or partitions of unreinforced masonry, including brick and terra cotta, often suffered very costly damage in the 1989 Loma Prieta earthquake. Note the steel framing (far right photograph) in this 1920s Oakland building.

Many old (typically pre-1940) office and other commercial buildings have partition walls built of hollow clay tile blocks. Such walls break apart easily and create hazards, as illustrated by this damage to the fire and emergency stairwells of a building in Oakland after the 1989 Loma Prieta earthquake.

Unreinforced masonry buildings

Larger unreinforced masonry (URM) buildings—a category that includes brick structures as discussed above—have long been recognized as some of the most hazardous in an earthquake. The 1933 Long Beach quake, which caused extensive damage to buildings of unreinforced brick and sand-lime mortar, brought an end to the construction of URM buildings in California, but not elsewhere in the earthquake prone areas of the United States.

In the October 1989 quake, the deaths at the Pacific Garden Mall in Santa Cruz and much of the damage in downtown Oakland occurred in URM buildings. Most of the deaths in that quake, aside from the collapsed Cypress freeway structure, were caused by URM buildings. In a larger or closer earthquake, many commercial URM buildings in the Bay Area will collapse.

Existing URM buildings have been the target of many hazard-mitigation ordinances, including California Senate Bill 547, enacted in 1987. That bill required cities and counties in seismically active areas to inventory buildings and come up with mitigation plans.

Older, non-ductile concrete frame structures are the most hazardous large structures in earthquake country. Both the telephone building in Spitak, Armenia and the I-880 viaduct in Oakland, California lacked structural details required by the current Uniform *Building Code. Several office buildings of this type in San Francisco, Oakland, and elsewhere came to within seconds of collapse on October 17, 1989. Some of the severely damaged buildings were designed and constructed as recently as 1981.*

Despite all the talk and good intentions, most California and all other U.S. cities have been slow to minimize the risks from these buildings. High retrofit costs, the trend toward historical preservation, politics, budget cutting, lack of concern by owners and employees and myriad other problems get in the way of strengthening or eliminating these potential killers. If you work in such a building, you are living with the worst possible risk in earthquake country.

Concrete-frame buildings

The second most dangerous structure is the older commercial concrete building known, in structural engineering jargon, as a nonductile concrete-frame building. The San Francisco and Los Angeles areas have hundreds of these, including one or two dozen highrises in San Francisco and many, many more in the Los Angeles area. A number of these buildings were severely damaged on October 17 to the point of near collapse. In fact, this was the type of construction used in the Interstate 880 double-decker Cypress structure that collapsed in Oakland, killing 42 people.

Concrete-frame structures generally use concrete beams and columns in somewhat the same manner as steel beams are used on steel-frame buildings. Designing adequate connections and reinforcing steel detailing for these much heavier building elements is, however, a far more difficult engineering feat.

In the 1971 San Fernando quake, which had a Richter magnitude of 6.5, many concrete-frame structures in high intensity areas suffered severe damage or collapsed. Engineers found several common design flaws; insufficient ties holding the vertical reinforcing steel together in columns, poor reinforcing of beam-to-column joints and numerous mundane engineering details.

Extensive modification of code requirements for these details were made in the 1973 Uniform Building Code (UBC), which governs earthquake design in the West, including California. Further refinements were made in later editions of the code.

Consequently, concrete-frame structures designed after these code revisions took effect should perform substantially better than those designed earlier. I, however, would not purchase or work in such a building. The limited testing of these buildings in the October 17, 1989 earthquake has yielded generally good results, but the real test of their performance must wait.

One of the most significant design problems for concrete-frame structures—and indeed for any structure—is a ground floor with large openings for garages or windows. Although esthetically desirable, these so-called soft-story designs with large openings on the ground floor leave little room for cross-bracing, thus weakening the structure's ability to withstand the lateral motion of an earthquake. The new 1988 building code restricts soft-story configurations and requires special design considerations when they are used.

Three examples of collapsed multi-story commercial non-ductile concrete frame buildings in Mexico City in 1985. Many comparably weak, older (typically pre-1973 buildings in California) concrete buildings can be found in San Francisco, Los Angeles, Seattle, Utah and elsewhere.

The steel frame of the San Francisco-Oakland Bay Bridge collapsed at one location because of inadequate connections between the beams sup- *porting the roadway and their supports. Any important structure should be evaluated and be strengthened if necessary.*

The best and worst types of construction

"Soft story" buildings are structures with many of the solid shear walls removed at the ground level to make room for garage doors or more windows (top photograph). The photograph in the center shows a damaged "soft story" building in the Marina district of San Francisco. Several such four-story buildings collapsed, as shown in the lower photograph. Hundreds of these buildings are collapse hazards throughout Southern and Northern California.

Concrete shear-wall buildings

Like steel buildings, these types, when properly designed, have a good history in past strong quakes, including Loma Prieta. Many of them, some dating to the 1910s, survived with no significant damage in the hardest hit areas, such as Santa Cruz and Watsonville. They are usually good investments (but certainly not always) and a safe place to work.

Concrete shear-wall buildings rely upon massive, stiff concrete walls, rather than frames, for their structural integrity. The walls are typically built together with a concrete frame and are designed to handle earthquake loads. The performance of concrete shear-wall buildings is highly dependent on the number of walls, their location within the building, their configuration, the size and number of openings in the wall, and reinforcement details.

Irregularly shaped shear-wall buildings and those with a "soft story" often perform poorly in earthquakes. In addition, buildings with walls distributed around only two or three sides are vulnerable to strong twisting forces. They have been severely damaged in past earthquakes.

The failure of the new Olive View Hospital in Los Angeles during the 1971 San Fernando quake is an instructive example. The hospital had been completed and dedicated only a few weeks before the earthquake, and it was supposedly designed and constructed in accordance with the latest building codes. It failed because the shear walls of concrete were eliminated on the ground floor to allow for more window space. In addition, the slim concrete supporting columns at the street level were inadequately reinforced with steel, and the combination of the heavy inertial load and the chaotic deflections of the ground floor shattered the columns and caused the entire structure to lurch to one side. Three of the four independent exterior stairwell structures totally collapsed because of the inadequate columns.

Many high-rise concrete buildings designed to standards similar to those of California prior to 1975 have also failed or completely pancaked in recent earthquakes in California, Alaska, Venezuela, Japan,

The reinforced-concrete Olive View Hospital in San Fernando was dedicated only weeks before the earthquake destroyed it, causing four deaths and several injuries. Three of the four separate stairwell structures also fell to the ground (one of them lies on the right),

and two smaller concrete buildings in the complex suffered partial collapses. Such failures in new, presumably well-designed structures during a moderate quake demonstrate weaknesses in the engineering application of contemporary building codes.

The reasons for the failure of the Olive View Hospital in San Fernando have been discussed earlier. What is interesting here is the differences in the performance of the two types of columns supporting the structures. The completely fractured corner column in the foreground had vertical steel reinforcements which were tied together with individual steel loops. The individual ties pulled apart, allowing the concrete core to burst.

Mexico City, Chile and Soviet Armenia. All of the failures are generally attributed to inadequate and outdated building code requirements, poor design, or a lack of careful supervision of the workmanship.

Concrete tilt-up buildings

The concrete tilt-up building is what we see in most modern industrial parks. The South San Francisco Bay's Silicon Valley and Orange County's high tech industry are mostly housed in such structures. They are cheap, easy and fast to build. They are the most common newer industrial park building in California and throughout much of the West.

Concrete tilt-up design came into general use in the early 1960s; today it's one of the least costly industrial and commercial structures to build. The concrete foundations and base slab are poured in place; next, the walls are poured in place, lying horizontally on the ground, and are then tilted up, like cards, on top of the foundation. Usually, a wood roof is then built, with only a few slender columns supporting it in the interior.

All this often makes for a risky investment and a dangerous place to work.

These buildings have become quite popular for speculative developments. In addition, the economics of tilt-ups make them likely to be built only to the minimum of

These modern concrete tilt-up, light-industrial buildings in San Fernando were two of many that were badly damaged by the quake. Similar buildings were damaged or collapsed in the 1987 Whittier and 1989 Loma Prieta earthquakes. In almost every case, one of the problems with the concrete structures was the poor design of the roof-wall connections—a very common weakness in larger concrete and masonry buildings with wood roofs and floors. Under the lateral ground motions of a quake, the heavy walls pull away from the roof or floor and break the connections. In the lower photograph, you can see the wood ledger which, with a few nails, was the only support for the roof beams. All buildings of this type should include the special steel connections that have been required since about 1975 but are often not built.

the required code, which may not be adequate. Further, many newer ones have been built to resemble frame buildings, replacing the concrete panels with glass.

During the 1971 San Fernando earthquake, many performed badly and partially collapsed. This poor performance was attributed to inadequate ties between the roof and walls, insufficient nailing of the roof plywood to the frame, poor engineering details at irregular design areas and bad design of the wall panels for lateral and vertical loads.

Following this poor performance, the relevant seismic requirements of the Uniform Building Code were modified in 1973. The 1976 UBC was again revised, with more stringent requirements. Tilt-up buildings designed to these new requirements should generally perform better than older structures, although several tilt-ups designed to 1976 (or better) requirements were extensively damaged in the Loma Prieta earthquake.

The best news about such buildings is that they can typically be strengthened and fixed for a very reasonable price. In fact, in the past few years, numerous California companies have gone through extensive programs to evaluate their tilt-ups and fix those found to be dangerous.

How safe are you?

The engineering technology exists to make all risky commercial buildings strong and safe. Some, such as tilt-up buildings, are easy to fix for a moderate price. Others, such as many unreinforced brick and older concrete frame buildings, can be very expensive to strengthen.

In the end, how safe you will be in the next big earthquake depends on you and your employer.

A collapsed tilt-up building in Hollister after the 1989 earthquake. In this case, stored pallets of tomato products fell against the poorly connected exterior walls and pushed them out. The addition of a few "hold-down" connectors, such as that illustrated below, would have prevented the damage. The strengthening detail is usually easy and inexpensive to add to existing buildings.

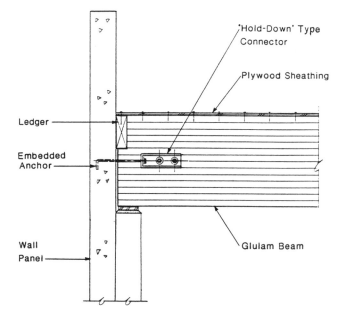

Ranking your workplace:

SAFEST OF ALL:
Steel-framed buildings (modern high-rises).

SECOND BEST:
Concrete shear-wall buildings; these rely on massive concrete walls rather than frames for structural integrity.

SOMETIMES OK:
Concrete tilt-up buildings (primarily if built since 1976 or retrofitted)—seen throughout the Silicon Valley and in many industrial parks.

HIGHLY DANGEROUS:
Nonductile concrete-frame buildings (the kind of concrete-frame construction used in the I-880 Cypress structure); often older buildings.

THINK ABOUT CHANGING JOBS:
Unreinforced brick buildings; most non-highway deaths on October 17, 1989 occurred in these.

CHAPTER SEVEN

Structural and architectural design and detailing for earthquake resistance

JUST AS THE VARIOUS PROTOTYPES OF "safety" cars can be austere and not very stylish, the most earthquake-resistant house would be a clumsy, bunker-like structure with a minimum of small and narrow windows and doors penetrating the walls. Numerous interior partitions dividing the house into small rooms would further strengthen the boxy structure. Obviously, such a house would not be very appealing, nor is it very common in structures built within the past 30 years. Until recently, when energy efficiency began modifying the architectural appearance of houses, the contemporary trend in design favored buildings without any visible means of support, and certainly such light and airy structures are much more attractive and better suited to the climate and life style of California and much of the West. Such buildings often have large glass areas, slender columns supporting broad-eaved roofs, multi-level floor plans, unusual geometric patterns and dramatic water and hillside sites.

Unfortunately, the design that makes these houses so attractive also incorporates many of the most obvious earthquake hazards. Engineers sometimes neglect to stress the importance of good detailing, and contractors do not usually have the knowledge to insist on proper earthquake-resistant design. Consequently, a large percentage of the building damage from earthquakes is directly attributable to poor design or detailing.

For example, the failure of a slender corner column supporting a heavy roof or the upper floor in a split level can cause damage not only to wall and large glass panels but also to the roof, the floor, the interior walls, the furnishings and the occupants of the building. In contrast, a sturdy simpler home with conventionally small window areas and numerous supporting walls might sustain some sheetrock cracks and chimney damage, but chances are very good that the house would remain intact and the damage would not be costly or dangerous to the occupants.

As this book has continually emphasized, the modern design requirements for houses and other small buildings in earthquake country must be accompanied by especial attention to the strengths of the load-bearing vertical supports and the connections among all the structural elements of the building. This chapter examines these factors in greater detail and suggests ways that poor detailing and design may be avoided in new construction or corrected in existing buildings. The chapter also discusses the special earthquake problems of older houses and of certain modern architectural features which have caused or have sustained disproportionate damage during recent earthquakes.

FOUNDATIONS

A good, reliable foundation is a *continuous, tied, wall foundation,* in which reinforced concrete forms a uniform length of support under the main load-bearing walls of the building. The concrete is reinforced with vertical steel bars securely tied together with horizontal steel bars that wrap around corners. Such tied foundations enable a building to move as a single integral unit during an earthquake so that the different components of the super-structure move together and damage is minimized.

A mat, or *floating foundation*—a reinforced-concrete slab resting directly on the soil—is ideal for buildings located on soft soils or other inferior ground, such as landfill. Full mat foundations, when well-reinforced with steel, have the advantages of rigidity and continuity—they provide continuous support to a structure and minimize the hazard from differential soil movements by bridging over the pockets of especially soft or loose soil in the ground. When foundations displace even slightly, the support of the building becomes uneven, causing severe cracking and warping of the floor. This can lead to col-

lapses in the frame. The damage can be similar to that caused by faulting directly under the house. Buildings on mat foundations (and on the pier or piling foundations described below) generally experience less of this type of damage during earthquakes. Much of the damage in the Marina district of San Francisco would not have occurred if thick mat foundations had been used over the soft fills of the area before the 1989 earthquake.

Drilled pier or *caisson-pile foundations,* which are steel or concrete pilings set deep in the ground, are generally used only on soft, weak or unstable soils. These foundations have a good record for endurance in large earthquakes. For example, much of the damage in the alluvial and filled areas of San Francisco in 1906 was caused by large ground settlements. However, the buildings on deeply submerged pilings did

This is an example of a well-tied and continuous wall foundation for a two-story house. Note the sill anchors (bolts) every few feet and the taller shear wall tie-downs which will connect the foundation directly to the plywood sheathed walls above.

Design and detailing for earthquake resistance

Foundation connections

A wood-frame building has little chance of surviving an earthquake without serious damage if its major support, the foundation, is poorly connected to the wood frame superstructure. One large jolt can easily break or misalign a weak sill connection, and this damage can, in turn, either knock the building entirely off its foundation or cause the collapse of studs and columns.

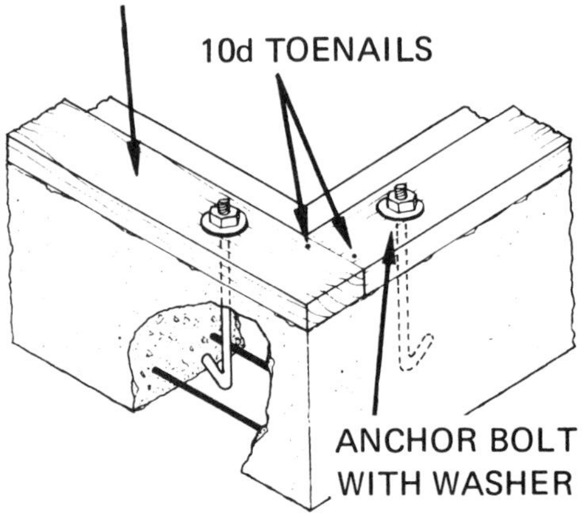

In new construction, the sill should be anchored with bolts which are embedded according to code in the concrete of the foundation. The bolts should be centered in the sill for maximum strength, and a washer should be used with the nut to allow a very tight connection without damage to the sill. Once tightened, the bolt should extend at least ⅛ inch above the nut. There should be such an anchor bolt at least every four feet for two-story houses and six feet for single-story houses along the sill and within 12 inches of the end of each sill piece. The joints between sill pieces should also be toenailed, as shown here.
In addition, the hold-down device shown here is recommended for the connections between the wall and foundation in plywood-sheathed walls with large openings (the front garage wall in a split-level, for example). The bolted connection above the sill dispenses the concentrated earthquake forces directly into the concrete of the foundation.

APPROVED PRESSURE TREATED
WOOD OR REDWOOD SILL

10d TOENAILS

ANCHOR BOLT
WITH WASHER

PLYWOOD SHEATHING OR SIDING
(CUT AWAY TO EXPOSE THE HOLDDOWN)

STUDS

BOLTS TO
FRAMING – SIZE
AS REQUIRED

STEEL BRACKET

SILL

BOLT TO FOUNDATION

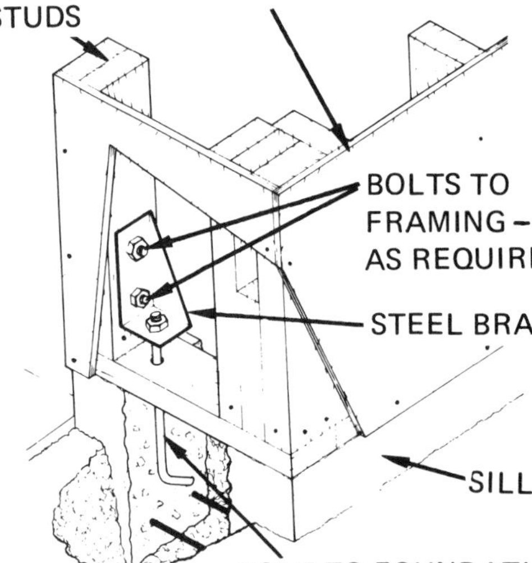

not settle with the alluvial or filled soils, and the damage to these buildings was substantially less. The same lesson was repeated in the October 1989 earthquake.

The quality and the earthquake resistance of these three types of foundations are governed by a few basic principles:

♦ The foundations should be supported by solid ground, and the major supporting segments of the foundation should rest on *uniform* ground conditions. For example, a portion of a foundation wall should not be partially supported on bedrock and partially on landfill material; for differential movements of the fill away from the rock during a quake can cause heavy damage to the foundation and to the structure it supports.

♦ Different types of foundations should not be used under one building—a combination of separate unconnected pilings with sections of continuous concrete-block wall, for example, could be risky unless the designing engineer had thoughtfully anticipated the earthquake hazard. Two different types of foundations will behave in different ways during the ground motion of a tremor, and uniform behavior is essential if a building is to withstand the earthquake stresses.

♦ The type of foundation required for a given site is determined primarily by the ground conditions under the building. A good bedrock base needs only the conventional continuous, tied concrete

foundation minimally required by most building codes, whereas very soft soil or loose fill may require special drilled pier or caisson footings. The selection of the proper foundation for the geology of your particular site should always be the decision of an engineer well-versed in earthquake hazard and in the ground conditions of your area.

♦ Faulty or insufficient connections between the foundation and the sill or between the sill and the studs and columns will drastically decrease the overall earthquake resistance of a building. The building can slip wholly or partially off its foundation. The sill connections are especially important and require some further discussion in the section that follows.

FOUNDATION CONNECTIONS AND BRACING FOR WOOD-FRAME BUILDINGS

One of the most common causes of damage to wood-frame buildings, which is also one of the easiest to fix, results from insufficient or poor anchorages between the sill and the foundation.

The Carnegie Institution report on the 1906 earthquake notes that many of the damaged single-family houses in San Francisco had "slipped from their foundations." Houses in almost all the cities on the northern coast of California suffered similar damage. On October 17,1989 this was the most common damage in Watsonville, Hollister, Santa Cruz, Los Gatos and the

Contemporary code requirements provide for some, but not always sufficient, connections between the foundation sill and the walls of a building. However, older buildings—some constructed before the mid- *1950s and most built before the 1940s—will often have no connections between the foundation and the frame. Obviously, it doesn't take much of a jolt to knock such a structure off its foundation.*

Design and detailing for earthquake resistance

Unless the foundations of very old buildings have been reconstructed to modern codes, it is very likely that they are resting on their foundations without any significant connections and bracing between the foundation and the structure. Witness this dramatically ruined Victorian house in San Francisco in 1906. The force of the fall from its foundation split the building in half.

An example of strengthened foundation connections in the Marina district of San Francisco, after the 1989 earthquake. The house has been sheathed with plywood on the exterior faces and anchor bolts (on the right) and hold-down devices (on the left) have been installed.

other towns near the epicenter or in severely shaken areas.

However, any enterprising homeowner can bolt down a house. It may take a day, or it may take three weekends. Or you can hire help. The importance of this detail cannot be over-emphasized. If the connection is inadequate, the building represents a very poor risk and a great danger to its occupants—especially when it is two or more stories high.

Existing building codes in most areas require firm anchorages between the sill and the foundation. For example, the San Francisco Building Code states that:

Foundation plates or sills shall be bolted to the foundation or foundation wall with not less than one-half inch bolts embedded at least seven inches into the masonry or concrete and spaced not more than six feet apart. Bolts shall be located within 12 inches of each end of each piece with a minimum of two bolts per piece. Washers are required under all nuts.

These code requirements are very good ones, although maximum spacing of four feet for the anchor bolts would add greater stability for a small increase in cost. The placement of a bolt within 12 inches of the end of each sill piece is especially important to ensure the stability of the sill.

If you carry out the recommended strengthening procedures, and if you also brace the crawl space walls with plywood (discussed next), your older wood-frame house will have an excellent chance of surviving the next strong earthquake without expensive damage. (Crawl space walls, also called cripple walls, are the short wood walls used to elevate the house above ground and allow access to the substructure and to utility lines.) If it is a single-story house, it probably will survive without any serious damage.

First, check whether the wood sill underneath the walls is bolted to the concrete foundation below. The sill is a thick (2- or 3-inch) wooden plank on top of the foundation to which the vertical studs of the house walls are nailed.

Bolting the house to its foundation

1. Lay out bolt locations. For the typical one story house, use ⅝″ diameter bolts at 4 to 6 feet on center.

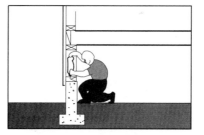

2. Drill holes through existing sill into the concrete foundations for 8½″ long expansion bolts, using carbide drill bits.

3. Use right angle drill for tight access places where the crawl space is low.

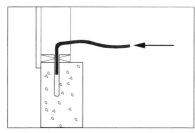

4. Blow all the dust out of the drilled holes using a rubber tube. Wear goggles and dust mask or respirator for protection from dust and debris.

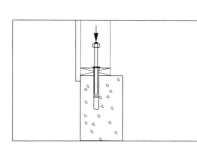

5. Insert expansion bolt with the washer and nut attached. Leave nut at top of bolt when tapping the bolt in place to protect the threads.

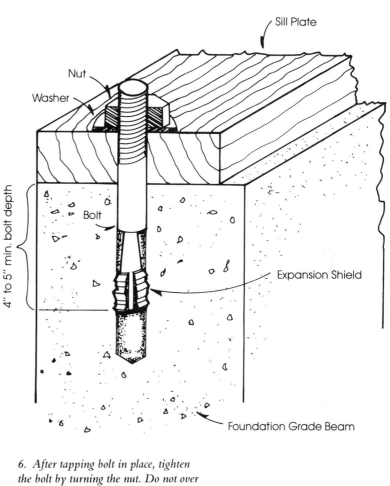

Sill Plate

Nut

Washer

4″ to 5″ min. bolt depth

Bolt

Expansion Shield

Foundation Grade Beam

6. After tapping bolt in place, tighten the bolt by turning the nut. Do not over tighten or bolt will be damaged.

Getting geologic and engineering help

There is a tremendous amount of misinformation about what constitutes professional help in evaluating and strengthening your house against earthquakes. And after most earthquakes, new "experts" spring up to give advice and lots of misinformation. But whether it's free, cheap or even overpriced, advice won't help if it's wrong.

Two professional groups are equipped to help: licensed geologists and engineers. These professionals are licensed by the state. Most others are either unqualified or inadequately qualified to dispense information that will one day affect your family's safety.

For example, after an earthquake a few years ago, I was asked this question: "You recently recommended bolting the wood sills of pre-1940 houses to their foundations for earthquake safety. I talked to a carpenter about this, and he told me it would be a waste of money. He said the holes for the bolts would have to be bigger than the bolts, and the bolts would pull out in a strong quake. The building inspector agreed. What should I do to counter the possibility of the bolts pulling out?"

This person talked to a carpenter who knows as much about earthquakes as the typical second-grader. Even more disturbing, the building inspector did not seem to know anything about earthquake engineering, either.

You should bolt the house to its foundations. The carpenter was thinking of the wrong type of bolts. Use expansion bolts, which are also called wedge bolts. These bolts are exactly the same size as the hole.

When you need help, seek either an engineer (civil, structural, soils or foundation) or a geologist. His or her advice can apply to a variety of problems—purchasing property, strengthening through structural alterations and additions to your house or building, or problems with unstable ground, landslides, settlement and the like.

Only engineers and some architects are trained in the fundamentals of earthquake engineering for small buildings. Carpenters, builders and contractors are not usually trained, and such laymen are not professionally qualified to give this advice. Some, of course, are interested enough to learn the basics.

All too often, laymen think that if a house is well built it will survive without damage. Unless specifically designed for quakes, however, a house may be sound but still vulnerable. An old brick house, for example, may be built very well, but unless it is reinforced for earthquake loads it can be damaged very easily.

Those qualified to help homeowners with the building itself are civil and structural engineers who specialize in earthquake engineering and structural design. Some civil engineers specialize in soils engineering; sometimes they are called foundation or geotechnical engineers. Many geologists are also highly qualified to give advice about earthquake safety—particularly about the stability of the ground on which the building rests.

I strongly urge everyone buying a house to seek both engineering and geotechnical advice about earthquake safety before making the purchase. Generally, you'll need two reports, because the expertise of structural engineers, soils engineers and geologists does not overlap. It is best to include a brief clause in the contract making purchase of the house contingent on these reports; as the buyer, who inserted the clause, you can remove it from the contract whenever you want. Allow yourself 5 to 10 working days to find an engineer. You might contact one when you start looking for a house.

If you're seeking an educated opinion rather than an escape clause, you will not usually need these reports in writing—something that can increase the cost dramatically. Just ask for oral advice and simple sketches that show you how to accomplish a specific, recommended strengthening detail.

In my opinion, the inspections are excellent investments. They can save you some serious problems in the event of an earthquake—or even prevent you from buying a house on top of a landslide.

To find an engineer, ask any architect or engineers you know, or call your city's engineering office, or check with your real estate agent (although he or she may say that such reports are unnecessary). You can also look in the Yellow Pages under "consulting engineers."

The best source for engineers in California is the Structural Engineers Association of California (SEAOC), which has prepared lists of engineers who conduct such evaluations. The addresses and telephone numbers of SEAOC's regional offices are:

♦ Structural Engineers Association (S.E.A.) of Northern California, 217 Second Street, San Francisco 94105. Telephone 415-974-5147

♦ S.E.A. of Central California, P.O. Box 161959, Sacramento, CA 95816-1959. Telephone 916-965-1536

♦ S.E.A. of San Diego, P.O. Box 26500, Suite 203, San Diego, CA 92126. Telephone 619-223-9955

♦ S.E.A. of Southern California, 2550 Beverly Blvd., Los Angeles, CA 90057. Telephone 213-385-4424 ▶

LIST OF RECOMMENDATIONS

1. FOUNDATION BOLTS (SEE DETAIL $\frac{D4b}{3}$)

2. BACK PORCH COLUMN BRACING (SEE DETAIL $\frac{D8}{4}$)

3. SHEAR BRACING OF CRIPPLE WALLS (SEE DETAIL $\frac{D9}{5}$ AND BLOCKING OF TOP AND BOTTOM SILL PLATE SEE DETAIL $\frac{D10}{6}$)

4. WATER HEATER (SEE DETAIL $\frac{D13}{7}$)

5. CHIMNEY (SEE DETAIL $\frac{D14}{8}$)

6. PORCH COLUMNS (SEE DETAIL $\frac{D15}{9}$)

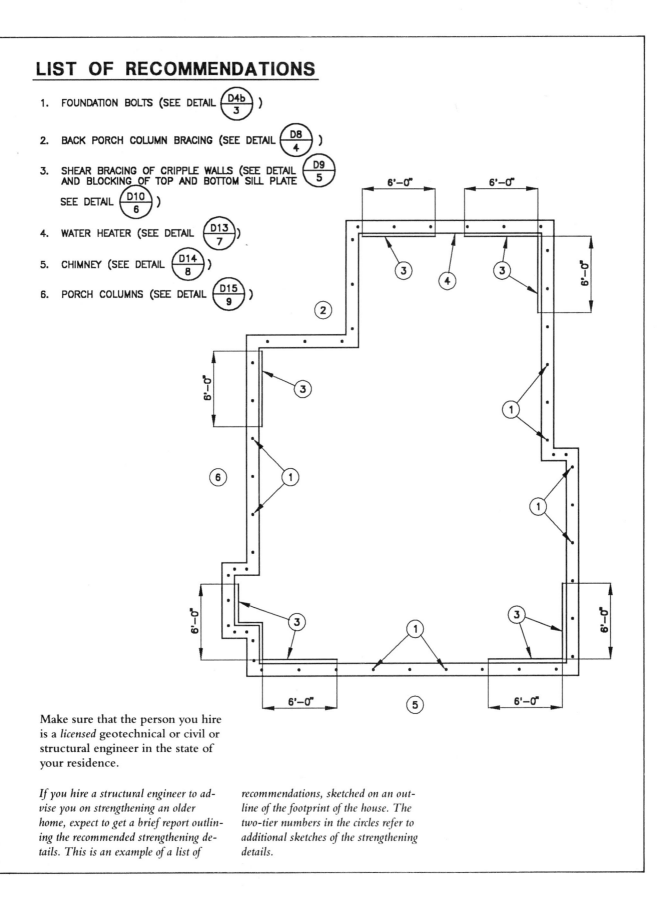

Make sure that the person you hire is a *licensed* geotechnical or civil or structural engineer in the state of your residence.

If you hire a structural engineer to advise you on strengthening an older home, expect to get a brief report outlining the recommended strengthening details. This is an example of a list of recommendations, sketched on an outline of the footprint of the house. The two-tier numbers in the circles refer to additional sketches of the strengthening details.

Design and detailing for earthquake resistance

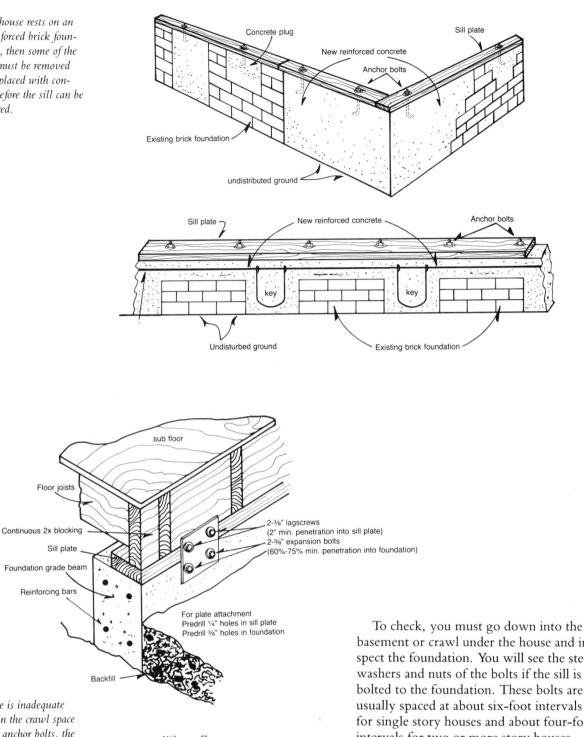

If the house rests on an unreinforced brick foundation, then some of the brick must be removed and replaced with concrete before the sill can be anchored.

Concrete plug

Sill plate

New reinforced concrete

Anchor bolts

Existing brick foundation

undistributed ground

Sill plate

New reinforced concrete

Anchor bolts

key

key

Undisturbed ground

Existing brick foundation

sub floor

Floor joists

Continuous 2x blocking

Sill plate

Foundation grade beam

Reinforcing bars

Backfill

2-⅜" lagscrews
(2" min. penetration into sill plate)
2-⅜" expansion bolts
(60%-75% min. penetration into foundation)

For plate attachment
Predrill ¼" holes in sill plate
Predrill ⅜" holes in foundation

If there is inadequate room in the crawl space to add anchor bolts, the sill can be attached to the foundation with sill plates. Each plate replaces an anchor bolt and is attached on the exterior of the house. The existing surfacing materials must be removed for this detail to work properly.

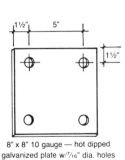

1½"   5"

1½"

8" x 8" 10 gauge — hot dipped
galvanized plate w/⁷⁄₁₆" dia. holes

To check, you must go down into the basement or crawl under the house and inspect the foundation. You will see the steel washers and nuts of the bolts if the sill is bolted to the foundation. These bolts are usually spaced at about six-foot intervals for single story houses and about four-foot intervals for two or more story houses. Most pre-1940 houses do not have such bolts. All post-1940 houses should have them, but you should check, just in case the contractor decided to cut costs or was negligent or uninformed.

If there are no sill bolts, they should be installed. Place bolts six to eight inches from all corners and about six to eight

Cripple studs are a very frequent cause of building failures during earthquakes. They are stable under earthquake stresses only when they are braced with shear-walls of plywood. Diagonal bracing, as in this damaged San Fernando home, is not sufficiently strong to withstand a large quake. Note also the fallen brick veneer.

The photograph at right shows the repairs to another San Fernando house. Note that repairs include plywood sheathing to reinforce the cripple studs that raise the floors of the split level home. Unfortunately, other houses in the area built a month or two after the quake carried on the faulty practice of bracing cripple studs only with diagonals.

inches from the ends of each sill board. Place a bolt at least every six feet for single-story homes, and every four feet for two-story homes on concrete foundations.

Use a wood bit to drill through the wood sill; then use a rotohammer with a carbide-tip bit for the concrete. You can rent this kind of drill in most rental hardware stores. When the space is too low for the drill, you can use a right-angle drill attachment to reduce the required height.

The sill bolt used for concrete is called a wedge bolt (or sometimes an expansion bolt). You can find these bolts at any major hardware supplier. Expect to pay from $3 to $6 apiece.

Contractors usually charge upwards of $15 per installed bolt, depending on the difficulty of installation. A typical house will need between 30 and 50 bolts.

Use 1/2-inch to 3/4-inch wedge bolts whenever you have access to the sill. The bolts should be seven inches or longer. Drive the wedge bolt through the sill and into the concrete, then tighten the nut on top of the sill.

The hole drilled into the sill and foundation does not have to be precise in its length, but it should be longer than the bolt. The diameter of the hole should provide a snug fit for the bolt. The hole should be cleaned by blowing out the debris inside with a small diameter hose or a straw.

If there is no access to the sill from the crawl space, the sill can be bolted from the exterior by uncovering the exterior coverings and by bolting flat steel plates into the sill and concrete foundations.

If the foundation is made of brick rather than concrete, consult a civil or structural

On several streets in
Watsonville, every house
failed during the 1989
Loma Prieta earthquake
(top left). All of the
damaged houses were
either not bolted down to
their foundations and/or
the cripple studs were not
braced with plywood. A
few houses (lower right
photo) survived—this
one had been bolted and
otherwise strengthened
shortly before the earth-
quake. It had no damage.

engineer specializing in earthquake-hazard
reduction. Usually, the engineer will recommend removing at least part of the
brick foundation and replacing it with a
concrete one. That can be quite expensive.

Weakly braced or unbraced underpinnings are the second most common weakness of older (pre-1950) houses, and some
newer houses that are supported on crawl
space walls. Typically these framed 2 x 4
walls extend two feet or less between the
concrete foundation and the flooring. They
are often called cripple walls. In some
houses, they are taller. In houses on sloping
ground they may be higher than eight feet.

A very high proportion of earthquake
damage to wood-frame houses in California in all earthquakes is from weak crawl
space walls. The weakest crawl space walls
are those that are covered on the exterior
of the house with lateral wood siding or

wall shingles. Those exterior finishes provide no effective lateral (or shear) strength;
they allow the crawl space wall to lean to
one side and collapse. Exterior stucco applied directly over the studs is a little
stronger than straight siding, but it is not
strong enough to prevent damage.

In the October 17, 1989 quake, several
hundred collapses occurred in the epicentral area—and most were easily avoidable.
Entire blocks of older houses in Watsonville collapsed. Most of these had crawl
space walls less than two feet high. Some
foundation sills were bolted and some were
not, but it did not matter, because the
crawl space walls collapsed.

In such houses, the weakness is in the
crawl space walls. Above, the house has lots
of walls to take up the force of the shaking.
In the crawl space, only the peripheral walls
have any strength; there are generally no

The cripple wall of a house in Watsonville failed in the 1989 earthquake (top and right). The cripples were not braced. The foundation of a neighboring house, left, had been removed and a new concrete peripheral wall constructed. The house had no damage.

other interior walls to help—only short columns on individual footings and a few framed walls, without any sheathing.

As usual, plywood is the recommended material for bracing and strengthening. Use ⅜-inch (or thicker) Structural 1 C-D plywood. (The drawing on page 129 shows the application of plywood bracing along the interior of the crawl space.)

Usually, it is recommended that at least eight linear feet of plywood bracing be added in each interior corner of the crawl space in each direction. Thus, if the crawl space is three feet high, you would need to strengthen your house with eight plywood sheets, each 3 by 8 feet long. It's better if the entire walls are braced.

If the crawl space is higher than four feet, then the plywood length on each face, in each corner, should be at least twice as long as it is high. Thus, if the crawl space is 5 feet high, you should use a total of eight sheets, each 5 by at least 10 feet. Again, it is better to brace all the walls.

These recommendations apply chiefly to houses on level or reasonably level lots, where the entire crawl space is accessible. If your house does not meet these qualifications, the needed strengthening may be more difficult; you might consider consulting a civil or structural engineer for further advice.

Before adding the bracing, of course, you should make sure that the house is bolted to its foundation.

The cost of the materials for bolting the foundation and bracing the crawl space walls is a few hundred dollars. If you hire a

Design and detailing for earthquake resistance

Two houses on Myrtle Street in Santa Cruz after October 17, 1989. The house on top had been recently renovated and had structural upgrades done at the same time. The house below had not been strengthened and came off its foundation. On one block of Myrtle Street, twenty-five old homes had cripple wall and foundation failures.

The plywood sheathing of the cripple wall of this house failed during the magnitude 6.0 Morgan Hill, California earthquake. The plywood failed because it was not properly nailed. The lower photograph shows the house during repairs, after it was leveled and new plywood was applied.

contractor, expect to pay upwards of $2,000 for a typical house and upwards of $8,000 for a large, difficult-to-fix house.

If everyone with an older wood house takes these two steps—bolting the sills and bracing the crawl space walls—I believe that as much as 70 percent of all serious earthquake damage to older wood-frame houses would be eliminated. I strongly urge you to do it.

Existing foundation damage

Existing foundation damage from ground settlement and, most often, rotting wood or termites is another common cause of building failures during a tremor. Older buildings especially are likely to have some foundation damage and should be carefully checked. When inspecting for foundation damage, give special attention to the condition of the wood connections. The foundation may have been laid or graded improperly so that it traps water and rots

Sheathing of cripple walls

1. Check the sill plate to be sure it has been adequately bolted to the foundation.

2. Check to be sure the sill plate and studs are the same dimensions (flush at face). If not, block between the studs and nail the blocks into the sill plate with six 16d nails per block to create a flush nailing surface for the plywood.

3. Measure the distance between the bottom of the sill plate and the top of the top plate. Measure the distance between the corner stud and the middle of a stud at 4' or 8' away to be sure a standard sheet will fit; if not, two sides of the 4' x 8' sheet will need to be cut. Check that the studs are square with framing square and use it to lay out cuts on the plywood.

4. Mark the center line of the vertical studs on foundation and above cripple wall to locate studs behind plywood for later nailing.

5. Locate all exterior ventilation grates with respect to some easy reference point so that they will not be covered with plywood.

6. Cut the plywood with a circular saw using a plywood blade.

7. Place each pre-cut section of plywood up to check fit. It may need to be trimmed; a jig saw can be used to trim the plywood without taking it out of the crawl space.

8. Tack the plywood up temporarily with a few nails. Using chalk line, snap a line on the plywood between the marks made in Step 4. Nail the plywood to studs and plates with 8d nails. The nails should be spaced 3" apart around the entire perimeter of each plywood panel and 6" apart in the middle of each sheet.

9. Measure and cut out a space with the same dimensions as the ventilation grates previously located using the jig saw.

10. Using a hole saw, drill two 1½" ventilation holes for each cavity between studs. The holes should be 2" up from the sill plate, 2" down from the top plate and centered between the studs.

11. Measure the next section to be cut and fit only after the previous section has been completely attached.

Note: In most single-story houses, it would not be necessary to sheath the entire cripple wall area. However, since this is a homeowner project, it would be less expensive to do the extra sheathing than to hire an engineer to advise you which areas should be sheathed.

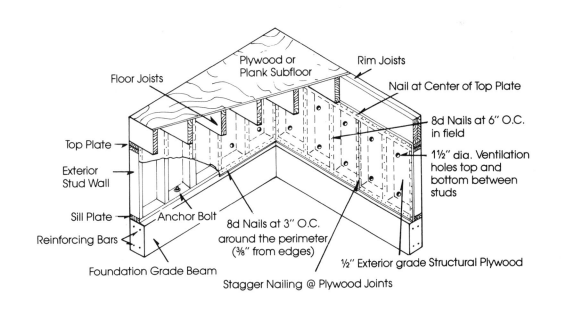

Floor Joists
Plywood or Plank Subfloor
Rim Joists
Nail at Center of Top Plate
Top Plate
Exterior Stud Wall
8d Nails at 6" O.C. in field
1½" dia. Ventilation holes top and bottom between studs
Sill Plate
Anchor Bolt
Reinforcing Bars
8d Nails at 3" O.C. around the perimeter (⅜" from edges)
½" Exterior grade Structural Plywood
Foundation Grade Beam
Stagger Nailing @ Plywood Joints

the wooden sill or columns. Poor insulation or an improperly placed dirt backfill may also retain or trap moisture and rot the wood connections. Termite damage to the sill or columns is another particularly hazardous factor. The buyer of a home should always insist on a termite clearance, even when it is not required.

Wide cracks (more than ⅛ of an inch) in foundation concrete are an almost certain sign of existing damage from ground settlement. (Do not confuse such cracks with the common "hairline" cracks which are caused by the shrinkage of concrete.) These wide cracks may also be indicative of further structural damage in the walls, so it is imperative that an engineer be con-

sulted. Existing foundation damage usually must be repaired, since it is not only an earthquake hazard but it may also lead to more serious damage to the structure simply in the course of time. The repairs can be expensive, and once you have learned from an engineer exactly what must be done, be sure to shop around with foundation contractors or pest control companies to get the most competent and economical work.

Houses on stilts and pilings

The construction of houses on stilts or pilings has made it possible for people to enjoy living on steep hills or over the water along bay shores and riverbanks. Such houses are very appealing, but they also can be very dangerous. As noted, the ideal foundation support for a house in a seismically active region is a continuous and tied wall of reinforced concrete or a reinforced concrete slab. Houses founded on a few slender supports are too seldom designed to carry the large lateral stresses of an earthquake. The earthquake risks for this type of building are compounded by the propensity of shoreline and steep hillside soils either to amplify earthquake intensities or to slide.

A house can be safely supported on slender columns only when the soil foundation is exceptionally stable and the columns and their piers below ground are specifically designed and braced for earthquake loads. For example, columns and floor joists of welded steel are one excellent solution for a steep hillside house. The columns must be imbedded in deep concrete pads and the floor joists must be thoroughly bolted and welded to the columns. Certain engineered pole foundations can also be used.

For the more conventional and less expensive wood columns, the safe choice is a shear-wall bracing system of plywood covering the entire length and breadth of the foundation.

Diagonal bracing is never adequate for timber stilts, and if you own such a house, you should certainly add continuous plywood sheathing as soon as possible. This is not a do-it-yourself type job, however.

Houses on stilts that are located on very steep hillside sites can be a poor investment, unless very carefully designed by a structural engineer.

This wood-frame building in Aptos, near Santa Cruz, collapsed during the 1989 earthquake. It was built on wood stilts on a very steep hillside.

Diagonally braced wood stilts are always extremely risky in earthquake country. The slender wood supports are simply not strong enough to withstand a large shock. Shear-wall bracing of plywood, applied over conventional studs, should be used instead for a steep site, as in the townhouses and the house under construction shown below.

Design and detailing for earthquake resistance

All of the houses supported by raised pilings along Bolinas Lagoon were shaken off their unstable foundations and dumped into the water during the 1906 quake. Despite the proximity of the San Andreas fault (the sand spit in the background was ruptured along the fault line), the same type of structures (and many of the same buildings) have been erected since 1906 all along the shore from Stinson Beach to Bodega. Pilings may provide adequate support only if they are securely tied to the building.

The services of an engineer are required to ensure that the design and mounting of the bracing complies with sound engineering principles.

Buildings partially or wholly on raised pilings are also very susceptible to severe damage. The slumping, liquefaction and high vibrational intensities experienced during a quake along shorelines and riverbanks can easily topple the pilings or simply shake the structure off these supports. If a house is supported entirely by pilings, they must be long enough and securely planted in the ground and *rigidly* tied to the understructure of the building. This work is best done by an engineer. When a portion of a building is supported on land and a portion is supported by a wharf structure, adequate ties between the two must be designed by an engineer. The ties will prevent the movement of the wharf and the consequent spreading and collapse of the pilings supporting the building. All buildings on raised pilings should be covered by earthquake insurance.

COLUMNS, WALLS AND SPLIT-LEVEL HOUSES

In general, the failure of wall supports, and particularly of the main corner columns, of a building is one of the most serious types of damage that might occur during an earthquake. Once an important wall fails or a column breaks or becomes disconnected, a chaotic sequence of further failures begins which can demolish the structure.

Wood-frame buildings

Wood columns fail most often because of the following deficiencies:

♦ The column is weakened by rotting because of poor drainage along the top of the foundation. Termite damage to the column is another common factor. If any rotted or termite-infested column bases are found in a home, the column should be replaced immediately, with careful provision for better drainage and thorough treatment of the wood against water or insect damage.

♦ The joists, sills and other horizontal structural members are inadequately tied to the column. This is by far the most common and troublesome weakness of columns in enduring earthquake forces. It is also the easiest and cheapest to correct. A pair of steel pins or steel angles are generally sufficient to strengthen these vital connections. The liberal use of these anchorages, either when building a new home or when reinforcing an existing structure, will add tremendous strength to the typical wood-frame building.

Wood-frame column connectors

There are numerous column anchorages available for wood-frame construction, and the use of these steel devices is highly recommended in building a house in earthquake country or in reinforcing the column connections in an existing structure. For exposed columns and beams, there are several anchoring devices which are designed to be concealed. Other types can be veneered or exposed and painted.

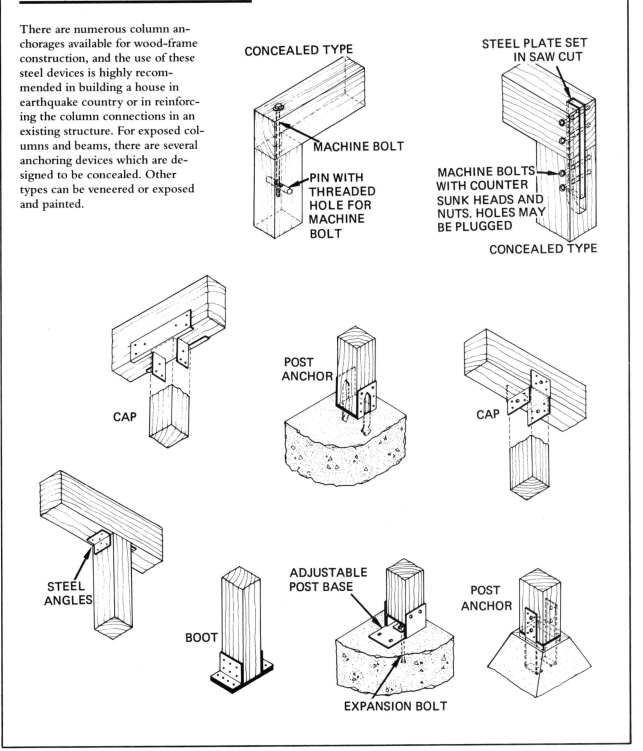

CONCEALED TYPE

MACHINE BOLT

PIN WITH THREADED HOLE FOR MACHINE BOLT

STEEL PLATE SET IN SAW CUT

MACHINE BOLTS WITH COUNTER SUNK HEADS AND NUTS. HOLES MAY BE PLUGGED

CONCEALED TYPE

CAP

POST ANCHOR

CAP

STEEL ANGLES

BOOT

ADJUSTABLE POST BASE

POST ANCHOR

EXPANSION BOLT

Split-level and multi-story houses or apartment buildings with garages located at ground level are a fairly recent development in building design. Most such buildings have been constructed since the early 1950s, and in the stronger earthquakes to strike populated areas of California since 1952, these buildings suffered a very disproportionate amount of the total damage, as did houses with lots of glass and commercial buildings, such as stores, with all glass fronts on the ground floor.

These buildings are often called "soft-story" buildings. The apartment buildings that collapsed in the Marina district of San Francisco on October 17, 1989 were all of this type.

The reason for the failure of these buildings is obvious. They are inherently weaker than conventional buildings because openings on the lower level weaken a portion of the wall area which must carry and resist earthquake forces. The garage level becomes, in effect, a foundation with only three walls. During an earthquake such a building tends to twist. But an essentially three-sided structure cannot withstand this twisting motion easily, particularly under the additional weight of another floor or two above it. If the walls of the garage do not eventually give way entirely, the top portion of the garage walls and the corners of the garage doors and windows can be severely cracked. In this case, the whole building is also susceptible to further damage or collapse if a strong aftershock should occur.

This type of damage has occurred most often to houses without adequate shear-wall bracing. All of the damaged homes illustrated here had stucco walls with interior wallboard and some diagonal bracing in the garage story; none of the garages was sheathed with plywood. Clearly, to minimize such damage and prevent collapses, the walls of the garage, and especially the front and back walls, should be strengthened with plywood sheathing. Wallboard sheathing and diagonal bracing are totally inadequate for this kind of stress. It is also very important to use steel holddowns or

The connections of columns to beams and to the foundation must be exceptionally strong if a building is to survive a large quake without serious structural damage. The "toe-nailed" connections in the photograph at top are extremely poor; the lateral motions of a tremor could easily detach the column and bring the whole structure down. Steel angles, such as that shown during construction at left, and various other steel anchoring and framing devices, should be used extensively—especially on the main supporting columns. Sturdy bolts will be placed in the framing device shown here; other devices may require only heavy nails.

These are two of numerous split-level and two-story homes in San Fernando in which the lower level garage walls were inadequately braced for the heavy load they had to support. Diagonal bracing is never sufficiently strong for this type of architecture. The right ground-level side of the first house also had diagonally braced cripple studs which contributed further to the devasta-tion. In the second photo-graph, note that the upper level of the house simply ripped away as it crushed the garage walls and the car inside. Nei-ther portion of the house seems to have suffered any other structural dam-age—a fact supporting the idea that plywood sheathing on the garage walls of a split level can mean the difference be-tween minor damage and costly destruction.

Most of the damage to houses in the Marina dis-trict of San Francisco was also due to weak lower floors (below). Typically, the basements of these houses were com-pletely open, without any structural cross walls (bottom right) and with no plywood bracing at the garage door or in the back. Plywood bracing such as that being applied (too late) on the house at right would have pre-vented the damage.

other anchoring devices to securely connect the plywood to the foundation sill and the floor joists above. Any columns which support intermediate floor joists should also be thoroughly connected with steel connectors.

Follow these guidelines:

♦ If the garage extends the entire depth of the house, so that there is no complete wall parallel to the garage door between the front and the back of the house, you need to build a new wall (with its own reinforced concrete footing) to block off part of the garage. In that case, make sure you hire an engineer to advise you.

♦ If a wall exists parallel to the garage door, separating the garage from another room in the back of the house, such as a family room on the lower floor, you should sheathe that wall with plywood.

Four different ways of strengthening weak two-story houses. All the photographs are from repair work in San Francisco's Marina. Top left—plywood sheathing is applied on all walls parallel to the street (weak direction of the house). At left center, plywood will be applied to the diagonally *sheathed wall and a new, back-up wall has already been built behind (with plywood sheathing on both sides). The two photos below show new steel frames at the garage opening (left) and in the middle of the garage (right). The steel frame is more expensive but does not take up any significant space.*

In these homes, the large plate glass walls are stabilized with steel frames, which take the place of plywood shear walls.

This very commonplace soft-story design for modern apartment buildings on the West Coast is both risky to the investor and unsafe for the occupants, unless proper measures are taken to strengthen the supporting walls and the connections between the walls of the different stories. With their essentially three-sided supporting foundation and thin columns, these San Fernando buildings were fortunate, indeed, still to be standing. A stronger shock or a few more years of inevitable deterioration in the structure would probably have meant the collapse of the buildings. All of the collapsed buildings in San Francisco's Marina in 1989 were of this type of design.*

Design and detailing for earthquake resistance

"Before and after" photographs of a soft-story concrete apartment building in Santiago, Chile after the 1985 magnitude 7.8 earthquake. A few concrete shear walls, properly placed on the ground floor, would have prevented the collapse.

First, remove the existing wallboard in the garage (this is usually a fire wall, and the wallboard is required). Apply ½-inch-thick structural grade plywood over the entire height of the wall, and over as much of the wall as possible. Try to use full 4-by-8 foot plywood panels. Apply them with the long side up.

Nail 8d (8-penny) nails at a spacing of about three inches along the entire periphery of each piece of plywood. Use six-inch spacing for nailing along the intermediate vertical studs, as illustrated. Such a wall is most effective if it is located about midway between the front and back exterior walls of the building. After nailing the plywood, apply wallboard over the plywood, as required by most local building codes.

Most often the side walls of the garage do not need additional bracing. They are much stronger than the front and back walls because they usually have no large openings such as doors and windows. It is a good idea, however, to add some plywood sheathing—at least one 4-by-8 foot plywood panel in each corner.

♦ Inside the garage, add plywood shear panels on each side of the garage door—between the door frame and the nearest perpendicular wall. Usually that space is less than three feet on each side. Use the some procedure as above. Sometimes a steel frame can be inserted behind the garage door.

♦ Special anchoring bolts, called hold-down bolts, should be added at the end of each plywood shear wall that is less than about six feet long.

If properly done, this strengthening can make the difference between no damage and partial collapse during a very strong earthquake.

Ongoing repair and strengthening of soft-story apartment buildings in the Marina. The building at top left had moved more than two feet to the left—it was pushed back and was shored-up, and awaits repairs. All the buildings in the top right photo have had or are having repairs—most were major. The lower photos show inserted, new steel frames, one braced, one ductile, on the ground floors of two severely damaged buildings. Other owners chose to sheath their buildings with plywood—another acceptable strengthening technique.

FLOOR AND ROOF DIAPHRAGMS

Most earthquake failures associated with the diaphragm members of a structure have occurred at their connections with the walls, rather than in the diaphragms themselves. The destructive forces of an earthquake are easily absorbed by these horizontal members, but their connections to the vertical supports are often considerably less durable. This is mainly a problem in masonry and tilt-up concrete buildings with wooden or steel framed roofs and floors. In the earthquake, the rigid masonry walls pull away from their connection with the diaphragms, and the unsupported roof or floors plummet.

The diaphragm connections in these buildings fail most often because of the ex-clusive use of a wood ledger—a framing beam which is bolted to the masonry walls. The floors and roof rest on and are nailed to this ledger. Such a connection is insufficient in earthquake country; the roofs and floors usually require the additional support of steel anchors or metal straps that tie the joists of the diaphragms directly to the wall.

These anchors and straps keep the diaphragms from pulling out from the ledger or from pulling the ledger out of the masonry. They also add considerable strength to the masonry or concrete walls and may help to prevent their collapse.

The most common problem with roof diaphragms in wood-frame buildings is a heavy roof. Mission-style clay-tile roofs, slate roofing and other heavy roofing materials require considerably more support and reinforcement to secure their connections during an earthquake. A clay-tile roof on a 1,500-square-foot building, for example, weighs about eight tons more than a roof of wood or asphalt shingles. The heavy-roof problem is especially hazardous with multi-story buildings because such buildings amplify the ground motion in the upper floors, causing much larger iner-

tial forces on the walls of the building. It is essential that the walls of a building topped by an exceptionally heavy roof be optimally strengthened with shear-wall bracing of plywood, so that the structure can support the roof during an earthquake. Even with such bracing, there is some risk of damage to or by the roof, and it is a good idea to carry earthquake insurance on the building.

Clay-tile, slate and other masonry or

Connections for masonry walls and wood diaphragms

The first two drawings show some of the detailing recommended for the connection of wood diaphragms and concrete masonry walls in new construction. The first is a steel joist anchor which is embedded in the masonry wall and, preferably, tied as well to the vertical steel reinforcing in the wall. The anchor

is then nailed to the underside of the blockings and joists of the roof and floors. The anchor should always be long enough to span at least three joists. Note also the anchor bolt, which is the conventional and code-required connection in all new concrete and masonry wall-wood diaphragm construction.

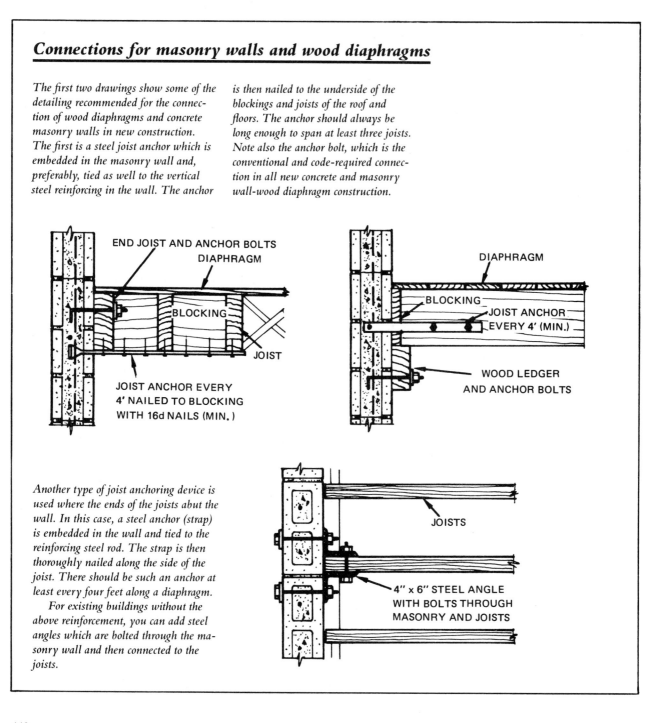

Another type of joist anchoring device is used where the ends of the joists abut the wall. In this case, a steel anchor (strap) is embedded in the wall and tied to the reinforcing steel rod. The strap is then thoroughly nailed along the side of the joist. There should be such an anchor at least every four feet along a diaphragm.

For existing buildings without the above reinforcement, you can add steel angles which are bolted through the masonry wall and then connected to the joists.

stone roofing materials are also in themselves especially susceptible to earthquake damage. Unless they are nailed to the roof, they tend to dislodge and fall during even moderate tremors that will leave the rest of the building completely unaffected. Besides being expensive to replace, these heavy roofing materials can be very dangerous to people running out of the building during the quake.

LARGE WINDOWS AND DOORS

Large doors and windows introduce weaker points in the structural frames of buildings. Much of the damage after an earthquake will be concentrated in the vicinity of these large openings. The cause for this damage is easy to understand: Where there are no openings in the walls, the earthquake forces are distributed evenly throughout the entire wall. A large hole in the structural frame interrupts the path of the earthquake forces and increases the stress to the area around the opening. The sharp corners of the opening also cause further stress concentrations which add to the damage.

A careful, plywood bracing system around the openings will be sufficient to redirect the earthquake forces back to the foundation and stiffen and strengthen the framing. The shear-wall bracing should be below, above and on both sides of the large windows or doors, and the sheathing on each side of the opening should be at least as wide as the opening itself in order to prevent cracking and other damage to the interior and exterior wall veneers.

Large plate glass panels, such as sliding glass doors and bay and picture windows or glass walls, present the additional hazard and costly damage of breakage during earthquakes. Plywood sheathing around

Buildings with heavy roofs, which includes clay-tile and slate roofing, require significantly stronger wall bracing. This building, at the Fukui, Japan, College of Engineering, vividly illustrates the whip effect caused by the combination of the heavy tile roof and the 1948 earthquake.

This single-story dwelling in Managua, Nicaragua, endured the heavy load of the tile roof and the strong tremor with only light damage in the 1972 earthquake. The strong walls and the low level of the building saved it from further damage. However, another disadvantage of tile roofing is shown here. Without careful anchoring, the tiles are easily thrown off the roof during an earthquake.

Large window and door openings are especially prone to earthquake damage (from the 1971 San Fernando and 1984 Morgan Hill earthquakes) because the openings interrupt the path of the earthquake forces and cause concentrations of stress around the openings and especially at their corners. Very often, the cracks that appear at these openings also indicate far more serious structural damage within the walls. Plywood shear-wall bracing should brace the walls surrounding large openings. The last photograph (bottom) shows the proper addition of plywood sheathing around all large openings on the ground floor of a house under construction.

such openings will prevent this damage by stiffening the walls and decreasing the wall distortions. However, some glass breakage in large windows and doors is virtually inevitable during strong quakes.

PARAPETS, ORNAMENTS, BALCONIES AND OTHER PROJECTIONS

Masonry parapets and other ornaments are usually the first components of a building to fail during an earthquake. Their positions at the tops of buildings, where the earthquake vibrations are most intense; the poor connections between the projections and the building; the cracking and general weakening caused by weathering and lack of maintenance; all contribute to the frequent failures of the architectural features.

In themselves, these decorative projections are not such a problem, because if they fall or break, an owner can simply eliminate them from the building and the repair costs will be moderate. However, when they fall, these heavy projections are also likely either to pull down a part of the supporting wall or to damage the lower portion of the building or other adjacent buildings. In addition, because these architectural features tend to be located above entrances, they are extremely hazardous to people running out of the buildings during a tremor.

Mainly for the latter reason, many but not all cities in California have passed retroactive building ordinances requiring the elimination or strengthening of hazardous parapets, ornaments and other projections on buildings other than private dwellings. Typically, a sufficient amount of time is allowed so that the problems can be eliminated in an orderly and thorough fashion and so that the owners can finance the repairs and meet some of the peculiar problems which inevitably arise. To date, most cities in California have not been responsible enough to see that the repairs are carried out. Fortunately, the repair and strengthening of hazardous projections are usually moderately inexpensive procedures. The most common method for strengthening building projec-

Masonry parapets, and other overhanging, unsupported architectural features, are highly subject to earthquake failure and are one of the most hazardous elements of earthquake damage. In the United States, many earthquake casualties result from falling masonry parapets, canopies and other exterior decorative features. The parapet and the top portion of this unreinforced masonry building in downtown Whittier collapsed in the 1987 magnitude 5.9 earthquake. Bricks from the building crushed the car in the foreground, but the driver narrowly escaped injury.

During the San Fernando quake, a parapet collapsed and fell through the ceiling of a classroom at Los Angeles High School. After numerous repetitions of this kind of damage to schools the California state and local governments took steps to replace or reinforce unsafe schools. However, many private schools, especially daycare centers, have not been checked or strengthened.

Design and detailing for earthquake resistance

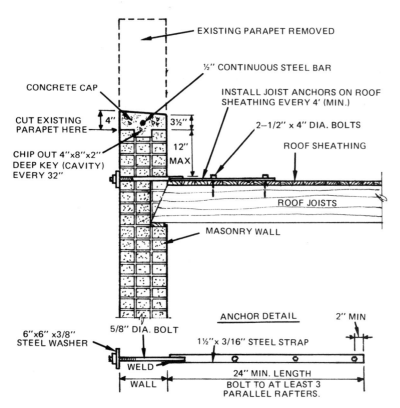

CONCRETE CAP

EXISTING PARAPET REMOVED

½" CONTINUOUS STEEL BAR

INSTALL JOIST ANCHORS ON ROOF SHEATHING EVERY 4' (MIN.)

CUT EXISTING PARAPET HERE

4"

3½"

2-1/2" x 4" DIA. BOLTS

ROOF SHEATHING

CHIP OUT 4"x8"x2" DEEP KEY (CAVITY) EVERY 32"

12" MAX

ROOF JOISTS

MASONRY WALL

6"x6" x3/8" STEEL WASHER

5/8" DIA. BOLT

ANCHOR DETAIL

2" MIN

1½" x 3/16" STEEL STRAP

WELD

WALL

24" MIN. LENGTH
BOLT TO AT LEAST 3 PARALLEL RAFTERS.

The reinforcement or removal of masonry parapets is an essential life-or-death obligation for property owners and city officers. One relatively simple method of reinforcement is shown here. The parapet is shortened, anchored with steel bolts and straps, and capped with concrete.

tions is their reinforcement with steel ties and anchors and/or the additional lateral supports of steel buttresses.

CHIMNEYS AND FIREPLACES

Exterior masonry chimneys are usually the most damageable and often the most damaging element of the typical wood-frame house. In fact, seismologists determine the intensities of a given earthquake partially by figuring the percentage of destroyed chimneys per unit area. In the 1906 San Francisco earthquake, San Mateo lost 92 percent of its chimneys; Redwood City, 96 percent; Belmont and San Carlos, 88 percent; Burlingame and San Mateo Hills (now part of San Mateo), 73 percent. In the 1971 San Fernando earthquake, most of the houses in the area were less than 15 years old, and their chimneys were reinforced with vertical steel bars in accordance with the local building codes. As a result, 68 percent of the chimneys in the highest intensity areas survived the quake without

damage. Certainly, if the chimneys had not been reinforced with steel, the percentage would have been close to zero.

Because a house and its masonry chimney are essentially separate and very different structures, they tend to respond to earthquake motions by pounding and pulling apart. Thus, chimneys must be tied thoroughly to the frame of the building, preferably with long steel straps that are embedded into the masonry and nailed to the joists of the various diaphragms of the building. These ties help to support the chimney and eliminate the possibility of pounding between the two structures.

Any masonry chimney pre-dating about 1960 is unlikely to have adequate ties to the building and should be expected to collapse in an earthquake.

If your brick chimney is somewhere in the middle of the roof and does not extend up more than three or four feet, the damage is usually not serious and repairs are relatively easy. If it is short and breaks at the roof line, it usually does not fall through the roof to cause serious interior damage.

More serious problems occur with chimneys on the side of the house. Newer chimneys, built during the past 30 years, are usually reinforced with steel. Such chimneys typically lean away from the house in a quake. If it breaks, it falls away from the house.

Older chimneys sometimes break away from the house, but since they often lack any reinforcement—or their mortar is weakened—they disintegrate more easily. In fact, this mode of failure is less damaging to nearby adjacent houses.

Long chimneys in houses with two or more stories are much more susceptible to damage, and they can do more damage if they fall on another part of the house, or on a neighbor's.

The most dangerous chimneys are those that extend five or more feet above the roof. The farther a chimney rises above the roof line, the farther it can fall. If it extends more than about five feet, it may go through the roof if it falls toward the house. This is likely when the roof is flat or has only a gentle slope. When the roof is very steep, broken

Masonry chimneys, old and unreinforced or poorly reinforced, are especially susceptible to damage, even in moderate earthquakes. The examples show shorter chimneys damaged by the 1971 San Fernando, 1983 Coalinga and 1987 Whittier, California, earthquakes. In the San Fernando quake, the falling old stone chimney destroyed a newer addition to the house. In Coalinga, center right and lower left, one of the chimneys was new, yet it did not have the necessary reinforcement. In the Alhambra home during the Whittier earthquake, at bottom right, the chimney fell through the roof, endangering the occupants.

parts of the chimney tend to slide down without breaking through the roof.

If the chimney is tall and in the middle of the roof, you should lay 1-inch-thick plywood either on the roof around the chimney (the preferred solution) or inside the attic around the chimney. The plywood should extend 1½ times the height of the chimney in each direction and should be nailed to the rafters.

Brick chimneys over doorways are hazardous because they may fall on someone leaving the house in panic. Train your family not to exit in a hurry, particularly through such a doorway.

It is difficult to reinforce an existing chimney properly without sizable expense. However, if your house has a very tall chimney, you should consider removing the portion above the roof and replacing it with a metal flue.

Anyone building a new masonry chimney anywhere in earthquake country should, above all, use the services of an engineer. A contractor does not have all the information necessary to construct an earthquake-resistant structure.

Tall masonry chimneys are probably the most dangerous feature of houses during earthquakes. Chimneys such as the one at right have little chance of surviving strong earthquakes. Tall chimneys fall apart even in moderate earthquakes, such as that in Seattle in 1965 (far right). The top photograph shows another chimney failure, in San Fernando, which caused extensive damage to a new house.

Peace of Mind in
Earthquake Country

Much better than the traditional brick and concrete chimneys are the prefabricated sheetmetal chimneys now available. These chimneys are very light, strong and flexible and will not collapse or cause any pounding damage. For a traditional appearance, the sheet metal can be encased in a masonry veneer, of course. Equally attractive and far more economical and functional would be a well-designed covering of wood or stucco.

Brick or other masonry fireplaces are also prone to earthquake damage. Thus, if you are building a fireplace, be certain that you or your contractor follow the procedure for anchoring exterior masonry veneer—that is, at least, one masonry anchor for every square foot of wall area supporting the brick or stone. If your home includes a fireplace, there are no simple measures you can take to ensure its stability in an earthquake. Chances are, if the fireplace is relatively new (built within the past 30 years), it will not collapse.

Because the heavy masonry chimneys are always subject to earthquake damage, even with the most thorough reinforcement measures, anyone constructing a chimney and fireplace in earthquake country would be wise to take advantage of the new and very safe prefabricated sheet metal units. One such unit is shown here for a single-story house. The strength, light weight and flexibility of the metal eliminates all of the traditional deficiencies of masonry chimneys. The metal units are also less expensive and require less construction time. A finished chimney is shown in the photograph at right.

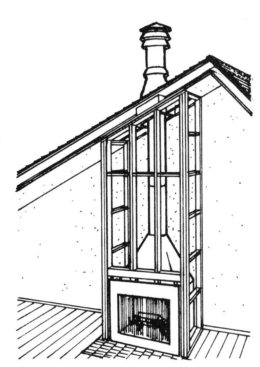

Chimneys over exits are dangerous. The only significant damage to this house was the collapsed tall chimney—which fell, practically intact, on the entrance steps. Fortunately, no one tried to run out of the house during the 1971 San Fernando earthquake—otherwise, they would have faced the only life-threatening situation in the house.

Design and detailing for earthquake resistance

Old buildings tend to suffer disproportionate earthquake damage either because the construction procedures or codes were inadequate at the time they were built or because age, poor maintenance and/or previous quake damage have weakened the structures. The large bungalow at center right was one of several hundred wood-frame dwellings which were thrown off their foundations by the Long Beach tremor. The house is of the same vintage and design as many homes in the Berkeley Hills near the Hayward fault. The Victorian house in Santa Rosa (lower right) also had foundation problems. The four-story, older building at top collapsed into a single-story pile of timbers, killing one person, in San Francisco's Marina. It, like several of its collapsed neighbors, had a weak (soft) ground floor. The photograph was taken three hours after the shock while the building across the street burned.

SPECIAL PROBLEMS WITH OLD BUILDINGS

The slow but steady evolution of the building codes has led to a gradual improvement in the earthquake resistant design of commercial and residential structures, particularly in California. This process was especially accelerated following the moderate but terribly destructive Long Beach earthquake in 1933. Up to that time, even some prominent geologists insisted that Los Angeles and the surrounding areas were in no danger from earthquakes and the building codes throughout Southern California reflected that attitude.

San Francisco, which had less excuse, was even more neglected. Soon after the scars of the destructive 1906 earthquake were removed, the business community of the city and its surrounding areas adopted the attitude that the fire, not the earthquake, destroyed the city. Eastern financial interests and insurance companies were familiar with great urban fires, and if the memories of the earthquake should be erased by San Francisco's leaders, the much needed funds for the city's rebuilding could be more readily attracted. The disaster became known, then, as the great San Francisco fire, and the local building codes regarding earthquake hazards were actually weakened in the years following the 1906 shock. Numerous large buildings built during the speculative 1920s were designed to dangerously substandard requirements, and these are some of the buildings which will probably cause the most spectacular failures during the next large shock. They will also account for a large proportion of the casualties. These are some of the buildings which suffered heavy damage in Oakland and San Francisco from the 1989 Loma Prieta earthquake. A few of them came perilously close to collapsing.

Old buildings, no matter how elaborate or costly, can be a very risky investment, and old masonry and concrete buildings present the additional problem of considerable danger to their occupants. Outdated design and engineering, outdated construction techniques, heavy construction materials, faulty connections and poor or dam-

aged foundations—all contribute to the costly damage typically sustained by old structures. In addition, lack of adequate maintenance over the years reduces the ability of many buildings to endure earthquake shocks. Rotted foundations or underpinnings, cracked mortar and plaster, and settled or distorted foundations, among many other features of neglect, all undermine the earthquake resistance of these buildings.

The minor Santa Rosa earthquakes in 1969 provided some interesting data on the relationship between the age of a building and its susceptibility to damage during an earthquake. Of 38 wood-frame dwellings badly damaged in the tremor, 29 had been built before 1920 and the other nine predated 1940. No wood-frame structures built after 1940 sustained considerable damage. The significance of this data should be obvious enough.

If you own or have your heart set on a home built before about 1950, then you should try and incorporate as many as possible of the earthquake-resistant details and remedies described in this book. First, have a civil/structural engineer examine the building and then faithfully carry out the recommendations. If you do, your new old home can be guaranteed a longer, more useful, and less costly and hazardous life.

While most older, pre-1940 houses in Coalinga were severely damaged, as shown in the top two photographs, the new single-story houses (above) typically escaped significant structural damage.

CHAPTER EIGHT

How to minimize interior, utility and other household damage

SOME INTERIOR DAMAGE IS INEVITABLE in a strong earthquake. Dishes will fall and break, taller furniture will topple, pipes may be ruptured. Generally, this type of damage can only be anticipated; to try to prevent it entirely would be to turn your household into a museum (or a motel room) in which everything is securely locked away or attached to the walls and floor. However, by anticipating the effects of an earthquake, you can at least minimize such damage and, in some cases, select among the household items that you wish to protect above all others. This chapter covers a miscellany of objects, utility components and interior features which are most typically subject to earthquake damage and which can be protected to some extent.

Electrical substations and other distribution nodes of the power grid tend to suffer severe damage, even in smaller earthquakes, because many of their porcelain components are weak. This damage occurred in San Fernando in 1971 and near Monterey in 1989. For planning purposes, do not count on having electricity in your house for at least 72 hours after a major earthquake.

UTILITIES

Obviously, the rupture of plumbing conduits during an earthquake can cause extensive interior water damage. Fortunately, this is not normally a problem because water lines are broken only when serious structural damage occurs. The gas mains should be thoroughly checked immediately following a strong quake. Keep in mind that leaking gas lines can explode into a fire hours after the shaking stops. If you smell gas and discover a broken gas line or gas leakage, shut off the main feeder valve and do not turn it on again without the assistance of a utility company employee.

If severe ground settlements or slides occurred in the vicinity of your property, the gas lines are very likely to be damaged. You will know there is such damage, of course, if the gas is not reaching your home. In this situation, the best course of action is (1) if possible, notify the utility company immediately; (2) prepare warning signs in the vicinity of the likely gas line breakage to keep other people away from the danger; (3) move yourself and your valuables a safe distance from the probable break.

Fire following an earth-quake is a very real possibility when structural failures in a building, particularly in the foundation area, are very likely to damage and sever gas pipes. The photograph at top left shows the ruptured gas line under the porch of a house that fell off its foundations in Santa Rosa in 1969. The same damage occurred to many houses in Watsonville in October of 1989. Note the broken gas meter in the house (which also fell off its foundation) at top right. One of its neighbors (lower right) was not as lucky and burned down from a gas ignition—all that is left are the front steps. Settlement of poor ground in San Francisco's Marina district broke numerous gas and water lines, incapacitating the fire protection system (lower left).

How to minimize household damage

How to shut off utilities, but only when necessary

GAS SHUT-OFF

1. Locate main gas shut-off (usually outside house) and all pilot lights.

2. Clear the area around the shut-off valve for quick and easy access in case of emergency.

3. A wrench (or specialty tool for turning off gas and water) should be attached to a pipe next to the shut-off valve or in another easily accessible but hidden location.

4. You may want to paint the shut-off valve with white or fluorescent paint so that it can be located easily in an emergency.

5. If you are concerned about your ability to turn off the main gas shut-off valve or are unsure if it is in proper working order (indication of rust, etc.) or do not know how to re-light your pilot lights, contact your local gas company. They can send a service representative to your house to show you the proper procedure and check the valve and pilot lights to be sure they operate properly.

WATER SHUT-OFF

1. Locate the main water service pipe into your house (probably in the front at the basement level). You will see a gate valve on the pipe. If you know you have leaks after an earthquake, you can shut off all water in your house with this valve. You may wish to paint the valve so it is easy to find in an emergency.

2. You can shut off all water to your property by finding the water meter box (usually at the street or sidewalk). Open the cover with a long screwdriver or specialty tool. The valve can be operated by a special tool or with a crescent wrench. If this box is inaccessible or you cannot find it, call your local water department.

ELECTRICAL SHUT-OFF

1. Locate main electrical shut-off.

2. Your house may be equipped with fuses or circuit breakers. If your house has fuses, you will find a knife switch handle that should be marked "MAIN." If your house has circuit breakers, you may need to open the metal door of the breaker box to reveal the circuit breakers (never remove the metal cover). The main circuit breakers should be clearly marked showing on and off positions. If you have any subpanels adjacent to the main fuse or breaker panel or in other parts of the house, be safe and shut them off too in an emergency.

NOTE: All responsible family members should be shown how to turn off utilities in case of emergency.

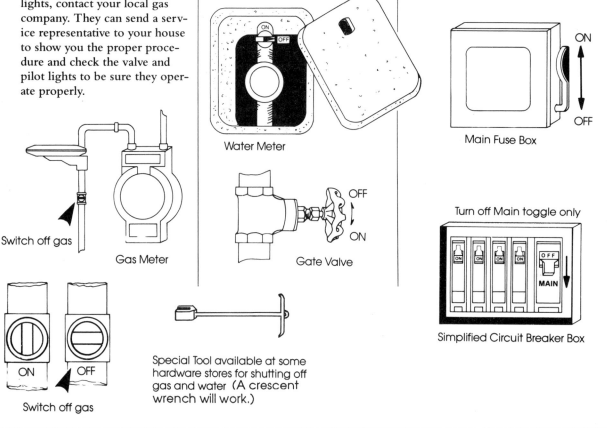

Switch off gas

Gas Meter

Water Meter

Gate Valve

Main Fuse Box

Turn off Main toggle only

Simplified Circuit Breaker Box

Switch off gas

Special Tool available at some hardware stores for shutting off gas and water (A crescent wrench will work.)

WATER HEATERS

Of all utility components, water heaters are most vulnerable to earthquake damage. Because they are quite heavy and often stand on supports unconnected to the floor, the heaters readily topple over. In order to avoid such unnecessary and sometimes hazardous damage, you should see that the water heater is bolted to the floor (many models provide bolt holes for this purpose). A toppled gas water heater can be a major fire hazard. When it falls, it tears out the gas line, allowing gas to escape freely. Any water heater, gas or electric, should be strapped to adjoining walls so it will not fall over.

The solution to this potential problem is quite simple. Brace the heater with at least two straps to two or more wood studs in the wall behind. If the wall is concrete, drill into the concrete. Place a lead expansion shield in each drilled hole, screw a screw-eye (¼ inch or thicker) into each shield and brace the water heater with light steel cable wrapped inside the screw-eyes. The entire operation probably will cost under $10, and those 10 bucks will buy you a lot of peace of mind.

AIR CONDITIONERS

Some thought should also be given to the location and installation of air conditioners. For example, it is not advisable to place them in the vicinity of a masonry chimney, which may collapse during a quake. The best location for an air conditioner is at ground level along the side of a building, where it is anchored to a low concrete mat foundation.

PLASTER AND WALLBOARD

The heavy plaster finishes in old houses, and particularly solid plaster ceilings, can represent a considerable hazard to furnishings and occupants. Plaster ceilings, for example, may weigh as much as eight pounds per square foot, which means that the ceiling of a small 15 by 15 foot room would weigh a ton or more. On the other hand, good quality plaster, like stucco, is surprisingly strong and will crack only under very heavy shaking and large wall deformations. Indeed, the combination of lath and thick plaster has a stiffening effect which can significantly increase the overall earthquake resistance of the walls.

Plaster, particularly cracked plaster in older homes, applied over lath backing, can be more easily damaged than sheetrock. This house in Whittier, Southern California lost much of its interior plaster in the 1987 earthquake.

Strapping your water heater

1. Strapping your water heater and making sure it is fitted with a flexible gas supply line will greatly reduce the danger of fire or explosion from a gas leak after an earthquake. If your water heater does not have a flexible gas supply line, contact a licensed plumber to install one. These instructions are for a *30-40 gallon water heater within 12" of a stud wall.*

2. Mark water heater at 6" down from top and about 18" up from bottom. Transfer these marks to the wall. Locate the studs in the wall on both sides of the water heater.

3. Drill a ³⁄₁₆" hole 3" deep through the wall sheathing and into the center of the wood studs at the four marks made in step 2.

4. Measure around the water heater and add 2" to the measurement. Using a hacksaw, cut the two 1½" x 16 gauge metal straps to this length for encompassing the water heater.

5. Mark 1½" from each end and insert in a vise or under a heavy object and bend the ends outward to approximately a right angle. Bend the straps into a curve.

6. Measure the distance from a point midway on each side of the water heater to the holes drilled in the wall. (Probably two different lengths.) Add 1½" to these measurements. Using a hacksaw, cut two pieces of conduit to each of these two lengths.

7. Using a hammer, flatten approximately 1½" at each end of the four pieces of tubing by laying the tube on a flat metal or concrete surface and striking with the hammer. Be sure you flatten both ends on the same plane. ▶

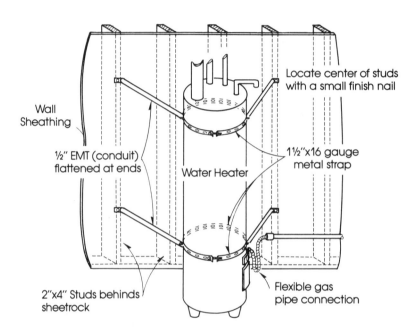

Wall Sheathing

½" EMT (conduit) flattened at ends

2"x4" Studs behinds sheetrock

Water Heater

Locate center of studs with a small finish nail

1½"x16 gauge metal strap

Flexible gas pipe connection

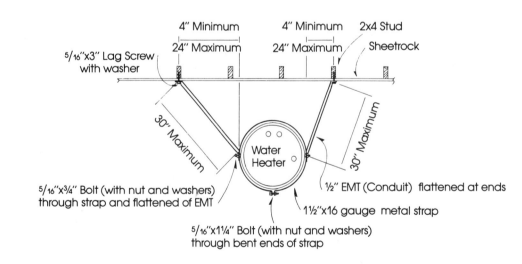

4" Minimum
24" Maximum

4" Minimum
24" Maximum

2x4 Stud
Sheetrock

⁵⁄₁₆"x3" Lag Screw with washer

30" Maximum

30" Maximum

Water Heater

⁵⁄₁₆"x¾" Bolt (with nut and washers) through strap and flattened of EMT

½" EMT (Conduit) flattened at ends

1½"x16 gauge metal strap

⁵⁄₁₆"x1¼" Bolt (with nut and washers) through bent ends of strap

8. Insert the flattened ends of the tubes, one at a time, into a vise or clamp. With the hammer and center punch make a mark ¾" from each end at the center of the flattened area of the tube. Drill ⅜" holes in the ends of all four tubes (8 holes). Be sure the tubes are clamped down while drilling. Bend each end to about 45 degrees.

9. Wrap the straps around the heater and insert a 5/16" x 1¼" bolt with washers into the bent ends. Tighten the nuts by hand. Insert 5/16" x ¾" bolts through the strap from the inside at the midpoint on each side of the water heater. Attach one end of each tube strut to a protruding bolt, add a washer and nut, and tighten by hand. Insert 5/16" lag screw in the opposite end of each tube strut and insert in the hole in the wall stud. You may need to tap the lag screw gently into the hole to start it, then tighten with crescent wrench.

10. Adjust the straps to the proper height and tighten all nuts snugly, but not too tight.

NOTE: You may wish to install an insulation jacket if your water heater is in an unheated space.

Interior damage can be very severe when houses fall from their foundations, or soft story buildings collapse partially. These examples are from the Marina district of San Francisco after October 17, 1989.

How to minimize household damage

The problem of falling or cracking plaster can best be avoided by being certain that the plaster is in good condition (no long cracks and no spots softened by water leakage). Further, if you own or will purchase an older house with plaster on inherently weak walls, such as a non-bearing partition wall, you should anticipate plaster damage in an earthquake.

Wallboard, also known as gypsum board and sheetrock, has replaced plaster in almost all construction since the early 1950s. When a house is properly stiffened and strengthened with plywood shear walls, or the house is a single floor, its wallboard is not easily damaged in an earthquake. In multi-story houses, however, the wallboard can be easily damaged

When wallboard is nailed directly to the studs of a main load-bearing stucco-exterior wall, there is considerable risk of damage such as this in a San Fernando home. Without plywood sheathing, these walls are subject to deformations which crack and throw off the wallboard.

if the house does not have shear wall bracing. That is why it is best to sheath with plywood the entire ground floor in a two story house, for example. At any rate, the damage to wallboard is usually not dangerous to occupants and is easily repairable.

FURNISHINGS

A strong earthquake is bound to cause some damage to furnishings, particularly to breakable items such as china, glassware, pictures and picture frames, lamps and art objects. Much of this can be prevented if you are willing to take the time.

If you don't want to bother with all your decorative objects, you should at least consider protecting (1) valuable paintings that might tear if they fall on furniture and (2) objects that might gouge expensive furnishings.

For example, paintings and other hung art objects should be attached to the wall with oversized threaded hooks, which can be screwed deep into the studs. For smaller frames, use regular but oversized hangers, and close the open hook to make it difficult for the wire to slip out during the earthquake.

Falling bookcases and books are common in earthquakes and can pose a serious hazard to occupants. Tall bookcases and other tall furniture with narrow bases easily fall. It is wise to attach such heavy furniture to wall studs with small steel angles or straps. It's also a good idea to arrange bulky books and other heavy objects on the lower shelves of a bookcase or cabinet. A lightweight bar, dowel or rim across the shelves is another protection for books, dishes or other objects displayed in high places.

Most of the damage to china and glassware occurs when cabinet doors fly open and the contents fall to the floor. The easiest and best solution is simply to have strong push latches on your cabinets. Whatever type of latch you use, the trick is to keep the doors closed against the force of the contents during an earthquake. Some hardware stores sell a special type of latch that opens only after the cabinet door is pushed from the outside.

Reducing interior damage

Cabinets: Install positive catching latches. Many variations are available at hardware stores.

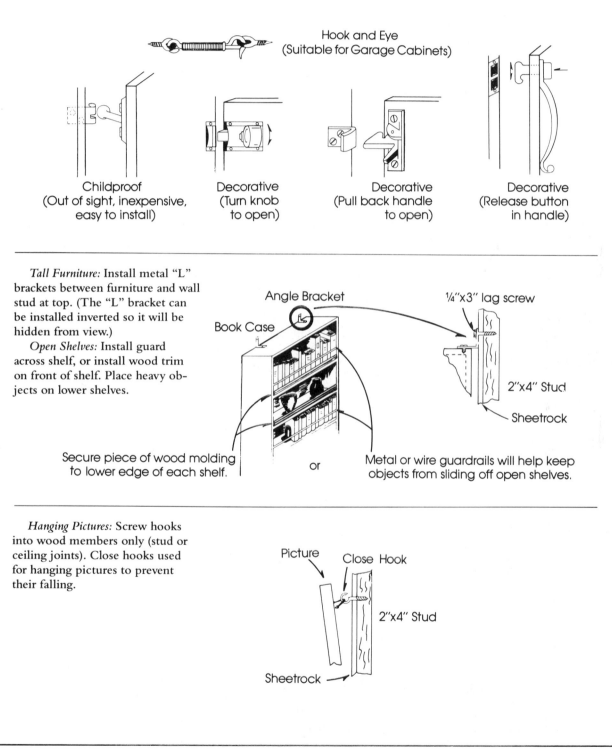

Hook and Eye
(Suitable for Garage Cabinets)

Childproof
(Out of sight, inexpensive, easy to install)

Decorative
(Turn knob to open)

Decorative
(Pull back handle to open)

Decorative
(Release button in handle)

Tall Furniture: Install metal "L" brackets between furniture and wall stud at top. (The "L" bracket can be installed inverted so it will be hidden from view.)

Open Shelves: Install guard across shelf, or install wood trim on front of shelf. Place heavy objects on lower shelves.

Angle Bracket

Book Case

¼"x3" lag screw

2"x4" Stud

Sheetrock

Secure piece of wood molding to lower edge of each shelf.

or

Metal or wire guardrails will help keep objects from sliding off open shelves.

Hanging Pictures: Screw hooks into wood members only (stud or ceiling joints). Close hooks used for hanging pictures to prevent their falling.

Picture

Close Hook

2"x4" Stud

Sheetrock

Some interior damage and vast disarray of objects and furnishings are inevitable in a large earthquake. This typical damage in a home in San Fernando can be minimized if you anticipate the effects of the quake and take measures to secure those belongings that are most breakable and valuable. Strong latches on cupboard doors; wire or angle anchors on tall, heavy furniture, valuable lamps and art objects and hanging light fixtures and pictures; dowels or rims on bookshelves— these and other common-sense measures can lessen the most heart-breaking kind of earthquake damage.

Views of interior damage of a hillside house after the Morgan Hill earthquake of 1984. The house itself had no significant structural damage.

Typical scenes of damage to office interiors from the 1987 Whittier (right), 1971 San Fernando and the 1989 Loma Prieta earthquakes. Suspended ceilings and light fixtures fall easily when they are not properly braced with diagonal wire, as required by modern codes. The majority of office buildings in California do not have up-to-date suspended ceiling bracing systems.

Valuable glass or other fragile objects, when not displayed, should always be kept in locked drawers or cabinets, preferably in a low-profile piece of furniture. Lower cabinets are far less likely to overturn during a large tremor.

Lamps and overhead light fixtures are common casualties of an earthquake, and in both cases a little discreet wiring or bolting can reduce the potential for damage.

One more note: It is extremely foolhardy to place beds anywhere near high heavy objects—a chandelier, for example, or tall heavy furniture or a large mirror. The first jolt of a strong earthquake may awaken you—but it may also plunge that heavy object into your bed seconds before you can move to safety.

It's also wise to place beds away from large glass walls or windows unless you have heavy curtains or blinds to protect you from falling glass. And, of course, savvy residents of earthquake country never hang pictures or anything else heavy on the wall behind the bed.

SWIMMING POOLS

Earthquake damage to swimming pools is usually related to ground disturbances in the vicinity. There is little you can do about this problem, of course, except to pick a sound geologic foundation for your homesite. The one hazard from swimming pools, especially on hillside sites, is the possible damage from sloshing and escaping water. In the larger California quakes, pools have often lost as much as 25 percent of their water from the sloshing caused by the earthquake motion. It is always best to locate a pool at an elevation lower than the house and as far away as possible from the house.

ANTENNAS

The worst location for a large and heavy antenna—a masonry chimney or a fragile cornice of the roof—is the place where most antennas are attached. Instead, they should be well-braced either to the middle of the roof, or, preferably, along the wall of the house.

FREE-STANDING AND RETAINING MASONRY WALLS

Masonry retaining walls and fences require good footings and some reinforcement and full grouting if they are to remain upright during a quake. Because they are heavy, inflexible and segmented, and because they have either no support (free-standing garden walls), or support on only one side (retaining walls), the walls can easily collapse without sufficient reinforcement and anchorage to a solid foundation. Collapse is not generally a hazard to life or property, of course, but the replacement of these walls is expensive, and the damage is easily avoided.

Reinforce all such masonry walls with at least ½-inch vertical and horizontal steel bars every two feet. The bars should extend the full height of the wall and should be fully grouted with poured concrete or good-quality mortar. In addition, *all* of the other cavities of concrete blocks should be grouted. The foundation for these walls should be embedded several inches into the ground. With brick walls, some horizontal steel reinforcement—about every two feet—is also required.

Concrete-block retaining and garden walls call for the same type of careful reinforcement that is required in constructing a concrete-block building. All of the garden walls in this block in San Fer- *nando Valley were toppled by the earthquake. Note that the columns remained intact when they fell, because they had been grouted with concrete. Had they also been reinforced with a steel rod* *that extended into the base, they and the whole wall might have remained upright as well. The blocks between the columns had neither grouting nor reinforcement.*

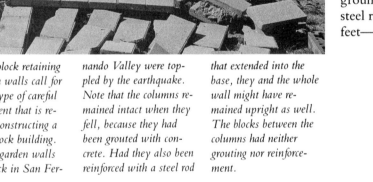

BEND ALTERNATE BARS

6" MIN.

10"

18" MIN.

24" OVERLAP

1/2" DIA. BAR MINIMUM

In reinforcing a concrete-block retaining or garden wall, the steel rods should be bent at the bottom end and these ends should then be embedded perpendicularly in a concrete-block or, preferably, poured-concrete base. The bend in every other rod should be placed in the opposite direction, so that the rods will pull against one another and remain anchored under the stress of the earth- *quake's lateral motions. The concrete base should be set at least 16 inches into the ground and a few inches of dirt should cover it. If the wall is fairly tall and the use of the lengthy steel rods would be awkward, you can use a shorter rod (called a "dowel") as the anchor and overlap it by about 24 inches with another rod that will extend to the top of the wall.*

PART FOUR

The other remedies— earthquake insurance and common sense preparations

CHAPTER NINE

Earthquake Insurance

*I*S EARTHQUAKE INSURANCE FOR HOME-
owners in California available on an
affordable basis? If it is, do you need
such insurance—how much and what
kind? In order to address these questions,
recent California legislation and insurance
market changes should be considered, before discussing what specifically is available
and at what price. Purchasing financial
protection should be the result of assessing
your financial risk—"exposure" in insurance jargon—and knowing what kind of
protection fits your needs.

THE CHANGING "RULES"

A legal theory known as "concurrent caus-
ation" holds that, under a so-called "all-
risk policy," such as the typical homeowners insurance policy, if a loss is attributable
to two perils (risks), one of which is *excluded* while the other is not, the loss *is* covered. In the past, earthquake damage may
have been required to be paid under policies without specific earthquake coverage if
a non-excluded contribution cause, such as
negligent construction, could be found to
have "concurrently" caused the damage.
Therefore, the pricing of normal homeowners policies has included a crossover
component for earthquake risk coverage
though the specific terms of the homeowners policy may have explicitly *excluded*
earthquake coverage.

As a result of this "concurrent causa-
tion" theory, the California legislature enacted legislation, effective January 1, 1985.

The stated intent of the legislature in enact-
ing Assembly Bill No. 2865 was "to make
clear that loss by or resulting from an
earthquake shall be compensable by insurance coverage only when earthquake protection is provided through a policy
provision or endorsement designed specifically to indemnify against the risk of earthquake loss, and not through policies where
the peril of earthquake is specifically excluded even though another cause of loss
acts together with an earthquake to produce the loss." Additional provisions of
this assembly bill required the promotion
of "awareness of earthquake insurance by
residential property owners and tenants by
requiring insurers to offer that coverage."
Further, in accordance with the provisions
of the bill, residential property coverage
insurers are now offering earthquake insurance to all residential policyholders.

The unofficial reports of a few major
companies indicate that approximately 15
percent of residential policyholders have
accepted this "additional" earthquake offer.
The previous acceptance level of earthquake coverage was approximately 7 to 8
percent. This dramatic increase in policyholders has not been greeted with enthusi-
asm by the insurance industry, however.
Some insurers have expressed concern that
their specific earthquake exposures were already as large as they considered prudent.
They are also concerned about "adverse selection"—the probability that a disproportionate number of owners of high-risk
homes have purchased the coverage the insurers have had to offer. Therefore, most

insurers have adopted some or all of the following actions:

1. Higher Deductible. Many insurers started using a 10 or 15 percent deductible on residential property. Previously, a 5 percent deductible had been a "standard" in the industry. Other insurers have adopted an approach of offering both a 5 and 10 percent deductible, at the option of the insured, with a significant price difference between the two.

2. Raised Rates. Because of the very low frequency of earthquake occurrence though high potential losses many insurers have adopted increased rates, presumably to help secure more adequate premiums to help cover potential losses. This has produced an extremely wide range of rates reflecting the varying perceptions of risk potential by the insurers.

3. Reviewed Homeowner Insurance Acceptability Standards. Because every policy insuring residential property must, by statute, be accompanied by an offer to provide earthquake coverage, some insurers have started to include the risk of earthquake damage in their considerations of accepting or rejecting applications for residential property insurance. An insurer which wishes to limit its earthquake exposure may elect to stop writing residential property policies on homes, for instance, with masonry construction, on homes located on landfill, hillsides, or in close proximity to known faults.

Since the Loma Prieta earthquake in October 1989, there has been a movement among some homeowners carriers to offer more favorable rates with somewhat lower policy deductibles; this is due to greater comfort with the residential risk through increased use of sophisticated technology for measuring potential losses and maintaining a better spread of risk. Also, certain mortgage lenders have begun sponsoring the offering of special earthquake coverage on a group plan basis, which holds the prospect of affordable coverage for those eligible.

Currently there are also legislative initiatives at both the national and state levels involving residential earthquake insurance. In both cases, they propose some form of government-sponsored insurance for homeowners. At this point there is no assurance that these proposals will become reality, or whether they will present an opportunity for significant protection for most homeowners.

COST FACTORS

Contrary to popular belief, earthquake insurance is now generally available throughout the West. The annual rate for a single-family wood-frame dwelling in the San Francisco or Los Angeles metropolitan areas varies from $1.00 or less to about $2.50 per $1,000 of coverage. Thus, the annual premium for $150,000 of insurance could be as low as $135—not an excessive amount considering the protection and peace of mind that the insurance may afford the homeowner. For higher risk buildings, of course, the rates will be considerably more expensive. For example, an unreinforced brick building in the same area might be rated as high as $11.00 per $1,000 of coverage, for an annual premium of $1,650 on a $150,000 policy.

Buildings located on other than firm, natural ground are sometimes penalized by a 25 percent or more increase in premium rates. Landfill, waterfront properties, landslide-prone areas and other poor ground conditions are included in this category. However, insurance underwriters rarely inspect either the building or the geologic foundation of small dwellings (under four units), and many such buildings are generally classified automatically as sound structures on solid soil foundations unless the area has a past history of landslide or seismic damage. This lack of inspection or soil investigation by insurers has been a distinct advantage to consumers with faulty buildings or building sites. However, anyone located in a well-known active fault zone will find it difficult to conceal that fact from insurers, many of whom are investing in systems to "map" high-risk locations.

Earthquake insurance rates are also based on the geographic location of the property in broadly-defined areas or zones. California, for example, is subdivided into zones for the purposes of insurance, and areas which experience fewer earthquakes are generally granted rates between 20 and 60 percent lower than higher-frequency areas. Overall, the different insurance zones are rather broad and arbitrarily chosen, so that pockets of expected high intensities in a low-risk zone are usually not penalized (although, as mentioned above, underwriters are beginning to employ the latest earthquake engineering technology to further identify higher-risk areas). Still, this is another favorable feature of earthquake insurance policies.

ing's replacement or rebuilding value at the time of the loss. In order to evaluate an insurance offer properly, it is most important to understand how this kind of deductible works. See the accompanying table for an example.

Deductible percentage

Assume you have earthquake insurance in the amount of $125,000 (the estimated cost to rebuild your home). A major earthquake occurs and your house and contents are severely damaged, but not totally destroyed.

Cost to repair your house	$ 75,000
Cost to repair or replace contents	$ 15,000
Additional living expenses	$ 10,000
Demolition and debris removal	$ 5,000
Total amount of loss and claim	$105,000
Your deductible (10% of $125,000)	$ 12,500
Insurer pays you	$ 92,500

Although many current or potential buyers of earthquake insurance are dismayed by the significant 5 to 15 percent deductibles involved, it should be recognized that the concept of catastrophic insurance is to cover infrequently experienced (but potentially very severe) damage. If it were designed for fixing superficial cracks, repainting or rebricking a facade, or patching a swimming pool, it would be very costly coverage, indeed. The most "cost efficient" approach for most homeowners is to take care of the relatively small losses themselves. Then they should only pay a relatively low premium for coverage in the less likely event of major damage to the structure itself.

POLICY DEDUCTIBLES

All insurance companies apply a deductible, expressed as a percentage of the build-

POLICY TYPES

Two types of earthquake insurance are available: (1) *straight earthquake insurance,* and (2) an *earthquake-damage endorsement*. Straight earthquake insurance is usually written as a separate "disaster" policy covering only those extraordinary losses caused directly by earthquake (or flood, *tsunami*, dam breakage, etc.). As of this writing, there is only one source of such coverage in California and presumably in other states. Such catastrophe coverage is offered through mortgage lenders and service companies to their existing and new mortgage holders on a special lower-cost group basis. The home must qualify as being built since 1950 (therefore it presumably meets acceptable earthquake-related building codes), located in a moderate earthquake intensity area, and not be much over 3,000 square feet in size. However, if qualified (and at least 70 percent of California houses are), the cost can be 40 to 60 percent less than most other earthquake coverages currently offered. It is often purchased as a companion to an existing homeowners or fire insurance policy, and operates much as the earthquake endorsement does.

The much more common earthquake-damage endorsement is merely an addendum to the standard fire or homeowners policy on a building, in effect extending the policy to cover the peril of earthquakes. The standard homeowners or fire policy for a home also covers *fire* damage caused directly or indirectly by earthquake, while straight earthquake policies usually exclude fire loss, relying on the underlying homeowners policy to cover fire losses—it was a requirement of the 1985 legislative change mentioned above that the homeowners/fire policy cover all fire losses, from any source.

In addition to this direct damage coverage on homes, both types of policies also provide for miscellaneous coverages. Some of these coverages are personal property, additional living expenses, rental value, and other types of special insurance coverage generally available with homeowners policies as well. These additional coverages are often offered at reduced rates when purchased in conjunction with the building insurance.

Both types of earthquake policies usually carry the following stipulations:

♦ An earthquake is defined as any one, or a series of, several shocks which occur in a given 72-hour period. Earthquakes or aftershocks which occur in the following 72 hours are considered to be a separate earthquake for insurance purposes. Thus, the deductible which the policies carry may be applied more than once for damaging shocks which occur at intervals greater than 72 hours.

♦ As deductible clauses are almost exclusively based on a percentage of the building's replacement or rebuilding value, the deductible is determined from the *replacement value* of the primary building/house (excluding the land and "appurtenant" structures like detached garages or swimming pools—although these are often covered) *before the loss*. It is important, then, that the coverage reflect the current costs for rebuilding the primary dwelling structure. An undervalued property would result in a lower deductible, but it might also be completely unrealistic in terms of the amount of money you would receive for replacing or repairing a badly damaged structure. Remember, the real devastating event financially for most home owners is the cost of a major rebuilding project. The goal of protection is to insure against this event.

♦ Window and door glass is generally not covered against earthquake damage. If such coverage is desired, it must be obtained in a plate-glass addendum to the standard fire policy or in a separate plate-glass policy.

♦ Losses caused directly or indirectly by explosions, floods or *tsunamis* resulting from an earthquake are not always covered by the earthquake policies. Be certain that you understand the range of coverage and consider the various earthquake risks to your property. If you live near the ocean shore in a sea-level site in Alaska, for example, *tsunami* coverage is probably essential.

The details of the coverage and of the rates should be discussed with your insurance agent or carrier, and you must be very careful to consider all relevant factors and understand the coverage afforded by your policy. The decision on whether to purchase insurance and how much coverage is necessary cannot be based entirely on broad generalizations. You should understand from this book that the geology of your site and the materials, design and structural features of your building are the important considerations. You have to thoughtfully weigh these factors, as well as the history of seismicity in your area. Certainly you have to consider your own financial situation. The remaining section of this chapter should help you in this important and very personal consideration of financial protection. It is worth generalizing in one sense, however, that some people are willing to risk their primary asset, their home, believing that the possibility of major damage is remote. Others elect to purchase protection for "peace of mind" against the possibility that mother nature will do the unexpected. An appreciation of your property risk and your capacity to absorb loss, coupled with the availability of affordable insurance, provide the ingredients for an intelligent choice.

HOW MUCH IS ENOUGH?

Earthquake insurance should be purchased by those homeowners who cannot afford or are unwilling to lose a major portion of their largest asset—the equity in their home. Most of us have a source of funds for repairing minor damage to our homes. But what if a loss of $25,000 or more occurs from an earthquake? Many homeowners would feel the financial pinch. The most intelligent approach to considering earthquake insurance, as with other kinds of insurance, is to buy coverage only when the lack of it will create a financial burden. In short, it is necessary first to decide at what level of loss—$25,000, $50,000, $100,000—the repair or rebuilding of your home becomes an unacceptable burden. This is an individual financial question, but we can look at a hypothetical case to help in making this judgment.

Let's assume . . .

1. That the cost of replacing your home, the Replacement Cost Value or RCV, is $130,000.

2. Now, let's assume that a major earthquake (8 + on the Richter Scale) occurs in your area and your home is damaged to the extent of either 10 percent of the RCV or, on the other extreme, totally destroyed. The dollar loss would be either $13,000 or $130,000 *in terms of the structure only.*

3. Valuable contents of your home may be damaged or destroyed, including furniture, fixtures, and appliances. This cost can be estimated as a percent of the house damage, say 20 percent or between $2,600 and $26,000.

4. Consider that there will be some dislocation of your family while the home is rebuilt. This could range from two weeks for minor damage to six months for a totally destroyed home (particularly when contractors will be in great demand). At a weekly cost of $500, for example, this cost could be $1,000 or $13,000.

Let's also assume . . .

You have $150,000 in equity in your home, and your furniture and personal possessions, including two cars, are valued at $35,000.

You have a money market account with $12,000, two IRAs worth $10,000, and securities valued at $25,000.

In total, your liquid assets (excluding pension fund and social security interests) amount to $232,000.

Now, how much is enough?

A generally accepted rule of thumb is that you should not risk more than 10 percent of your liquid assets, or about $23,000 in our hypothetical case.

The conclusion that can be drawn in this hypothetical case is that minor earthquake damage can be borne without insurance coverage, but the potential damage from a major earthquake far exceeds safe financial guidelines. This in turn suggests that most homeowners should have earthquake coverage. The coverage should recognize the ability of the homeowner to assume some of the loss, up to $23,000 in this example, in return for lower-priced catastrophe coverage that meets the critical financial need.

Adding up the earthquake damage in both the minor and major damage scenarios, we find:

	Minor Damage	Total Destruction
Structure	$13,000	$130,000
Contents	2,600	26,000
Living Expense	1,000	13,000
Estimated Total	$16,600	$169,000

How to behave before, during and after a quake to protect your family, yourself and your property.

BEFORE AN EARTHQUAKE

The most important measures in preparing for an earthquake are: (1) Make your building and its contents as stable and earthquake-resistant and well-insured as possible, using common sense, the help of a civil/structural engineer, and the text of this book as your guide. (2) Think about and discuss with your family, neighbors and co-workers the likelihood and the effects of the next big earthquake, and consider what you and the others would and should do in your home, at work, in your car or in any other place when the tremor strikes. Conscious pre-planning will enable you to react calmly and effectively during the emergency. In addition, you should make the following preparations:

- Set aside a flashlight, a battery-powered radio, extra batteries, a working fire extinguisher, a first-aid kit and a few days' supply of canned food and plastic-bottled water.

- Have some knowledge of first-aid procedures. Medical facilities are always overloaded after a disaster.

- All responsible family members should know what to do to avoid injury and panic. They should know the location of the main gas and water valves and the electrical switch, and they should understand the safety measures to be taken in protecting themselves, small children and the building.

- Support legislation and government-agency planning that will strengthen buildings, eliminate hazards and prepare emergency and public-safety organizations for fast and effective action.

DURING AN EARTHQUAKE

The most important thing to do during an earthquake is to remain calm. If you can do so, you are less likely to be injured and those around you will also benefit from your coolness. Think about the possible consequences before making any moves or taking any actions.

If you are inside a building, stand in a corner or in a strong, preferably interior doorway, or if you can, get under a sturdy desk or table. Watch for falling plaster, bricks, suspended ceilings, light fixtures and tall, heavy furniture. Stay away from windows, large mirrors and masonry chimneys and fireplaces. In tall office buildings, it is best to get away from windows or glass partitions and watch out for falling ceiling debris. In factories, stay clear of heavy machinery that may topple or slide across the floor.

Do not rush outside if you are in a store, office building, auditorium or factory. Stairways and exits may be broken or littered with debris and are likely to become jammed with panicky people. The power for elevators and escalators often fails. In addition, many deaths and injuries in an earthquake result from falling debris around the exteriors of commercial and public buildings. Unless you are in an especially dangerous building, such as an unreinforced brick building or a nonductile concrete frame building, it is usually better simply to wait until the shaking has stopped before exiting the buildings. Then, choose your exit with care and as you leave, move calmly but quickly and watch for falling debris and collapsing walls.

If you attempt to leave a house during the quake, be wary of collapsing chimneys or porch canopies and watch for fallen electrical wiring. Once you are outside, or if you are outside when the quake strikes, stay well away from high buildings and from masonry walls. Watch for falling power poles, lamp posts and power lines. Remain in an open area until the ground motions have ceased, and do not re-enter your house until you are certain that the quake is over and the walls are stable. If there is obvious and serious damage to the house, you should stay out of it or enter it very carefully and only long enough to turn off the utility valves. An aftershock or the damage itself might cause further collapse.

If you are in an automobile during the earthquake, stop in an open area away from tall buildings and overpasses and remain in the car until the quake is over.

AFTER AN EARTHQUAKE

After the quake, the first thing to do is to check for injuries among the people around you. Seriously injured persons should not be moved unless they are in immediate danger of further injury. First aid should be administered. Your next concern should be the danger of fire. Check the gas lines, and if there is any likelihood of leakage, turn off the main gas valve, which is usually near the meter. If there is a possibility of damage to the gas lines outside of your building, put up warning signs, notify your neighbors and the emergency authorities and stay well clear of the fire and explosion hazard until it has been checked by a serviceman. Do not use electrical appliances if there is a possibility of gas leakage, because the sparks could ignite the gas.

Check the water and electrical lines next, and turn off the main valve or switch if there has been damage. Be especially careful of any damage to the wiring. Also, since there is likely to be shattered glass and other debris after a quake, put on shoes before you begin to inspect the damage. There is always a danger of falling debris long after the quake, so be cautious in moving about or near a building. Particular attention should be given to the roof line and chimney.

Do not use the telephone unless you have a genuine emergency. The lines are always overloaded during a disaster, and your unnecessary call could be responsible for blocking an emergency call by someone else. Do not go sightseeing; the streets must be kept open for emergency vehicles. Use the radio to obtain information and damage reports.

Stay away from beaches and other low-lying waterfront areas where *tsunamis* could strike after the quake. Your radio will broadcast any alerts regarding the danger of sea waves. Also stay away from steep, landslide-prone areas, since an aftershock may trigger a slide or avalanche.

Small children often suffer psychological trauma during a quake and should be comforted and attended at all times. An aftershock may panic them if the parents are absent. Pets also suffer trauma during an earthquake.

If the water is off, emergency drinking and cooking water can be obtained from water heaters (be careful of broken glass particles) and from toilet tanks, melted ice cubes and canned vegetables. Do not flush your toilet until you are certain that you will not need the water stored in the upper tank. If the electricity is off, use the fresh and frozen foods first before they spoil. Save canned and dried food for last. Use outdoor barbecues or fireplaces for cooking. With the latter, however, be certain that the chimney is undamaged. Check especially at the roof level and in the attic,

---

Preparedness planning

Be prepared—what you do immediately following an earthquake may prevent injuries and significant financial loss.

Preparing for an earthquake takes two forms—physical preparation (equipment and supplies) and mental preparation (knowing what to do).

I believe that the average home, with a few simple additions, has the supplies and food on hand to last up to 72 hours. State and local officials advise residents that outside help after a large, damaging earthquake may take up to 72 hours. Based on experience, if you live in an urban area, you should expect help within 24 hours following an earthquake. However, immediately following an earthquake help from local fire and police departments will not be available. Be prepared to administer first aid or put out a small fire. Listed below are a few suggestions and hints on how to best utilize the resources at hand.

- Water—The water heater (30-40 gallons) for a family of four should contain enough water to last 4 days. The upper toilet tank can provide up to 7 gallons of water. Ice cubes in the freezer and liquid from canned food can be used. I recommend keeping purification tablets on hand rather than trying to store extra water.

- Food—Most houses have ample food on hand for several days. Use food in your refrigerator and freezer first. If there is no power, frozen food will keep 3 days in an unopened freezer.

- First Aid—Most homes have the necessary items to handle routine accidents. A first aid kit and a book on first aid should be kept in a central location. Take a first aid and CPR course from the Red Cross.

- Fire Extinguishers—Have one or more fire extinguishers. Learn how to use them! Have your fire extinguishers serviced annually to be sure they are working properly.

Develop a family plan

Develop a plan for your family to use during an earthquake. Discuss it fully and conduct a drill. Draw a floor plan of your house and locate the following:

☐ Safest place in the house

☐ Most dangerous places

☐ Exits and alternative exits

☐ Utility shut-off valves

☐ Flashlights and batteries

☐ First aid kit

☐ Fire extinguishers

☐ Food and water supplies

☐ Batteries and transistor radio

You should also:

☐ Make special provisions for elderly or disabled family members.

☐ Make evacuation plans for your children's school or day care.

☐ Identify resources in your neighborhood. Find someone in your neighborhood to watch out for your house. Know the skills of your neighbors (doctor, engineer, etc.).

☐ Identify a person outside the immediate area to coordinate family contact. While local lines may be down, long distance lines will function sooner.

☐ Make special provisions for pets. Pets will not be allowed in shelters and will need to be confined in a safe room in your house.

for unnoticed damage could result in a fire if you use the fireplace.

Finally, be prepared for strong and possibly damaging aftershocks and do not remain in or near a building that might be further damaged. Masonry buildings are especially susceptible to aftershock damage, and it is a good general rule simply to stay away from such buildings until they have been declared safe by an expert.

After an earthquake

☐ Check for injuries, give first aid, and cover the seriously injured with blankets to prevent shock. Do not attempt to move seriously injured persons unless they are in immediate danger.

☐ Turn on a battery-operated or car radio and listen for information on what to do.

☐ Do not attempt to drive anywhere. Roads may be damaged or blocked with debris. Freeway overpasses may be down. Use will be restricted to emergency vehicles only.

☐ Plan for strong aftershocks. Stay out of already weakened and damaged homes.

☐ Wear shoes to protect your feet from broken glass and debris.

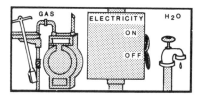

☐ Don't take unnecessary risks. If you notice any damages, turn off gas, electricity, and water. Do not turn back on until each has been properly inspected.

☐ Do not touch downed power lines or objects in contact with power lines.

☐ Do not expect the telephone to work. Do not try to use the telephone unless it is an emergency.

Appendices

The faults and earthquakes of the western states

MAJOR PORTIONS OF ALASKA CALIfornia, Nevada and Utah and smaller sections of Washington and Oregon are interlaced with hundreds of faults, many known to be active. Some of the most heavily faulted areas contain the largest urban settlements in the West, including Los Angeles, San Francisco, Oakland, and Salt Lake City. Other large cities, such as Seattle, Portland and Anchorage, are near major fault zones and have experienced damaging earthquakes in the past.

This appendix contains brief descriptions of the larger and more important faults in the West and includes brief accounts of some of the most damaging earthquakes recorded along these fault zones. The descriptions here are not in-

tended to be used as the sole aid in locating your property with regard to the nearest fault zone. This is no more than a general summary of existing information on the location and activity of major faults. Small but active faults and branches of the major fault zones and some major faults are not included.

ALASKA

The earthquake history of sparsely settled Alaska is very spotty, although there are partial records dating back to the late 1700s. One fact, however, is certain. Of all 50 states, including California, Alaska has experienced by far the largest number of *great* earthquakes. In the past 90 years, for example, eight shocks have exceeded mag-

Major earthquakes of Alaska

Date (GMT)	Region	Richter Magnitude
September 4, 1899	Near Cape Yakataga	8.3
September 10, 1899	Yakutat Bay	8.6
October 9, 1900	Near Cape Yakataga	8.3
June 2, 1903	Shelikof Strait	8.3
August 27, 1904	Near Rampart	8.3
August 17, 1906	Near Amchitka Island	8.3
March 7, 1929	Near Dutch Harbor	8.6
November 10, 1938	East of Shumagin Islands	8.7
August 22, 1949	Queen Charlotte Islands (Canada)	8.1
March 9, 1957	Andreanof Islands	8.2
July 9, 1958	Southwestern Alaska	7.9
March 28, 1964	Prince William Sound	8.4
February 4, 1965	Rat Islands	7.8
February 28, 1979	Mount St. Elias, Southeastern Alaska	7.7
May 7, 1986	Kadak Island	7.7

nitudes of 8, the largest (8.6) near Yakutat in 1899, the next largest (8.5 and 8.4) in the Aleutians in 1957 and in Prince William Sound in 1964. By comparison, during the same time span, California has experienced only one earthquake with a magnitude greater than 8—the famous quake of 1906.

Many of Alaska's large earthquakes have been concentrated along the Aleutian Islands, including the most recent large earthquake, the magnitude 7.7 Adak Island shock of 1986. In fact, the entire Pacific coast of Alaska and the Aleutian archipelago, with its many active volcanoes, lie along a particularly active section of the Circum-Pacific Seismic Belt. There are several fault systems in the state, some larger, more dramatic and certainly no less active than California's San Andreas fault system.

It would be futile to describe all of these known faults and all of the important earthquakes which have shaken Alaska, for the state is very lightly populated and, gen-

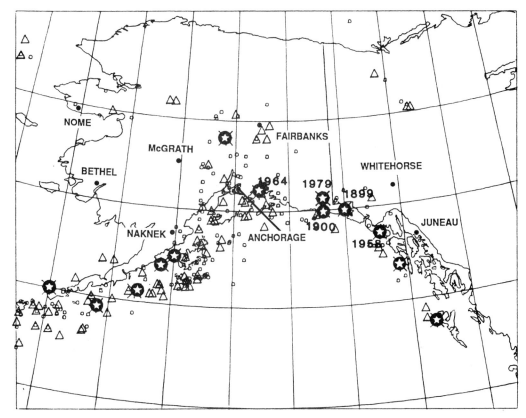

Epicenters of Alaskan earthquakes for the period 1899-1979. Triangles represent earthquakes with magnitudes between 6.5 and 7.5 and stars represent magnitudes of 7.5 or larger.

erally, the hazards to life and property are few. Fortunately, no *known* faults bisect the larger towns and settlements of the state. However, all of these populated areas are located in the vicinity of major faults, and the huge 1964 tremor vividly demonstrated the destruction that can occur on the periphery of a large fault zone.

It is reasonable to assume that every building constructed in the more populated sections of the state, and particularly along the southern coastal areas, will experience a strong earthquake in its lifetime. The two largest cities of Alaska—Anchorage and Fairbanks—and the capital, Juneau, are in particularly high seismic areas, and Fairbanks has an especially long earthquake history. In regard to the latter city, three tremors stand out. On July 22, 1937, Fairbanks suffered severe shaking and considerable minor damage from an earthquake of magnitude 7.3 centered about 25 miles

away, near Salcha Bluff. Another magnitude 7 earthquake, accompanied by numerous foreshocks and aftershocks, shook the city on October 15, 1947. On June 21, 1967, Fairbanks experienced a series of three earthquakes, all with magnitudes less than 6.

The great Prince William Sound (Anchorage) earthquake of March 28, 1964 was the cause of immense property damage and a number of deaths in Anchorage and along the southern coast of Alaska. The total damage probably exceeded $800 million (1964 dollars). The Good Friday quake is well documented. Numerous references describe the damage in minute, exacting detail. Maps pinpoint the more severely affected locations, the numerous landslides triggered by the earthquake, and the extent of the inundation and property damage caused by the *tsunamis* that struck along the coast.

CALIFORNIA

California has the dubious distinction of having more earthquakes than all other states combined, with the exception of

Major faults and historical earthquakes of California.

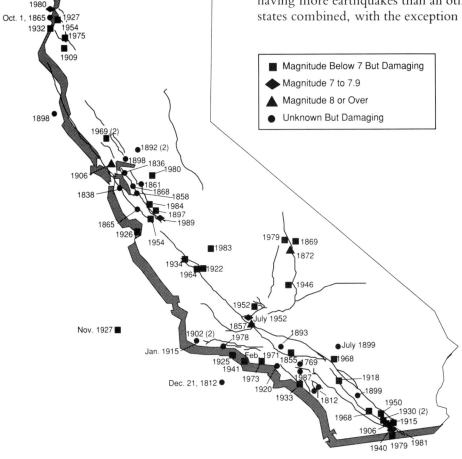

Alaska. The state is crossed by numerous faults, many known to be active. It is interesting to note that the largest cities in the state were founded in the immediate vicinity of the largest and most active of the fault zones. The table here lists the prominent earthquakes which have disturbed the state since the first recorded shock of July 28, 1769, and most of these quakes are also discussed briefly in this text. Voluminous information exists on many of these earthquakes and faults. For the best and most authoritative sources, see the listings in Appendix B.

San Andreas fault

The San Andreas fault is certainly the best known fault in the United States and very probably in the world. It is also the most intensively studied. The connection between earthquakes and surface faulting was first understood following the 1906 San Francisco earthquake, and, therefore, the San Andreas was the first fault to draw the attention of American geologists. The fault zone and the most recent traces of fault ruptures have been mapped in great detail by several agencies, including the U. S. Geological Survey and the California Division of Mines and Geology. The geologists had a considerable task, for the San Andreas extends almost the entire 1,000-mile length of California and then continues through Mexico into the Gulf of California.

Seismic activity along the fault has increased in the last decade, culminating in the Loma Prieta earthquake of 1989. As a result of frequent earthquakes, there have been large gains in scientific knowledge. Various segments of the San Andreas fault have been recognized to behave differently. The fault is described here mainly in those sections that cross larger populated areas.

**Prominent earthquakes in California, 1769 through 1989
(Intensity VII and above)**

Date	Region	Richter Magnituide	Mercalli Intensity
July 28, 1769	Los Angeles region		
October 11-31, 1800	San Juan Bautista		VII
November 22, 1800	San Diego	6.5	VII
June 21, 1808	San Francisco	6.5	VIII
December 8, 1812	Orange County	7.0	VIII-IX
December 21, 1812	Off coast of Santa Barbara	7.0	X
June 10, 1836	San Francisco Bay	6.8	IX-X
June 1838	San Francisco region	7.0	X
July 10 or 11, 1855	Los Angeles County		VIII
January 9, 1857	Near Fort Tejon	8.0	X-XI
November 26, 1858	San Jose	6.0	VIII
November 12, 1860	Humboldt Bay		VIII
July 3, 1861	Near Livermore	6.1	VIII
October 1, 1865	Fort Humboldt—Eureka area	5.5	VIII—IX
October 8, 1865	Santa Cruz Mountains	6.3	VIII—IX
October 21, 1868	Hayward	6.8	IX—X
March 26, 1872	Near Lone Pine, Owens Valley	8.3	X—XI
April 19, 1892	Vacaville	6.4	IX
April 21, 1892	Winters	6.2	IX
April 4, 1893	Northwest of Los Angeles	5.4	VIII—IX
June 20, 1897	Near Hollister	6.2	VIII
March 30, 1898	Mare Island	6.0	VIII
April 14, 1889	Mendocino area	6.4	VIII—IX
July 22, 1899	San Bernardino County	6.5	VIII
December 25, 1899	San Jacinto—Hemet area	6.6	IX

continued ▶

Prominent earthquakes in California, 1769 through 1989
(Intensity VII and above)

Date	Region	Richter Magnitude	Mercalli Intensity
▶ *continued*			
July 27 & 31, 1902	Santa Barbara County	5.5	VIII
April 18, 1906	San Francisco region	8.2	XI
April 18, 1906	Brawley, Imperial Valley	6.0	VIII
October 28, 1909	Humboldt County	6.4	VIII
January 11, 1915	Los Alamos	5.5	VIII
June 22, 1915	El Centro—Calexico— Mexcalli area	6.3	VIII
April 21, 1918	San Jacinto—Hemet area	6.8	IX
June 21, 1920	Inglewood		VIII
March 10, 1922	Cholame Valley	6.5	IX
June 29, 1925	Santa Barbara area	6.3	VIII—IX
October 22, 1926	Monterey Bay	6 to 6.9	VIII
August 20, 1927	Humboldt Bay		VIII
November 4, 1927	West of Point Arguello	7.5	IX—X
February 25, 1930	Westmorland	5.0	VIII
March 1, 1930	Brawley	4.5	VIII
June 6, 1932	Humboldt County	6.4	VIII
March 10, 1933	Near Long Beach	6.3	IX
June 7, 1934	Parkfield	6.0	VIII
May 18, 1940	Imperial Valley	7.1	X
June 30, 1941	Santa Barbara-Carpinteria area	5.9	VIII
March 15, 1946	North of Walker Pass	6.3	VIII
July 29, 1950	Imperial Valley	5.5	VIII
July 21, 1952	Kern County	7.7	XI
August 22, 1952	Bakersfield	5.8	VIII
April 25, 1954	East of Watsonville	5.3	VIII
December 21, 1954	Eureka	6.6	VII
October 23, 1955	Walnut Creek/Concord	5.4	VIII
March 22, 1957	Daly City	5.3	VII
April 8, 1961	Hollister	5.8	VII
April 8, 1968	Northeast San Diego County	6.5	VII
October 1, 1969	Santa Rosa	5.7	VII-VIII
February 9, 1971	San Fernando	6.6	VIII-XI
February 21, 1973	Point Mugu	5.9	VII
August 1, 1975	Oroville	5.8	VIII
August 13, 1978	Santa Barbara	5.7	VII
August 6, 1979	Gilroy/Hollister	5.9	VII
October 15, 1979	Imperial Valley	6.6	IX
January 24, 1980	Livermore	5.5	VII
January 27, 1980	Livermore/Danville	5.8	VII
May 25, 1980	Owens Valley/Mammoth Lakes	6.1	VII
May 25, 1980	Owens Valley/Mammoth Lakes	6.0	VI
May 25, 1980	Owens Valley/Mammoth Lakes	6.1	VII
November 8, 1980	Eureka Offshore	7.0	VII
May 2, 1983	Coalinga	6.7	IX
April 24, 1984	Morgan Hill	6.2	VIII
July 8, 1986	Palm Springs	6.0	VII
July 21, 1986	Chalfant Valley	6.1	VII
October 1, 1987	Whittier Narrows	5.9	VIII
November 23, 1987	Superstition Hills	6.2	VI
November 24, 1987	Superstition Hills	6.6	VIII
October 17, 1989	Loma Prieta (Santa Cruz Mountains)	7.1	IX

Northern San Andreas fault: Eureka and Cape Mendocino to Bodega Head

For the purposes of this book, the northern section of the San Andreas fault zone is limited to the area from Cape Mendocino, just south of Eureka and Humboldt Bay, south to Bodega Head, which is approximately 50 miles up the coast from San Francisco. The entire length of this northern section of the San Andreas fault broke during the 1906 earthquake, including, it is believed, all of the submarine sections. This extensive surface faulting in 1906 would indicate that the entire coastal area of this section of California will be affected by intense shaking during future large earthquakes. In particular, the inroads of the fault across coastal lands and the long narrow valleys further inland that parallel the route of the fault are most hazardous. Some of the most severe damage from the 1906 shock was experienced in Fort Bragg, Healdsburg, Petaluma and other towns located in these parallel alluvial valleys.

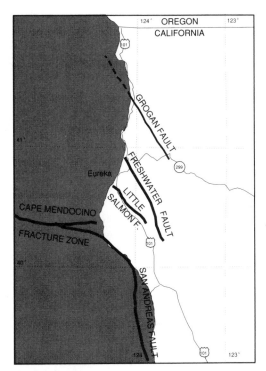

Faults of Northern California in the general vicinity of Eureka and Humboldt Bay.

At its northern end at Cape Mendocino, the San Andreas fault bends sharply to the west and merges into the Mendocino fracture zone. Because of this abrupt bend, the coastal area between Mendocino and Eureka is especially active. Prior to 1906, the Eureka area experienced at least three destructive earthquakes—in 1860, 1865 and 1898—and the 1865 shock was severe enough to damage every building in the Eureka and Fort Humboldt area. There were two other moderate tremors in 1909 and 1927, and a much larger quake on June 6, 1932. The 1927 shock, located about 30 miles off the coast, a little northwest from Eureka, caused limited damage in both Eureka and Ferndale. The Eureka earthquake of 1932 left very few brick chimneys standing in Eureka, which was most severely hit, and triggered numerous landslides around Humboldt Bay. The magnitude 6.4 shock was also felt as far south as San Jose and north to Coos Bay, Oregon. Another large earthquake jolted the area on December 21, 1954. It had a magnitude of 6.6 and caused extensive damage throughout Eureka and around all of Humboldt Bay. Recently one of the largest earthquakes ever to occur along the north coast of California struck on November 8, 1980. The magnitude was 7.0 but it was located well off-shore so that damage was only moderate in Eureka.

The immediate Eureka area is also affected by two lesser faults, called the Freshwater fault and the Little Salmon fault. The fault nearest to Eureka proceeds in a straight line between Freshwater and Indianola, where it enters Arcata Bay. The faults present only a minor threat of surface ruptures, but all buildings within the vicinity of the fault should be designed to withstand the high vibrational intensities of inevitable future earthquakes.

San Francisco Bay section, San Andreas fault: Bodega head to San Juan Bautista (see also the Hayward and Calaveras faults)

The San Francisco Bay section of the San Andreas fault extends from Bodega Head, about 50 miles north of San Francisco, to San Juan Bautista and Hollister, some 80 miles south of San Francisco. The fault al-

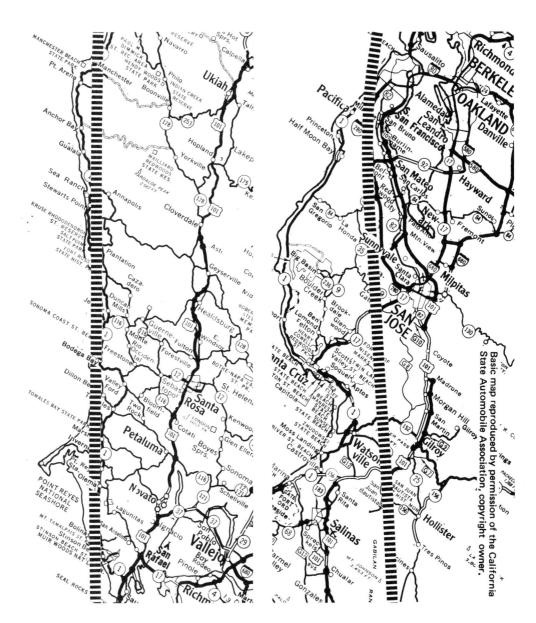

ternates between the sea and the land until it re-enters land at Mussel Rock, just south of San Francisco, for its long course through California to the Sea of Cortez in Mexico. In the offshore areas, the fault zone is never more than about three miles from the coast.

Southwest of San Francisco, the fault slices through urbanized Daly City and San Bruno, passes within a few miles of the airport and the densely settled sections of San Mateo, Belmont, San Carlos and Redwood City, then crosses suburban areas— Woodside, Portola Valley and Los Trancos Woods—and continues into the sparsely settled Santa Cruz Mountains. Thus, the

San Andreas fault parallels the entire San Francisco Bay Area, including the Santa Clara Valley and San Jose. From Saratoga south the fault can be traced as a nearly straight line to San Juan Bautista. Along the way, it comes to within ten miles of Santa Cruz and three miles of Watsonville. A little farther south, the Salinas area is also exposed to high earthquake risks.

A number of active subsidiary faults— among them the Zayante, Seal Cove and San Gregorio faults—parallel the San Andreas through the San Francisco peninsula. These minor faults are probably less risky than the San Andreas itself, but you would be well-advised not to locate a building di-

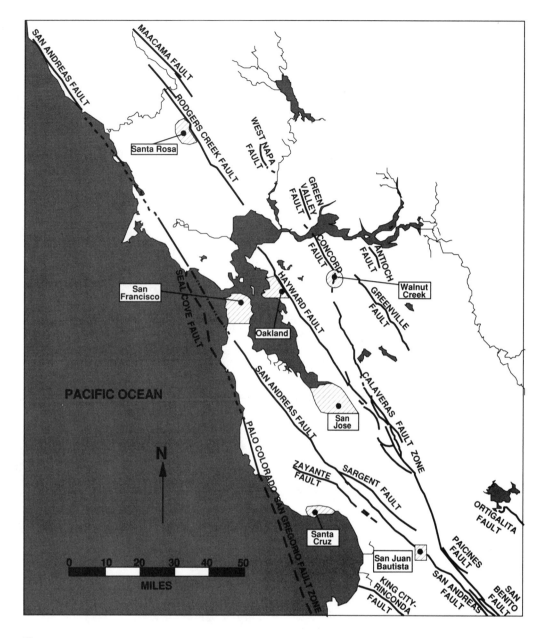

Faults of the San Francisco Bay Area.

rectly over or within a few hundred feet of any of these faults. In the event of the next major San Andreas quake, these subsidiary faults could also move simultaneously.

Numerous damaging earthquakes have occurred in the San Francisco Bay Area along the San Andreas fault. The earliest known record is of a series in the vicinity of San Juan Bautista during October of 1800. Friars at the mission reported themselves so terrified by the numerous strong shocks, sometimes as many as six in a day, that they spent the nights out-of-doors in the mission carts. The thick adobe walls of all the buildings at the mission were dam-

aged. Another strong earthquake, with an estimated magnitude of 7, occurred on the peninsula in June of 1838. Contemporary accounts of the quake describe a long fissure reaching from San Francisco to a point near Santa Clara. The ground motion was severe in the harbor of San Francisco and in San Jose and Santa Clara. Damage was reported in Redwood City and as far away as Monterey.

A series of smaller earthquakes between 1850 and 1865 damaged different sections of the Bay Area, including San Jose, Santa Clara, Santa Cruz, Santa Rosa and San Francisco. The shock of the October 8,

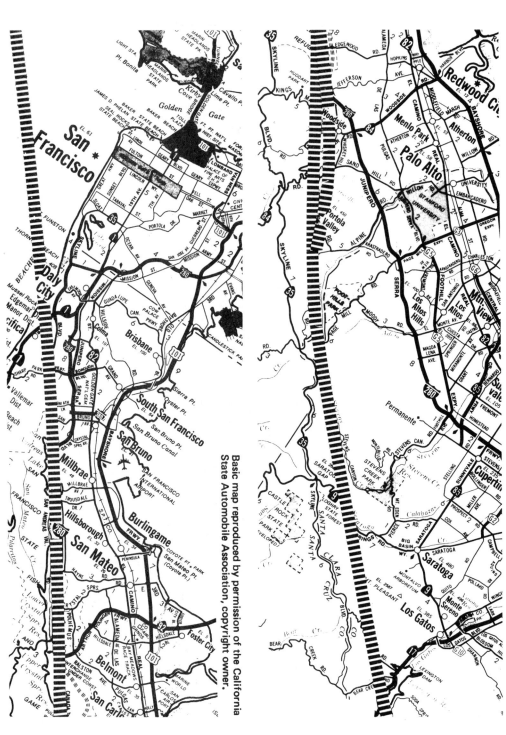

Basic map reproduced by permission of the California
State Automobile Association, copyright owner.

1865 quake, which apparently was centered in the Santa Cruz mountains, was the most damaging of this period.

The San Francisco earthquake of April 18, 1906 is one of the world's most famous and significant earthquakes. It gave birth to the sciences of seismology and earthquake engineering; it was the first earthquake in the United States to be carefully studied and to have the large amounts of surface faulting recorded; it was also the first truly great earthquake to strike a major American metropolitan area. San Francisco alone suffered damage estimated variously between $350 million and $1 billion (1906 dollars), and several towns along the fault, notably Santa Rosa and San Jose, suffered proportionately greater damage.

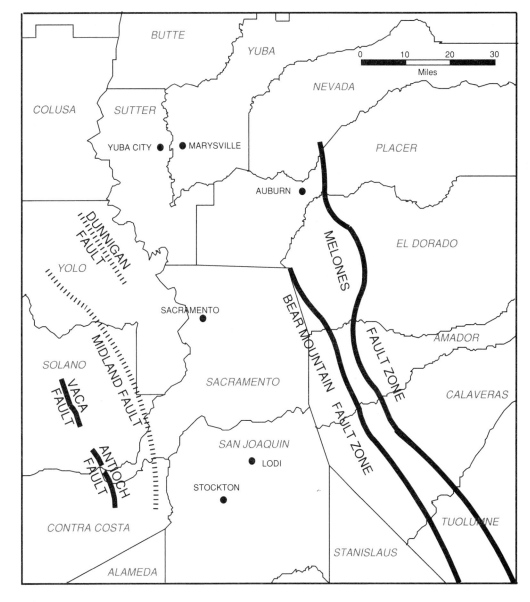

Faults of Central California between Modesto, Sacramento and San Francisco.

Total fatalities in San Francisco were between 500 and 1,000, and there were an additional 300 fatalities in other areas. New data suggest that the fatalities may have been much higher.

The earthquake had a magnitude of about 8.2, generating high vibrational intensities that caused great damage all along coastal Northern California and far into Central and Southern California. The shock was felt in all of the surrounding states, over a land area of about 375,000 square miles. The 270 miles of surface and submarine faulting stretched along the coast from Point Delgada and Fort Bragg to Hollister. Horizontal displacements of

15 feet occurred near Olema. The earthquake was followed by thousands of aftershocks.

Two other notable San Andreas earthquakes caused limited damage to several communities south of San Francisco. The July 1, 1911 earthquake was centered near Coyote in Santa Clara County and damaged San Jose, Gilroy and Morgan Hill. The October 2, 1934 earthquake was centered on the fault near Colma and caused considerable damage in that city and in Daly City, South San Francisco and the Portola district of San Francisco. Until 1989, the most damaging recent earthquake was the one March 22, 1957, when a minor, magnitude 5.3 shock was centered in Daly City, just off Mussel Rock. Generally, the San Francisco Bay section of the San Andreas fault had been quiet since the disastrous shock of 1906.

On October 17, 1989, during rush hour at the beginning of the third game of the World Series in San Francisco, a magnitude 7.1 earthquake struck the Bay Area. Fortunately, it was centered more than 60 miles south of San Francisco in the lightly populated Santa Cruz Mountains. Nevertheless, coastal cities from Santa Cruz to Watsonville, three to ten miles from the fault, were heavily damaged. Older, unreinforced buildings, poorly designed elevated freeways, and structures founded on weak soil, were devastated as far away as downtown Oakland and San Francisco. Estimates of total damage are greater than $10 billion, with $2 billion of that for San Francisco alone. There were 62 fatalities, a remarkably low number considering the time of day and size of the earthquake. Most of the deaths were caused by the collapse of the Cypress Street section of elevated freeway in Oakland. More than 2000 buildings were destroyed or severely damaged. Eighteen thousand homes were damaged and 500 were destroyed. The San Francisco Bay Bridge was closed for one month, and two elevated freeways in San Francisco were severely damaged.

The earthquake strongly confirmed a point that engineers and geologists have been emphasizing for several decades: Even at locations away from known active faults, weak and water saturated soils, such as filled land along the Bay or in river bottom areas, can settle or collapse during major earthquakes.

The Loma Prieta earthquake occurred along one of the six fault segments in California that scientists had identified as most likely to produce major earthquakes in the next 30 years. In addition, two moderate quakes with magnitudes 5.1 and 5.2 ruptured the same area 2 and 15 months earlier. This has encouraged seismologists to watch for signs of an impending major earthquake on the San Francisco peninsula segment of the San Andreas fault, which is immediately north of the 1989 rupture.

Central San Andreas fault: San Juan Bautista to Tejon Pass
(see also the Santa Ynez fault and the White Wolf fault)

The central section of the San Andreas fault is nearly straight as it stretches between San Juan Bautista and Tejon Pass, north of San Fernando Valley. The fault is clearly visible through this section. The narrow fault zone valley passes near Parkfield, goes through Cholame, passes Taft, and intersects the traces of the Garlock-Big Pine fault at Fraser Park near Tejon Pass. The section of the fault north of Cholame is not known to have experienced any major faulting or earthquakes during recorded history. However, the area has had numerous small earthquakes, and certain sections show signs of slow, creeping fault displacements. In addition, several shocks have caused minor surface faulting near Parkfield and Cholame.

The San Luis Obispo earthquake of April 11, 1885 is sometimes attributed to the central section of the San Andreas, but the shock may have occurred on the Nacimento fault, which parallels the San Andreas nearer to San Luis Obispo. Property damage was concentrated near San Luis Obispo, although Visalia and Monterey were also shaken substantially.

Several other minor shocks, all with magnitudes between 5.5 and 6.5, have damaged some buildings and caused limited faulting along this section of the fault. These include the Stone Canyon earthquake of March 2, 1901, centered northwest of Parkfield, the Cholame Valley earthquake of March 10, 1922, the mildly damaging earthquake at Parkfield on June 7, 1934, the Hollister shock of April 8, 1961, and a second Parkfield earthquake on June 27, 1966. Five remarkably similar magnitude 6 earthquakes have struck Parkfield with an average of 22 years between shocks. Scientists are predicting a magnitude 6 quake in the area by 1993. Hundreds of instruments have been placed near the San Andreas fault at Parkfield to measure vibrations, stretching and tilting of the ground, changes in water levels in wells, and other earthquake effects.

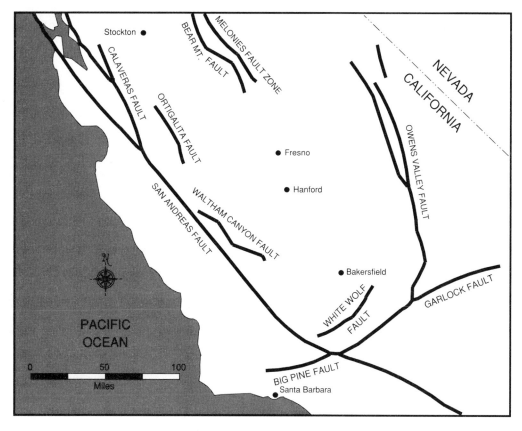

The central San Andreas fault, from San Juan Bautista and Hollister to Tejon Pass.

None of the Parkfield earthquakes, excluding that of 1885, caused serious damage. However, that is directly attributable to the low population density of the area and not to a "characteristic" mildness of the shocks. A severe earthquake along this central section of the San Andreas fault is expected at any time.

Los Angeles section, San Andreas fault: Tejon Pass to San Bernardino (seealso the Sierra Madre fault zone)

Between Tejon Pass and the San Bernardino area, the San Andreas fault experienced very large displacements during the great Fort Tejon earthquake of 1857. It was the strongest of Southern California's history, and with an estimated magnitude of about 8, it is generally ranked third, behind the Owens Valley shock of 1872 and the San Francisco earthquake of 1906, in the history of the state. Another major earthquake along this portion of the fault would pose a very great hazard to much of Southern California.

The epicenter of the 1857 earthquake was in the vicinity of Fort Tejon, on the Tejon Pass through the Tehachapi Mountains. Surface faulting is estimated to have extended about 225 miles, from the vicinity of Cholame to San Gorgonio Pass, north of Palm Springs. Some of the displacements may have been as large as 30 feet. Most of Southern California was violently shaken, but the damage was slight, of course, because of the sparse population. However, all of the regions along this fault segment reported severe vibrational intensities, and these areas now include Los Angeles, the San Fernando Valley, San Bernardino, Riverside, Lancaster, Bakersfield and Fresno, as well as the southern San Joaquin Valley and the Southern California desert. Because they are founded on thick alluvial soil and located near the fault, the cities of Lancaster, Quartz Hill and Palmdale must expect especially heavy shaking during a major shock along this section of the San Andreas.

The Los Angeles section of the San Andreas fault has experienced numerous

*The Los Angeles section
of the San Andreas fault
from Tejon Pass to San
Bernardino.*

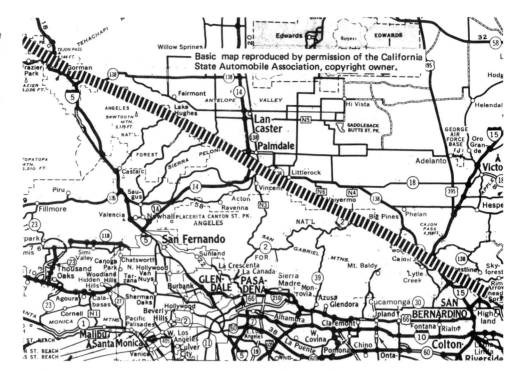

earthquakes in addition to the severe Fort Tejon tremor. Among them, the earthquake of July 22, 1899, which was centered near Cajon Pass, had a magnitude of about 6.5. The maximum intensities for that shock ranged from VII (damaging) to IX (destructive) in the area of the fault in the San Bernardino Mountains, an area which today continues to be rapidly developed. During this Cajon Pass tremor, the road in Lytel Creek Canyon was blocked by debris slides in many places, while the Cajon Pass road was filled with debris for a distance of half a mile. San Bernardino, Highland and Patton were damaged extensively, and some damage was also reported in Riverside, Redlands, Pomona, Pasadena and Los Angeles.

The southern end of this section of the San Andreas cuts near Cajon Junction and enters the San Bernardino Valley near West Highland, where it splits into two branches, the North Branch and the main South Branch. The North Branch later merges into the Mission Creek fault; the South Branch follows the foothills of the San Bernardino Mountains. A number of shorter, subsidiary faults of unknown activity follow the main trace of the fault through Del Rosa, Highland, Harlem Springs and East Highland.

As a whole, this segment of the San Andreas fault presents very high earthquake and landslide risks, and the purchase or development of property in the fault zone itself would be unwise. Any property within several miles of the fault zone should be thoroughly investigated for its foundation geology and seismic hazards, and structures should be carefully planned or strengthened.

Southern San Andreas fault (the Banning fault): Bernardino to El Centro (see also the San Jacinto and the Imperial faults)

South of San Bernardino, both branches of the San Andreas fault break up into a multiplicity of parallel, merging and diverging faults over much of south-central California. The Mill Creek fault is the southern extension of the North Branch of the San Andreas fault below San Bernardino. This fault passes through Fallsvale, merges into the Mission Creek fault, crosses San Gorgonio Pass, continues through Desert Hot Springs, until it meets the Banning fault at Thousand Palms. The South Branch of the San Andreas parallels the North Branch, and merges into what is called the Banning fault, which passes near Palm Springs, and then converges again with the North

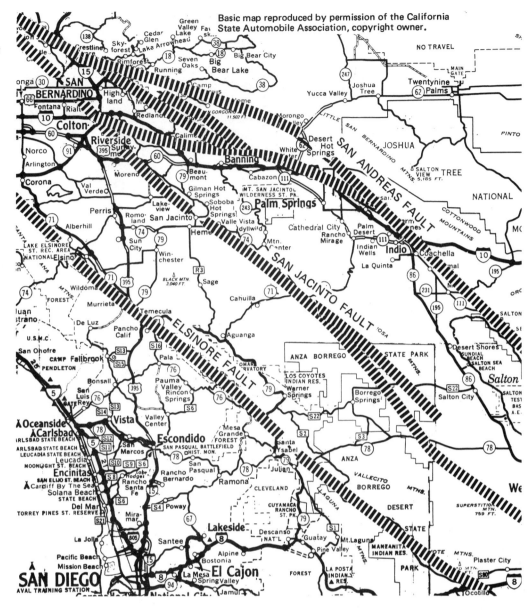

The southern San Andreas fault and the San Jacinto and Elsinore fault zones.

Basic map reproduced by permission of the California State Automobile Association, copyright owner.

Branch/Mission Creek fault at Thousand Palms in the Coachella Valley. The southward continuation is called the Coachella or Indio segment of the San Andreas fault. It passes the Salton Sea along its eastern shores and continues along the eastern boundary of the Imperial Valley and into Mexico.

Numerous earthquakes have been recorded along this southern section of the San Andreas fault zone. The Desert Hot Springs earthquake of December 4, 1948 is the most damaging earthquake to have occurred in the area in the recent past. This quake had a magnitude of about 6.5 (simi-

lar to the San Fernando earthquake of 1971), and the maximum intensities were felt in the Desert Hot Springs-Mecca area. The region was very sparsely populated then, and the light damage was mainly concentrated in the towns of Twentynine Palms and Indio. A similar or larger earthquake today would cause significant damage to the greater Palm Springs area.

A moderate quake of magnitude 5.9 struck the area on July 8, 1986. It was centered about ten miles north of Palm Springs causing some damage to adobe buildings and an electrical switchyard north of the city.

Hayward Fault (see also the Rodgers Creek fault and the Calaveras fault)

The Hayward fault along the eastern side of San Francisco Bay is one of the major active branches of the San Andreas fault system. Because this fault is very active and stretches through one of the most densely populated areas of California, it has been studied and mapped in considerable detail.

The southern end of the Hayward fault is between Warm Springs and Milpitas, along the Alameda-Santa Clara county lines. Further south, the fault merges into the Calaveras fault zone, another major branch of the San Andreas system. The Hayward fault passes through virtually every city on the eastern shores of San Francisco Bay before it enters the bay at Point Pinole near San Pablo. It emerges from the bay in Sonoma County and continues toward Petaluma along the Petaluma Valley. The fault then appears to merge into two other zones, the Rodgers Creek and Healdsburg faults, which continue north past Santa Rosa to Healdsburg.

The Hayward fault has been the cause of several destructive earthquakes including the Hayward earthquake of June 10, 1836, which was one of the largest ever to occur in Northern California. According to a recent study of that quake, fissures opened along the fault from San Pablo to Mission San Jose, and the tremors caused havoc in the settlements in Monterey and Santa Clara. In another great quake in 1868, the fault ruptured for about 20 miles, from Warm Springs to the vicinity of Mills College in Oakland. Horizontal displacements along the trace were up to three feet, and every building in the village of Hayward was either severely damaged or completely demolished. Numerous structures in San Francisco, particularly in the filled areas of the bay, were also destroyed or damaged. San Leandro, Oakland, San Jose and other nearby towns suffered damage.

Another earthquake on October 7, 1915 was centered in the vicinity of Piedmont, where most of the damage occurred, but the shock was felt as far as Sebastopol and Santa Clara. On May 16, 1933, the fault erupted again, reaching intensities of VIII in the vicinity of Niles and Irvington, where all chimneys were knocked down and numerous dwellings were damaged. The most recent damaging earthquake along the Hayward fault occurred on March 8, 1937 in the Berkeley-Albany-El Cerrito area.

The Hayward fault presents one of the greatest earthquake hazards in California. It stretches through a densely populated area. It is imperative that any property owner or prospective owner in this area carefully examine his or her property according to the standards outlined in this book.

Because strain has been accumulating on the Hayward fault since the large earthquakes of 1836 and 1868, it is possible that a repeat of those quakes could occur at any time. Scientists have estimated that there is more than a 40 percent chance of a similar magnitude 7 earthquake on the Hayward fault in the next 30 years and more than 67 percent chance for such an earthquake in the San Francisco Bay area. The Loma Prieta quake has not reduced this estimate; if anything, it has increased the chances. Given the high population along the Hayward fault today and the large number of older buildings and vulnerable structures located adjacent to the fault, a repeat of the 1836 or 1868 earthquake is what many disaster planners fear the most.

Rodgers Creek and Healdsburg faults

The Rodgers Creek fault and the Healdsburg fault are linked continuations of the Hayward fault. This fault zone follows the straight front of the hills along the eastern side of the Santa Rosa Valley from San Pablo Bay and Petaluma, passes through downtown Santa Rosa and Healdsburg, and continues to the northwest about 10 miles.

The first damaging earthquake on the Rodgers Creek/Healdsburg fault was a magnitude 5.1 shock in 1893. Some building damage occurred in Santa Rosa and the shock was felt as far east as Sacramento and to the south in Alameda. Then in 1969, a pair of earthquakes of magnitudes

5.6 and 5.7 struck Santa Rosa. Damage was severe in the downtown area where 21 buildings were damaged beyond repair and 53 others required major repair work.

Today, Santa Rosa is densely populated and one of the fastest growing suburban cities in California. A major earthquake today on the Rodgers Creek fault would be far more disruptive than the 1969 shocks.

Calaveras fault zone and the Concord, Pleasanton, Green Valley and Antioch fault branches

The Calaveras fault is another major, active branch of the San Andreas fault system. It splits off from the San Andreas a few miles south of Hollister and runs in an almost straight line through Morgan Hill and the Calaveras Reservoir, south of Fremont, where it intersects the Hayward fault and continues north-northwest past Sunol and along Interstate 680 through Dublin, San Ramon, Danville, Alamo and the Lafayette-Walnut Creek area. From here, one branch of the fault passes through Vallejo and into Solano County, the other branch passes Pleasant Hill, crosses Martinez and the Carquinez Straits, and disappears in the eastern outskirts of Vallejo. Particularly in the northern section, in the vicinity of Martinez and Vallejo, the Calaveras is most appropriately called a fault zone; for it consists of a series of several smaller faults. The Calaveras fault is at its most active in the city of Hollister, where regular creep has been measured for the past three decades.

A number of earthquakes have occurred along the Calaveras, but none has approximated the magnitudes and intensities of earthquakes along the nearby parallel Hayward fault. The strongest recorded tremor on the fault occurred on July 3, 1861 and is known as the Amador Valley earthquake. The epicenter of the shock is believed to have been in the Livermore Valley near Dublin, where about five miles of surface faulting was reported. Damage from this quake was reported throughout the Amador, Livermore and San Ramon valleys.

Two other damaging earthquakes have been recorded in the northern section of the fault: The Mare Island earthquake of March 30, 1898 had a magnitude of about 6 and was very damaging to the Vallejo area; the Walnut Creek earthquake of October 23, 1955, with a magnitude of 5.4, was centered between Walnut Creek and Concord, probably on the Concord fault branch. It caused considerable damage to chimneys and other brick structures at Martinez, and extensive minor damage.

The Pleasanton fault is a minor break which parallels the Calaveras fault through Pleasanton. It is apparently active. A recent study by the U.S. Geological Survey has also determined that the Concord branch of the Calaveras is showing significant creep in the Concord area and presents some risk to recent housing developments in Ignacio Valley. Because grading operations of the developments have virtually eliminated any natural features of the landscape that once marked the location of the fault, there is some uncertainty about its exact position there.

Recent studies by geologists from the California Division of Mines and Geology and the U.S. Geological Survey have also discovered active fault slippage along the Green Valley fault, which is a possible extension of the Concord fault west of Fairfield. It is possible that the powerful and very destructive Vacaville-Winters earthquakes of April 21, 1892 were centered on this fault. Future development north of Concord and Suisun Bay must consider the risks introduced by this active branch of the Calaveras fault zone.

Recent research by the Geological Survey has also discovered apparent creep along a related and previously unmapped fault which passes through the central area of the town of Antioch. The creeping fault appears to be the cause for curb and sidewalk offsets throughout the town, and some structural damage to several buildings. The earthquake record of the area also strongly supports the likelihood of fault movements. Among the numerous earthquakes, mostly small, which have occurred in the area, that of May 1889 caused the greatest damage in Antioch and the town of Collinsville. The Geological Survey concludes that other quakes along the fault are likely.

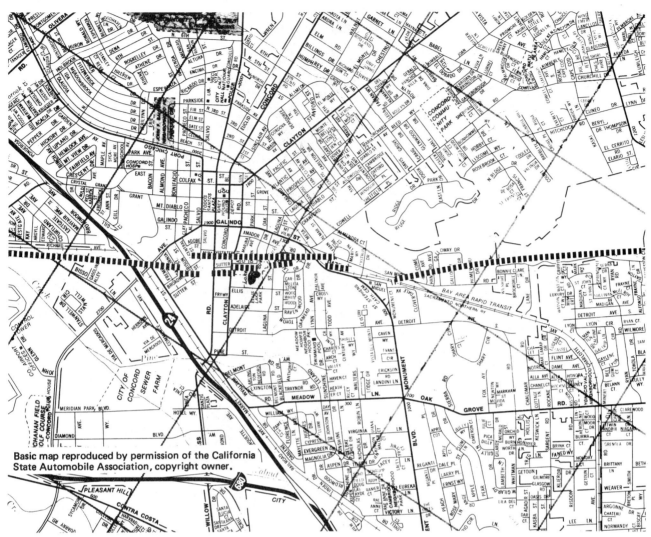

Approximate location of the Concord fault through the Concord area.

The southern end of the Calaveras fault from south San Jose to Gilroy and Hollister has a long history of moderate-sized quakes. The largest was a magnitude 6.5 earthquake that caused locally strong damage in the south San Jose area in 1911. In recent years there has been a flurry of activity beginning on August 6, 1979, with the magnitude 5.9 Coyote Lake earthquake. More recently, the damaging magnitude 6.2 Morgan Hill quake struck on April 24, 1984. There were no fatalities but 280 homes and 20 commercial buildings were damaged.

In this rapidly developing corridor that includes San Jose, Morgan Hill, San Marino, and Gilroy, all homes and businesses are close to the fault and therefore at high earthquake risk.

San Jacinto fault

The city of San Bernardino, like San Francisco and Oakland, has the dubious distinction of being surrounded on both the east and west by the San Andreas fault and its parallel subsidiary branches. One of these subsidiary fault zones, which bounds the southwest side of San Bernardino, is the San Jacinto fault, considered by many geologists the most active in California. Numerous sizeable tremors have been centered on the fault and have caused extensive surface faulting. The first significant earthquake recorded on the San Jacinto fault was on Christmas Day in 1899, with an estimated magnitude of 6.6. It was centered near Hemet and San Jacinto, where the vibrational intensities were highly de-

Peace of Mind in Earthquake Country

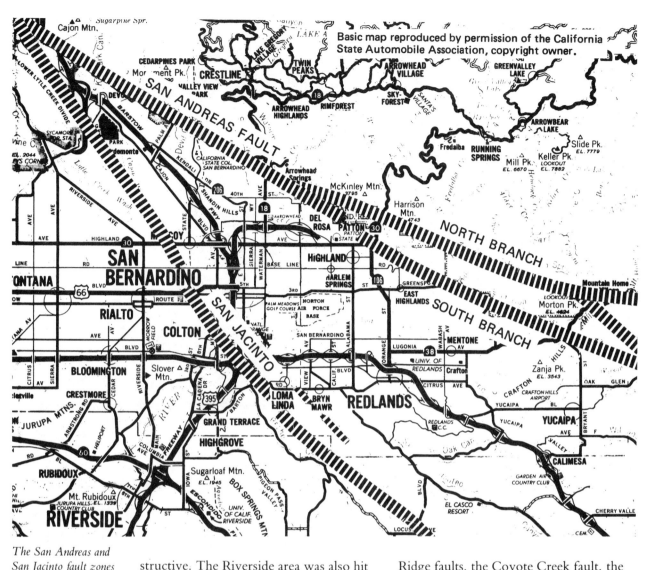

The San Andreas and San Jacinto fault zones through the San Bernardino and Redlands areas.

structive. The Riverside area was also hit hard by the earthquake, and it was strongly felt as far south as San Diego. The most recent shock along the fault was the Borrego Mountain earthquake of 1968.

The San Jacinto fault starts between Cajon Pass and San Bernardino, crosses Colton, Loma Linda, San Bernardino and Bryn Mawr, and continues into the San Jacinto Valley, the Borrego Valley and into the Colorado River Delta in Mexico. There is also some possibility that the San Jacinto merges with the very active Imperial fault. The fault zone never follows a single linear pattern but instead proceeds as a series of overlapping and parallel fissures which include such fault segments as the Glen Helen fault, the Claremont fault, the Casa Loma fault, the Clark and Buck

Ridge faults, the Coyote Creek fault, the San Felipe Hills fault, the Superstition Hills fault, the Superstition Mountain fault, and several others. The Coyote Creek fault is particularly active and presents a serious threat to the Borrego and Clark valleys.

The magnitude 6 Southern California earthquake of September 19, 1907 is believed to have been centered on the San Jacinto fault, since it was felt most strongly at San Bernardino and at San Jacinto. San Bernardino experienced three large shocks at that time, and numerous landslides were reported in the hills and mountains along the fault. Another large shock with an estimated magnitude of 6.8 and an epicenter along the San Jacinto was the San Jacinto earthquake of April 21, 1918. The greatest damage occurred in the business district of

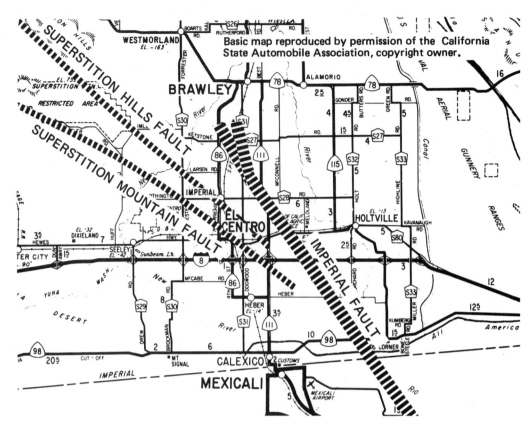

San Jacinto, where only two buildings remained standing.

The Borrego Mountain earthquake (April 8, 1968) had a magnitude of 6.5. Since the epicenter was located in the sparsely settled area west of the Salton Sea, the quake caused very little damage. However, the Coyote Creek fault, a subsidiary branch of the San Jacinto, experienced surface breaks for about 30 miles, and for the first time following any earthquake, investigators found evidence that several nearby faults, including the San Andreas and the Imperial, had experienced some faulting as a result of the San Jacinto tremor. This phenomenon indicates that anyone living in or very near a fault zone also risks property damage from an earthquake on a different, adjacent fault.

Several other notable earthquakes have occurred along the San Jacinto fault zone: San Bernardino, 1923, magnitude 6.25; San Jacinto, 1937, magnitude 6; Brawley, 1942, magnitude 6.5; and Coachella, 1954, magnitude 6.2. Because of low population densities in the affected areas, they caused little damage.

Two more recent earthquakes jolted the Superstition Hills area at the southernmost end of the San Jacinto zone on November 23 and 24, 1987. The magnitudes were 6.2 and 6.6. A total of 94 people were injured and damage occurred far to the south in Mexico.

Imperial Fault

The Imperial fault is one of the numerous traces of the San Andreas fault zone in Southern California. The fault became known for the first time following the major, magnitude 7.1, El Centro (Imperial Valley) earthquake on May 18, 1940, when it ruptured for approximately 40 miles from Brawley to Volcano Lake in Baja California. The trace of the Imperial fault rupture was about five miles east of the towns of Imperial, El Centro and Calexico. The epicenter of the earthquake was in the vicinity of El Centro. All of the towns in the area were heavily damaged, and the intricate irrigation system of the Imperial Valley was heavily damaged by displacements of up to 19 feet.

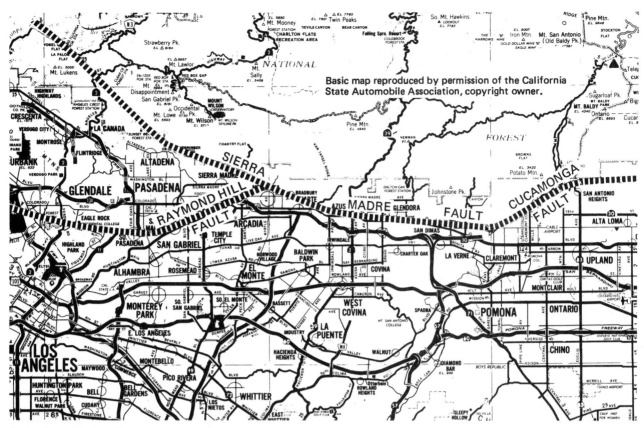

Approximate location of the Sierra Madre fault zone.

Several other earthquakes have disturbed the serenity of the region. The Imperial Valley earthquake of June 22, 1915 was centered in the Calexico-EI Centro area and hit Calexico very hard. The quake had a magnitude of approximately 6.3 and intensities up to IX. It is uncertain whether the shock was focused on the Imperial fault or on the nearby San Jacinto fault zone. On October 15, 1979, a magnitude 6.7 earthquake on the Imperial fault struck the El Centro area. This earthquake was almost a repeat of the 1940 earthquake.

Sierra Madre fault zone and the lesser faults of the San Fernando Valley

The Sierra Madre fault zone is one of the major geologic features of the Los Angeles Basin, outlining the base of the San Gabriel Mountains and the northern edge of the San Fernando Valley. California's first recorded earthquake in 1769 was apparently on this fault. The Sierra Madre fault zone starts a little northwest of Altadena and follows the San Gabriel foothills through Sierra Madre, Monrovia, Duarte, Azusa and Glendora. There it turns east, where it

becomes the Cucamonga fault, and continues along the foothills.

Branching off and running parallel to this fault are many other lesser "local" traces, which include the San Fernando fault responsible for the 1971 earthquake. The San Fernando is surrounded by a number of other faults, such as the Santa Susana fault, the Granada Hills fault, the Mission Hills fault, the Northridge Hills fault, the Verdugo fault, the La Tuna Canyon fault, the Park fault, the Chatsworth fault and the Olive View fault. Although they are not all active, it is important to keep in mind that the small San Fernando fault and the other minor faults in the valley must be viewed together as a fault zone of major significance.

The San Fernando fault was really defined for the first time as a result of the 10 miles of surface ruptures accompanying the 1971 earthquake. It can be subdivided into two general areas: the Sylmar segment and the Tujunga segment. The Sylmar segment lies almost entirely within the heavily populated Sylmar-San Fernando area. It is characterized by numerous ground breaks forming a zone up to one mile wide. The

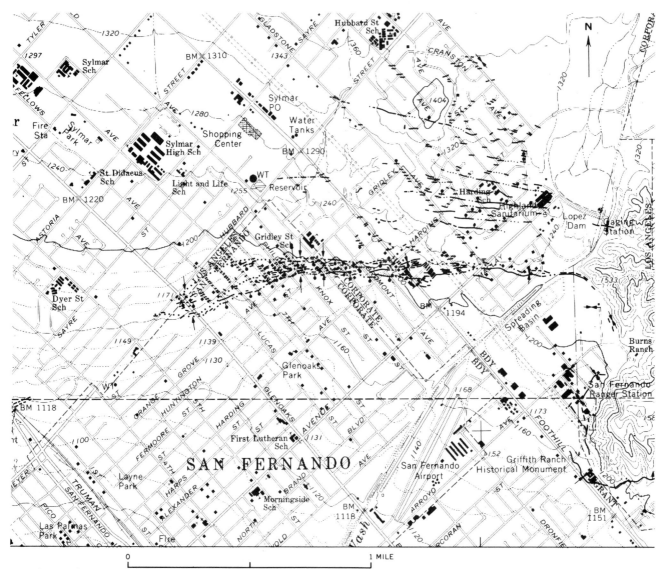

The most destructive
segment of the San Fer-
nando fault during the
1971 earthquake.

Tujunga segment generally follows the
foothills of the San Gabriel Mountains to
the east of San Fernando, along the Tujunga Valley, and consists of only one or two
parallel breaks.

The Raymond Hill fault is another short
fault which transects the area between
South Pasadena and Monrovia and finally
joins the Sierra Madre fault. The fault trace
is in the general vicinity of San Marino,
Temple City, Sierra Madre and Arcadia.
The fault is believed to be active, but it has
not moved in the past 200 years. Nevertheless, it is probably capable of generating an
earthquake similar to the 1971 San Fernando; and like all of the small faults in the
area, it presents a serious hazard which

must be considered in the design, construction and purchase of buildings in the area.

Newport-Inglewood fault zone

The Newport-Inglewood fault zone is one
of the major faults of the Los Angeles area
and is probably its most dangerous fault
because it crosses the entire Los Angeles
basin through its most populated districts.
The fault has been the source of numerous
earthquakes, including the second most destructive earthquake in Southern California, the Long Beach tremor on March 10,
1933. The Newport-Inglewood fault is
parallel to the San Andreas, with the major
trace beginning just north of Culver City.

*Peace of Mind in
Earthquake Country*

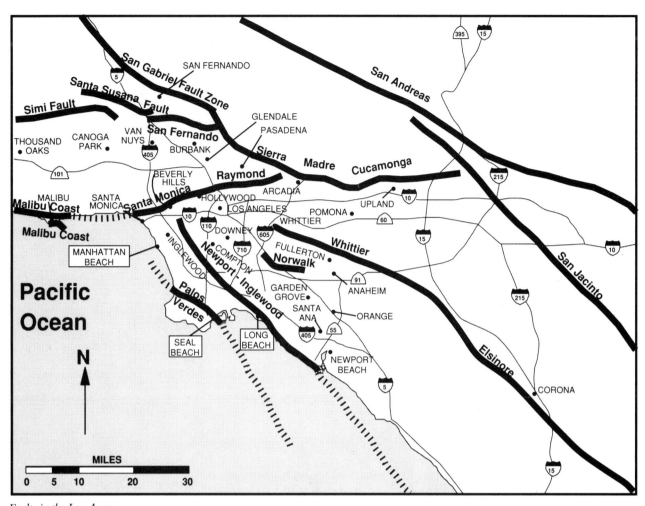

Faults in the Los Angeles area. The darker lines outline the better known and the most active of the faults.

It crosses the Baldwin Hills, Inglewood, the Dominguez Hills and Signal Hill, then parallels the coast along Seal Beach, Sunset Beach and Huntington Beach and enters the Pacific near Newport Beach. The southern end of the fault is not known, but some geologists have suggested that it may continue as far south as San Diego. It is difficult to follow the trace of the fault through much of this area, since most surface details are covered by developments and thick alluvium.

The 1933 Long Beach shock was moderate, with a magnitude of 6.3 and maximum intensities of VIII to IX. There was no known surface faulting. Nevertheless, this quake caused about 120 fatalities and more than $50 million in property damage. The epicenter was near Newport Beach, and the most heavily damaged cities were the coastal cities, primarily Long Beach. The town of Compton was nearly leveled.

It is estimated that, overall, about 20,000 dwellings and 2,000 apartment houses, stores, office buildings, factories, warehouses, theaters and churches were damaged. The reason for the disproportionate damage was that the quake was centered in a heavily populated area, built up without any regard for the dangers from earthquakes.

Several small earthquakes have caused lesser degrees of damage to the area since 1933. Typical examples are the tremors of October 21 and November 14, 1941. The latter caused damage to the towns of Torrance and Gardena. In addition to earthquakes, the failure of the Baldwin Hills Dam on December 14, 1963 is attributed to the slow creeping movements along the section of the Newport-Inglewood fault below the reservoir. The Newport-Inglewood fault is regarded as one of the more active zones in California.

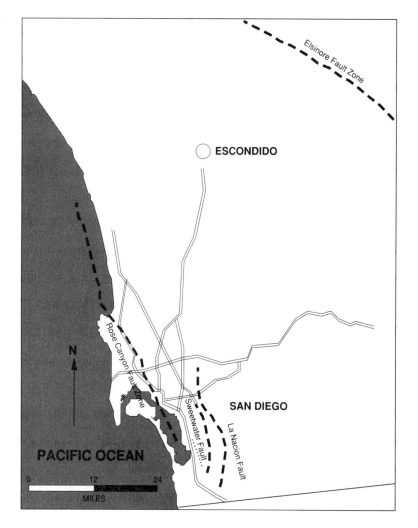

Rose Canyon fault

The Rose Canyon fault parallels the coastline, offshore north of San Diego before coming ashore at La Jolla. From there it trends southward along the east side of Mission Bay, passes through downtown San Diego, and down the center of San Diego Bay. The fault is 40 miles long and is thought to be capable of a major (magnitude 7) earthquake although the probability of such a quake is lower than for the Newport-Inglewood fault. The only major earthquake on record for San Diego is a magnitude 6.5 quake that occurred on November 22, 1800. The missions of San Diego and San Juan Capistrano were damaged but little else is known about the earthquake. It probably was centered on the Rose Canyon. In 1862 a moderate quake shook the area that is now downtown San Diego and there were several other moderate shocks in the 1800's, but there has been no important local seismic activity in this century.

Norwalk fault

The known segment of the Norwalk fault extends for only about five miles from the Norwalk, Cerritos and Artesia areas, through La Mirada and Buena Park into Fullerton. However, because this small fault is believed to be active and is situated in a densely populated urban area, it must be taken seriously as a hazard to life and property. The last damaging earthquake attributed to the Norwalk fault occurred on July 8, 1929. It was a mild tremor with a magnitude of about 4.7. Because much of the damage was concentrated in the Whittier area, and because the Norwalk fault

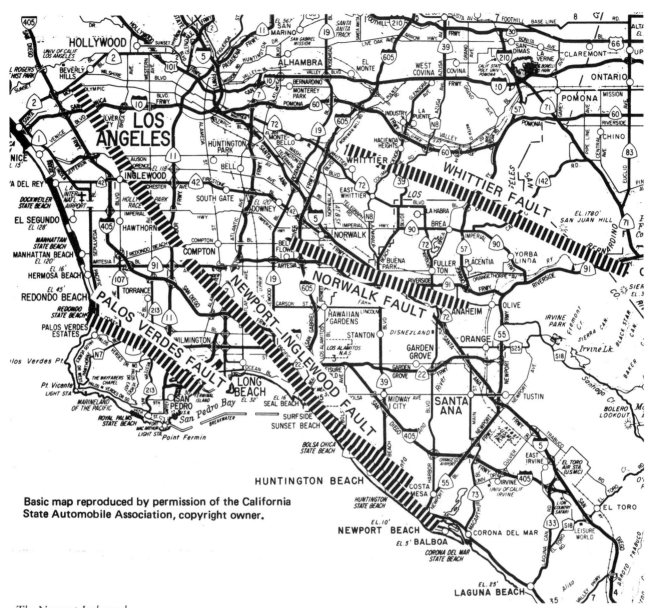

Basic map reproduced by permission of the California State Automobile Association, copyright owner.

The Newport-Inglewood fault zone, and the smaller Palos Verdes, Norwalk and Whittier faults.

was unknown at the time, the shock was blamed on and named for the Whittier fault, which extends along the base of the Puente Hills.

Numerous smaller earthquakes have occurred along the Norwalk fault since 1929, but none has been very damaging. However, according to Professor Richter, "There is good reason to suppose that the Norwalk fault is capable of producing an earthquake of the magnitude of the Long Beach earthquake." Because the fault is located in a generally flat area with an alluvial soil foundation, the effects of such an earthquake will probably be similar to

those produced by the costly and destructive San Fernando earthquake of 1971.

Elsinore and Whittier faults

The Elsinore fault is one of the longest in Southern California. It parallels the San Jacinto fault, some 20 to 25 miles to the west, and follows a nearly straight course for 150 miles through Lake Elsinore, Murietta, Temecula, Palomar Mountain and toward the Mexican border. A secondary branch passes through Aguanga, Oak Grove and Warner's Hot Springs. The fault appears to be active, although only one moderate earthquake with a magnitude greater than 6 is known to have occurred over its length. That earthquake, and a series of related smaller aftershocks, was in May of 1910. The quake was strongest in the vicinity of Lake Elsinore, but it was also felt over most of Southern California.

The Whittier fault is the northern extension of the Elsinore fault, joining the Elsinore south of Corona. It runs along the base of the Puente Hills, crossing numerous towns including Whittier, La Habra, Brea, Fullerton and Yorba Linda. The history of the fault is at best sketchy, since the same general area is affected by the active Norwalk fault.

The activity of the Whittier fault was verified dramatically on October 1, 1987, when a magnitude 5.9 shock struck the populous San Gabriel Valley area. Then, three days later, a magnitude 5.3 aftershock occurred. The two earthquakes caused $220 million in direct damage to 10,500 residential and commercial structures. The city of Whittier was particularly hard hit.

Santa Ynez fault zone and related faults of the Santa Barbara region

The southwestern corner of Santa Barbara County, which includes the cities of Santa Barbara, Montecito, Carpinteria, Goleta and Gaviota, is an intensely active earthquake area affected by a group of interrelated faults. The longest fault is the Santa Ynez, which can be traced from eastern Ventura County west to the town of Gaviota, where it enters the Santa Barbara Channel. The fault zone is apparently the cause for the uplift of the Santa Ynez Mountains, which rise more than 4,000 feet to form the picturesque backdrop for Santa Barbara.

The Santa Ynez fault zone is paralleled by a number of other faults, several located along the coast, others entirely submerged in the Santa Barbara Channel and a few crossing the Channel Islands off the coast of Santa Barbara. Currently it is believed that the offshore faults that lie parallel to the coastline are the most active and have produced all of the major earthquakes that have damaged Santa Barbara. This was

substantiated on August 13, 1978 when a moderate 5.7 magnitude quake occurred just offshore of Goleta.

At least six earthquakes have caused significant damage to Santa Barbara, and four had epicenters close to the city, presumably on the nearby faults. The earliest, in 1812, destroyed the Santa Barbara Mission, as well as the Mission Purisima Concepcion, some 10 miles northeast of Point Arguello. It also caused a *tsunami* along the north coast of the Santa Barbara Channel. It is estimated that the earthquake had a magnitude of 7. Nearly a century later, on July 27, 1902, a smaller shock was centered near Los Alamos, where tremors were felt for more than a week. Every house and chimney in the area was damaged, and the town of Lompoc suffered extensive property loss.

The best known Santa Barbara earthquake, that of June 29, 1925, had a magnitude of 6.3 and severely damaged much of the town, particularly the business district. Another forceful earthquake, magnitude 7.5, occurred two years later on November 4, 1927. The tremor was centered near Point Arguello, and its effects were most pronounced in the Lompoc, Surf and Honda areas. However, damage was widespread for many miles, and the shock also caused a six-foot *tsunami* in the channel. Another damaging earthquake occurred on June 30, 1941. This magnitude 6 earthquake was centered in the Santa Barbara Channel, about five miles south of the coast, between Santa Barbara and Carpinteria.

Malibu Coast fault and Anacapa fault

The situation along the Malibu Coast fault is similar to the coastal earthquake zone at Santa Barbara. The Malibu Coast fault closely parallels the coast for about 25 miles from Leo Carillo Park on the west to at least Malibu Beach. The Anacapa fault runs parallel to it about 3 to 5 miles offshore in Santa Monica Bay.

Past movements on these two faults have produced the abrupt, spectacular hills and cliffs of the Malibu coastline. Moderate earthquakes in recent decades have shown that these faults are probably still active.

In 1973 a magnitude 6 earthquake struck in the vicinity of Point Mugu at the far western end of the Malibu Coast fault. Buildings were damaged in the Oxnard-Port Hueneme area. That quake and a smaller magnitude 5.2 shock that caused widespread but minor damage at Malibu in 1930 called attention to the activity of the faults. A swarm of small jolts, beginning January 1, 1979, with a magnitude 5.0 quake, on the Anacapa fault also caused damage in Malibu.

White Wolf fault

The existence of the White Wolf fault had been known by geologists since its general trace was plotted as early as 1906, but the fault was not considered to constitute an earthquake threat. Then on July 21, 1952, it suddenly and unexpectedly erupted, causing the major, magnitude 7.7, Kern County earthquake and miles of surface breaks. This tremor remains the largest earthquake in California since the 1906 San Francisco earthquake and the largest earth-

quake in Southern California since the great Fort Tejon earthquake of 1857. The effects of the shock on structures in Kern County are described and pictured throughout this book. It caused ground movements of up to two feet in a horizontal direction and up to about four feet in a vertical direction. The entire Bakersfield area and much of Southern California suffered extensive property losses.

The White Wolf is traceable for only about 34 miles, extending between Highway 58 and Interstate 5, just south of Arvin. Much of the fault line is invisible, particularly in the vicinity of Wheeler Ridge and up to Sycamore Canyon. From there, until Bealville, the fault outlines the edge of the Tehachapi Mountains.

Owens Valley fault

On March 26, 1872, Owens Valley, east of the Central Sierra, was shaken by what may have been the greatest earthquake in California history. In effect, the earthquake struck the western United States, for it was felt throughout California and as far east as Salt Lake City. The earthquake is estimated to have been magnitude 8.3, a little larger than the 1906 quake. Extensive faulting occurred in a number of short parallel fractures all across the long narrow valley, from Haiwee Reservoir north 100 miles to Big Pine. The ground surface displacements were immense. In some locations, particularly between Lone Pine and Independence, there were up to 23 feet of vertical and 20 feet of lateral shifts.

Despite the low population density of the area about 60 people died, mostly from the collapse of adobe buildings. In a summary of his observations of the earthquake, the editor of the *Inyo Independent* wrote on April 6, 1872:

Severe and appalling as this great convulsion of the earth unquestionably was, it is a settled Conviction with all here, that not a person would have been killed or hurt had their houses all been made of wood.

Further on, he recommended to his readers that they ". . . forever eschew adobe,

The White Wolf and other faults in the Bakersfield and Tehachapi areas.

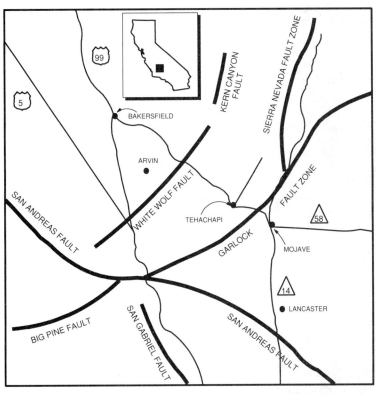

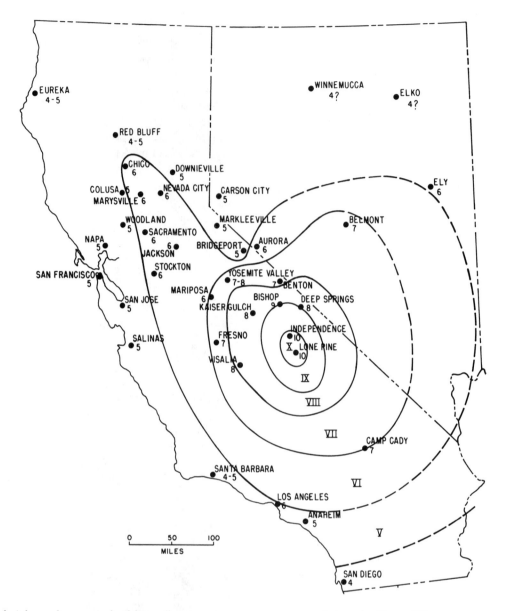

EUREKA
4-5

WINNEMUCCA
4?

ELKO
4?

RED BLUFF
4-5

CHICO
6

DOWNIEVILLE
5

ELY
6

COLUSA 5
MARYSVILLE 6

NEVADA CITY
6

CARSON CITY
5

WOODLAND
5

MARKLEEVILLE
5

BELMONT
7

NAPA
5

SACRAMENTO
6

BRIDGEPORT
5

AURORA
6

JACKSON
6

STOCKTON
6

YOSEMITE VALLEY
7-8

BENTON
7

SAN FRANCISCO
5

MARIPOSA
6

BISHOP
9

DEEP SPRINGS
8

SAN JOSE
5

KAISER GULCH
8

INDEPENDENCE
10

X LONE PINE
10

SALINAS
5

FRESNO
7

IX

VISALIA
8

VIII

VII

CAMP CADY
7

SANTA BARBARA
4-5

VI

LOS ANGELES
6

ANAHEIM
5

V

0   50   100
MILES

SAN DIEGO
4

brick, and stone in buildings."

The Owens Valley fault remains the most active zone in the system of faulting that is responsible for the formation of the Sierra Nevada ranges and the hills and low valleys to the east. Indeed some of the fissures which opened in the 1872 earthquake were reactivated by new tremors in the 1960s and 1970s.

NEVADA

Most earthquake activity in Nevada is concentrated along a series of faults extending in a northerly direction from California's Owens Valley to Winnemucca. The area of

greatest activity, the Reno-Winnemucca-Tonopah triangle, also contains a major portion of Nevada's population. A number of large earthquakes have struck this area in the past 75 years, all accompanied by significant fault displacements and strong vibrations that affected hundreds of thousands of square miles. However, because of the very low population density of most of the area, damage until now has generally been low.

The largest of the quakes in this century, the 1915 Pleasant Valley earthquake, was centered along a fault on the eastern side of the valley, which lies south of Winnemucca. The magnitude 7.6 shock was felt at

Reno, but damage was concentrated in the Kennedy, Winnemucca and Lovelock areas. Surface faulting of about 22 miles accompanied the tremor. Another tremor exceeding magnitude 7.3 struck Cedar Valley, a practically uninhabited area, in 1932. The shock caused spectacular faulting, extending about 38 miles with a width of four to nine miles. Some heavy structural damage was sustained at Hawthorne, Luning and Mina. The Excelsior Mountains earthquake (magnitude 6.3) in 1934 brought damage to much of the same area, including Mina and Marietta.

The year 1954 stands out in the earthquake history of Nevada. Four earthquakes with magnitudes between 6.8 and 7.3 struck throughout the western part of the state. Three separate tremors occurred east of Fallon, causing extensive damage in the Fallon-Stillwater area, and the last of these, that of August 23, 1954, was accompanied by 11 miles of surface faulting. Another major earthquake, of magnitude 6.8, hit the Frenchman's Station-Dixie Valley area east of Fallon later that year. Spectacular faulting broke the surface for about 55 miles, with vertical fault movements exceeding 20 feet and horizontal slippage of about 12 feet. The fault scarp crossed U.S. Highway 50 east of Frenchman and may still be seen today, some three miles south of the highway. The most significant damage from the latter earthquake occurred in California, where a Sacramento water reservoir partially collapsed.

The more densely populated Reno-Sparks area has felt a number of earthquakes. None have been particularly destructive, but a few were uncomfortably close. The largest shock in the vicinity of Reno was that of April 24, 1914, with an intensity of about VII. The quake lasted for 10 seconds and caused some light structural damage. Two other earthquakes, in 1942 and 1953, caused limited damage.

OREGON

Oregon holds the distinction of having the least number of earthquakes of the four states nearest the Pacific Ocean. During the period between 1841 and 1980, a total of only 19 earthquakes in Oregon had intensities greater than V. A few California earthquakes have caused some damage along the southern portions of the state, and *tsunamis* inundated some coastal areas as a result of the 1964 Alaska quake.

The most active earthquake areas of the state include Klamath Falls, Grants Pass, Salem, Portland, The Dalles, Milton-Freewater and Baker. The largest earthquakes (intensities of VIII) in Oregon occurred in Port Orford in 1873, in Portland in 1877 and 1880, and in Milton-Freewater in 1936. Earthquakes with intensities of VII were also recorded in Umatilla in 1923 and in Portland in 1962. The latter occurred on November 5, 1962. The epicenter was located about two miles southeast of Hayden Island, near the Columbia River. The maximum intensity was VII and damage was minor in the city, consisting mainly of shattered chimneys, broken windows, cracked plaster and damaged furnishings. A number of aftershocks, none of them damaging in Portland, followed the main shock.

Despite this encouraging record, the Portland area in particular is in an area of moderate activity. According to Dr. George O. Gates of the U.S. Geological Survey, "Portland . . . is within the Circum-Pacific Seismic Belt, and there is no reason to believe it could not be subjected to strong seismic shock at some time in the future." According to two other experts, J. H. Balsillie and G. T. Benson of Portland State University:

Of the 240 earthquakes felt in Oregon between 1841 and 1958, 51 were reported in the Portland area. Although this proportion may reflect population distribution in part, Portland is certainly among the more active seismic areas in the state. In the last few years, about one shock has been felt in the Portland area per year.

Local earthquakes are common in the Portland metropolitan area and may threaten the coast from Coos Bay south to Brookings. The Oregon Department of Geology and Mineral Industries feels that the threat of earthquakes is significant and recommends that local earthquakes of magnitude from 6 to 6.5 be used as a standard for the design of buildings.

Although many faults have been identified to date, no fault in western Oregon has been proven to be capable of rupturing in an earthquake. An example of such a fault is the Portland Hills fault which runs along the east face of the Portland Hills through the city of Portland. The trace of the fault in Portland is most clearly outlined from the west bank of the Willamette River at the south end of Suavie Island to about Vaughn Street.

The largest danger from earthquakes to Oregon may be from a very different source. Recent research of offshore faults indicates that Oregon may be threatened by great earthquakes, with Richter magnitudes of 8 to 9, along the Cascadia subduction zone. That is a major fault system that runs from Northern California to southern British Columbia some distance offshore, and extends beneath the coast and coastal

ranges of the Pacific Northwest. The zone is similar to the offshore fault zones that strike Chile, Mexico, Japan and Alaska. But there is one major difference. Whereas earthquakes strike often in those subduction zones, the Cascadia may generate earthquakes much more infrequently—about every 500 years. Studies of coastal marshes in Oregon and Washington show repeated pre-historic events of sudden coastal subsidence accompanied by *tsunamis,* most recently in the 1600's. For further discussion, see the section on Washington in this appendix.

UTAH

Utah is in a highly active seismic belt. The main faults in Utah are aligned north-south through the central part of the state, where about 85 percent of the population lives. In the period from 1850 through 1963, for example, nearly 300 earthquakes were felt in

Faults through the more populated areas of Utah.

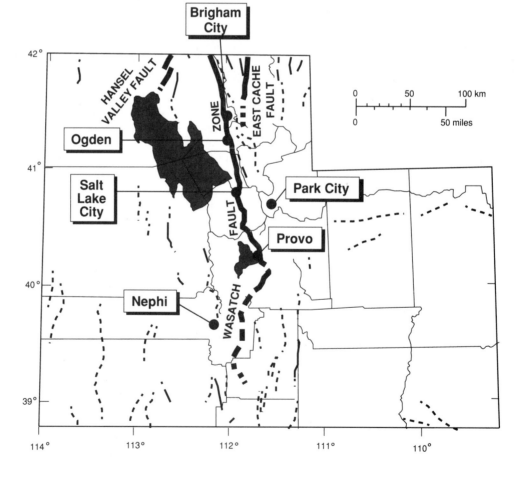

*Peace of Mind in
Earthquake Country*

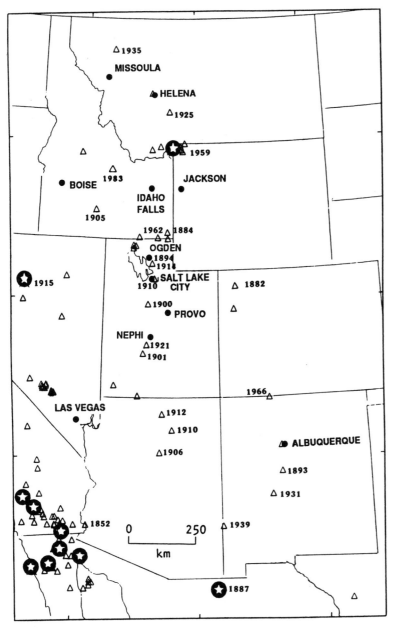

Epicenters of the region around Utah. The triangles represent earthquakes with maximum intensities of VII and VIII. The star represents an earthquake with a maximum intensity of IX or greater.

♦ Sevier fault zone.

♦ Hurricane fault zone, extending southward from the Cedar City area to the Grand Canyon.

The Wasatch fault zone is one of the nation's most dangerous, active faults. It is very fortunate that no major destructive earthquakes have occurred along its length during the course of Utah's short history. The fault crosses the most heavily populated parts of Utah, starting north of Brigham City, bypassing Logan, and continuing through the Brigham City, Ogden and Salt Lake City areas. Further south, it passes near Provo and continues south of Nephi. The entire Salt Lake City area in particular presents one of the highest earthquake risks in the United States. Unlike many of the large cities in California, which are similarly crossed by an active fault system, almost all of Salt Lake City has been developed without regard for the earthquake hazard. Code requirements for construction and zoning plans for fault traces and other geologic hazards have only recently been implemented. Numerous residential and commercial buildings are located directly across the Wasatch fault. In addition, because the city is situated on a deep alluvial valley at the foot of the Wasatch Range, it could be subject to very high vibrational intensities that could literally level the many masonry buildings in the city. Since about 60 percent of the buildings, including houses, in the city are of unreinforced masonry, much of the building stock can be destroyed. Unless such buildings are reinforced, much of Salt Lake City could resemble the destroyed areas of Armenia after the disastrous earthquake there in 1988.

Another hazard associated with the Salt Lake area, as well as Ogden and other cities affected by the Wasatch fault zone, involves the numerous landslide-prone hillsides along the scarps of the fault.

Like most other faults of comparable length, the Wasatch is actually a series of separate smaller faults. For example, the active East Bench fault is a branch of the Wasatch system. It forms the boundary between the East Bench and the valley bot-

the state, although only about 38 caused any property damage.

Five of the longest and most active fault zones in Utah are the following:

♦ Wasatch fault zone, extending for about 200 miles along the western foot of the Wasatch Mountains between Malad City, Idaho and Fayette, Utah.

♦ Hansel Valley fault zone, north of the Great Salt Lake.

♦ East Cache fault zone, along the eastern margin of Cache Valley in northern Utah.

*Earthquake fault map of
a portion of Salt Lake
County, Utah. Note the
East Bench fault through
the heart of Salt Lake
City.*

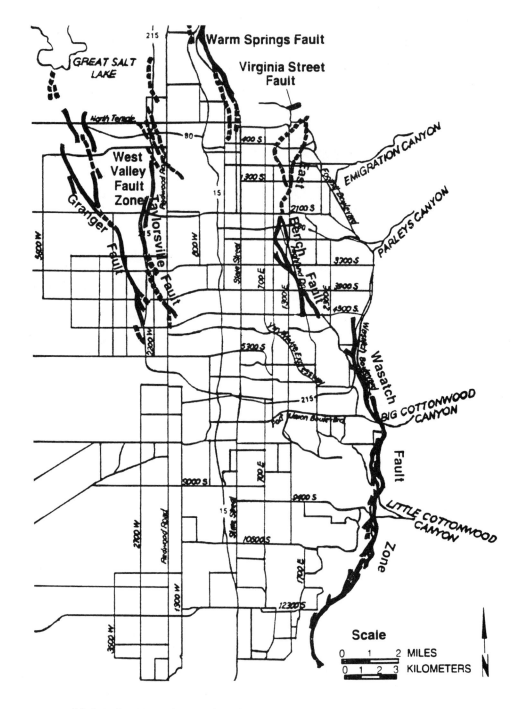

tom areas of Salt Lake City. The north end
of the fault is in the vicinity of 13th East
and 1st South Streets. From there, it can be
traced northeasterly through Federal
Heights, an expensive residential district.
In the opposite direction, the East Bench
fault proceeds in a southerly course across
highly developed sections of Salt Lake
City. Another branch of the Wasatch system, the Warm Springs fault, is located at

the northern end of the city, at the boundary of Davis and Lake counties.

The largest earthquake in the recent history of Utah happened in 1934. The shock
on March 12, 1934, known as the Hansel
Valley earthquake, was centered near Kos-
mo, at the north end of the Great Salt
Lake, and therefore caused little damage
despite its magnitude, 6.6, and high intensities. On November 13, 1901 an earth-

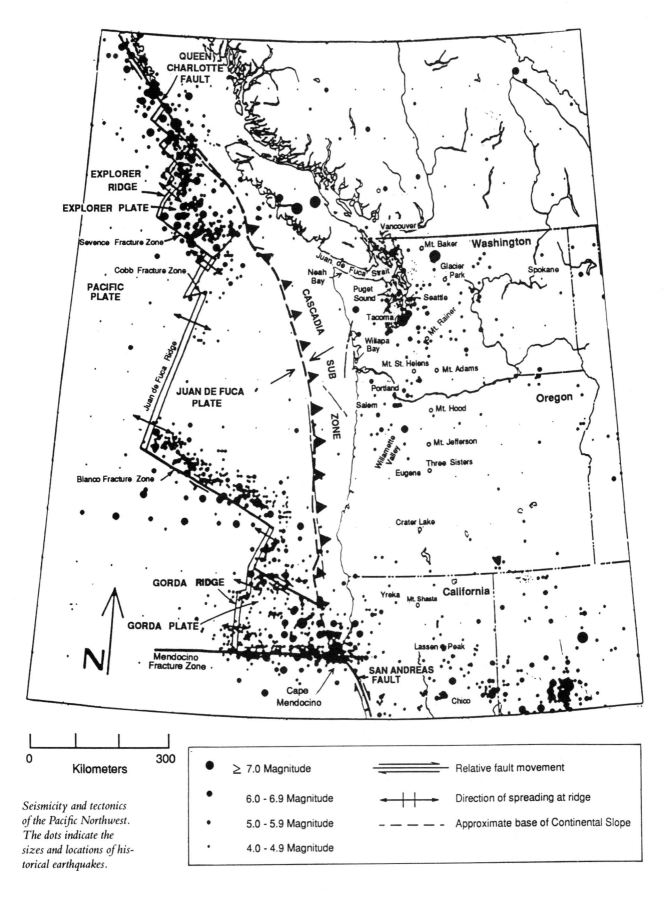

QUEEN
CHARLOTTE
FAULT

EXPLORER
RIDGE

EXPLORER PLATE

Sevence Fracture Zone

Cobb Fracture Zone

PACIFIC
PLATE

Juan de Fuca Ridge

JUAN DE FUCA
PLATE

Blanco Fracture Zone

GORDA RIDGE

GORDA PLATE

Mendocino
Fracture Zone

Cape
Mendocino

N

Vancouver

Juan de Fuca Strait

Neah
Bay

Puget
Sound

Tacoma

Willapa
Bay

CASCADIA SUB ZONE

Mt. Baker

Glacier
Park

Seattle

Mt. Rainer

Mt. St. Helens

Portland

Salem

Mt. Hood

Willamette Valley

Mt. Jefferson

Three Sisters

Eugene

Crater Lake

Yreka

Mt. Shasta

Lassen Peak

SAN ANDREAS
FAULT

Chico

Washington

Spokane

Oregon

California

Seismicity and tectonics
of the Pacific Northwest.
The dots indicate the
sizes and locations of historical earthquakes.

0	Kilometers	300	

● ≥ 7.0 Magnitude

• 6.0 - 6.9 Magnitude

• 5.0 - 5.9 Magnitude

· 4.0 - 4.9 Magnitude

⟶ Relative fault movement

⟵|—|⟶ Direction of spreading at ridge

– – – Approximate base of Continental Slope

quake possibly comparable in size to the 1934 earthquake caused considerable damage near Richfield, about 140 miles south of Salt Lake City. The Elsinore area, several miles south of Richfield in the Sevier Valley, was struck by two earthquakes each of about magnitude 6.0 on September 29 and October 1, 1921. The earthquakes caused considerable damage to the towns of Elsinore, Richfield and Monroe.

Numerous smaller earthquakes have caused varying degrees of damage. The August 30, 1962 Richmond (Cache Valley) Northern Utah earthquake, which was centered in Cache County, caused significant damage on the east side of Cache Valley from Logan to Lewiston. The greatest damage occurred at Richmond. The last earthquake that caused significant damage in the Salt Lake City area was a magnitude 5.2 shock on September 5, 1962. It was located about 10 miles southwest of the city's downtown area.

WASHINGTON

Nearly 1000 earthquakes have been recorded in the state of Washington. The greatest number were in western Washington, in the Puget Sound area, which contains much of the population of the state. The Olympia, Seattle, Port Angeles and Sultan areas are the most active districts in this part of the state. On the eastern side of the

Cascades, the Chelan-Wenatchee area is the most active district, but the Spokane and Walla Walla areas have also had several earthquakes of moderate intensity.

Scientists believe that the probability of a great earthquake, such as the 1906 San Francisco disaster, occurring near Puget Sound is small. However, the probability of a great earthquake occurring offshore, along the Cascadia Subduction zone and affecting the Puget Sound area is quite real. As discussed briefly in the section on Oregon in this Appendix, the major offshore faults are capable of generating earthquakes with Richter magnitudes greater than 8. The last such event is believed to have occurred in the 1600s. Further, such large events are currently expected to recur about every 500 years. Such an earthquake could be similar to the large, magnitude 8+ earthquakes that regularly strike Chile, Mexico, Japan and Alaska. If that is the case, Puget Sound and much of coastal Washington, as well as southern British Columbia and Vancouver, could be subjected to long-duration strong ground motion. That motion would be far more destructive than any recorded earthquake in the state. Because of the poor soils under much of Seattle, effects on taller or larger buildings could be similar to those in Mexico City in 1985.

The first recorded Washington earthquake occurred on June 29, 1833 in Thurston County, near the southern end of

Important earthquakes of Washington and Oregon

Date	Region	Richter Magnitude	Mercalli Intensity
December 14, 1872	Near Lake Chelan, WA	7.0	IX
October 12, 1877	Cascade Mountains, OR		VIII
March 7, 1893	Umatilla, OR		VII
March 17, 1904	NW of Seattle		VII
January 11, 1909	North of Seattle		VII
December 6, 1918	Vancouver Island, B.C.	7.0	VIII
January 24, 1920	Straits of Georgia		VII
July 16, 1936	Freewater, Northern Oregon	5.7	VII
November 13, 1939	NW of Olympia	5.8	VII
April 29, 1945	SE of Seattle		VII
February 15, 1946	NNE of Tacoma	6.3	VII
June 23, 1946	Vancouver Island, B.C.	7.2	VIII
April 13, 1949	Between Olympia and Tacoma	7.1	VIII
April 29, 1965	Between Tacoma and Seattle	6.5	VIII

Puget Sound. The four largest earthquakes since then were in 1939, 1946, 1949 and 1965. The Olympia earthquake of November 12, 1939, had a magnitude of about 5.8 and brought minor damage to Centralia, Elma and Olympia. No structural collapse of buildings was reported. Other small areas of intensity were noted in Tacoma, Auburn, Kent and Port Orchard. The Puget Sound earthquake of February 14, 1946 registered a magnitude of about 5.8 and was centered about 20 miles north of Olympia. The tremor caused several deaths and moderate property losses, mostly in Seattle. The most severe damage in Seattle occurred in industrial buildings on filled ground in the Duwamish River valley, along the former tidal areas at the south end of Elliott Bay, and along the waterfronts of the city.

The Olympia earthquake of April 13, 1949 was the largest earthquake on record for the state, with a magnitude of 7.1. Eight people were killed and many more were injured. The earthquake was centered between Olympia and Tacoma along the southern edge of Puget Sound. Numerous areas were damaged extensively, including Seattle, Tacoma, Auburn, Castle Rock, Centralia, Chehalis, Olympia, Puyallup and many smaller settlements.

The Puget Sound earthquake of April 29, 1965 is the most recent damaging tremor in the area. The magnitude of the earthquake was approximately 6.5, the center about 13 miles southwest of downtown Seattle. The damage pattern of the earthquake closely resembled that of the 1949 shock but was less severe. Again, much of the damage was concentrated in the "poor land" areas of Seattle, including the filled and low alluvial lands along the rivers and the sound. Buildings which had been damaged in 1949 often sustained additional damage in 1965.

None of the known earthquakes in the state of Washington has been accompanied by surface faulting. However, the most earthquake-active areas of the state, particularly those located in the Puget Sound lowlands, are covered in places with hundreds of feet of soft glacial deposits, and this glacial cover has effectively prevented surface investigations of possible faulting during the past earthquakes. Several faults are known to exist in the state. For example, the Tolt River earthquake of 1932 is believed to have been caused by a major fault which borders the western edge of the northern Cascades. But again, the fault is covered by thick layers of sedimentary deposits, so there was no evidence of surface faulting. Generally, then, there seems to be no known danger of surface faulting in the state. The earthquake hazard, which is considerable, arises primarily from ground motions and from amplification of the earthquake intensities in soft alluvial soils.

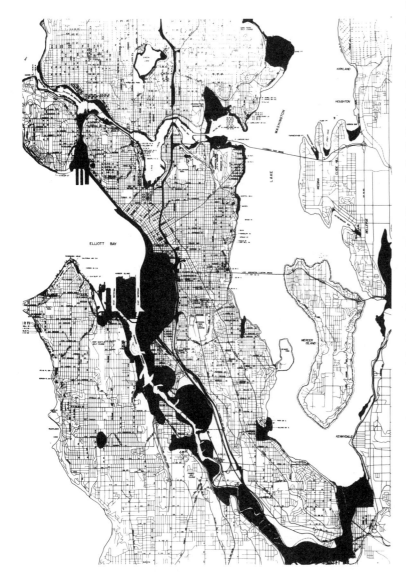

High intensity zones of Seattle. The darkened areas have suffered, or are expected to suffer, greater earthquake damage because of the geologic foundations—loose soils, filled lands, old river beds, etc.

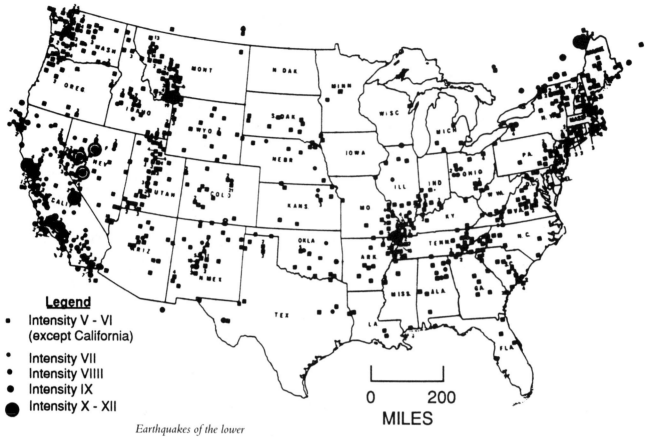

Legend
- • Intensity V - VI (except California)
- ‥ Intensity VII
- ⁘ Intensity VIIII
- ● Intensity IX
- ● Intensity X - XII

Earthquakes of the lower 48 states through 1976.

THE OTHER STATES

The earthquake epicenter map of the United States shows that no part of the country is free of earthquakes. Some states, such as Florida, Texas or North Dakota, have experienced very few tremors. The majority, however, have had strong, damaging earthquakes during the 200-year history of the country. Much literature exists on the seismicity of the United States. This section very briefly summarizes two of the largest earthquakes to strike east of the Rocky Mountains since 1800. My purpose in including this material is to remind the reader that the earthquake hazard is not limited to the West. In fact, because so little has been done to protect those who live east of the Rockies, many in the East, South and Midwest face high earthquake risks.

The New Madrid, Missouri Earthquakes of 1811 and 1812

During the winter of 1811-12, three great earthquakes struck about 100 miles north of Memphis, Tennessee and 120 miles south of Saint Louis near New Madrid, southern Missouri. These shocks are believed to be the largest in North America—excluding Alaska—since Europeans settled the continent. The earthquakes are summarized as follows:

Main Shocks	Richter Magnitude	Mercalli Intensity
December 16, 1811	8.6	XI
January 23, 1812	8.4	X-XI
February 7, 1812	8.7	XI-XII

These were followed by about five aftershocks with magnitudes between 7 and 8,

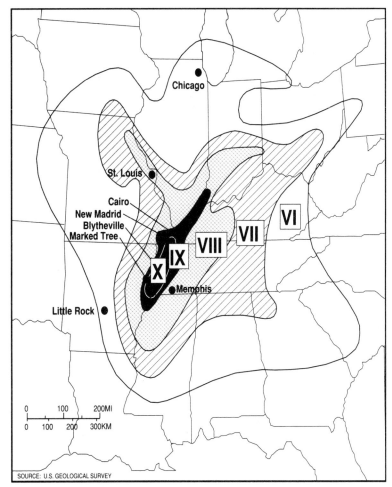

Probable intensity map and areas with significant damage (intensity VI or more) for a repetition of the December 16, 1811 earthquake centered near New Madrid, Missouri. It had a magnitude of about 8.6.

ten earthquakes with magnitudes between 6 and 7, and about 2,000 earthquakes during that winter that were strong enough to be felt in Louisville, Kentucky, approximately 200 miles away.

At the time, the central United States was lightly settled, and only a few substantial buildings were affected. However, the damage to land in the region was dramatic, with widespread ground failures.

A repetition of one or more of these earthquakes today would affect more than a million buildings—practically all of which are designed without earthquake resistant features. The accompanying figure shows the area that would be affected by a repetition of the December 16, 1811 shock. Damaging intensities, those above VI, would occur in much of the Central United States. Very damaging intensities,

VIII and above, would also affect a large area. Among the hardest hit cities would be Memphis and Saint Louis.

The following are likely recurrence intervals of major earthquakes:

Richter Magnitude	Recurrence Interval in Years
6.0	70–120
7.0	100–300
7.5	200–400
8.5	500–900

The table shows that a magnitude 7.0 earthquake would have been expected to occur within 100 to 300 years of 1811. That means that we are probably overdue for a magnitude 7.0 shock in the same region. In fact, we are approaching the period in which we might reasonably expect an earthquake with a magnitude of 7.5.

The above probabilities are based on sparse data. The important point is that much of the population of the United States lives in a known earthquake region. Sooner or later they may experience a disaster comparable to the Armenia earthquake of 1988.

The Charleston, South Carolina Earthquake of 1886

The largest and most destructive earthquake to strike the Southeast region of the United States occurred on August 31, 1886. It was centered about 15 miles northwest of Charleston, South Carolina. The first shock lasted about 35 to 40 seconds and was followed by a strong aftershock within about eight minutes. The earthquake had a magnitude greater than 6.5 and less than about 7.7. Charleston, and its surrounding area, experienced intensities greater than VIII. Structural and geological damage was widespread. The shock was felt as far away as Chicago, Saint Louis and New York.

A similar shock today would find a densely populated region with buildings generally built without provisions for earthquake loads. Very damaging intensi-

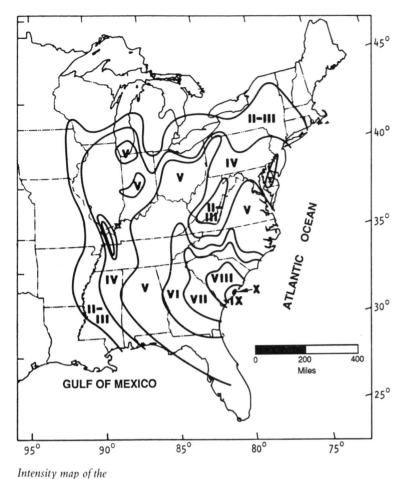

Intensity map of the
1886 Charleston, South
Carolina earthquake.

ties would affect most of South Carolina. Serious damage would extend to at least North Carolina and Georgia.

A comparison of the area severely affected by the 1811-12 New Madrid and 1886 Charleston earthquakes and those similarly affected by the 1906 San Francisco and 1971 San Fernando earthquakes shows clearly the relative earthquake hazard and resultant risk east of the Rocky Mountains. Because of differences in the rock underlying the West, the Central and Eastern United States would feel high intensities over much greater areas. Thus, an earthquake such as the magnitude 7.1 Loma Prieta earthquake would be damaging over a ten times bigger area if it occurred east of the Rockies. Large earthquakes may happen more often in the West, but they would affect much larger and less prepared areas elsewhere.

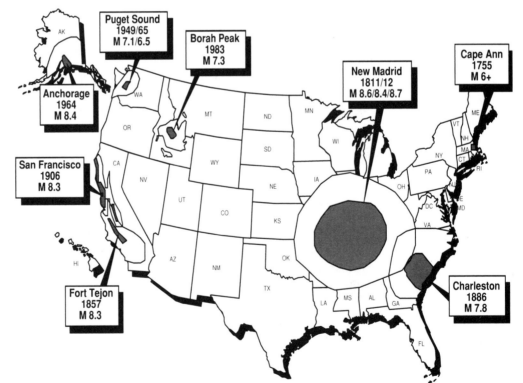

Comparison of damage
areas for several earth-
quakes. The intensities
shown are VI to VII and
VIII.

*Peace of Mind in
Earthquake Country*

Earthquake, fault, geologic and landslide information sources for selected western states

EARTHQUAKE, FAULT, GEOLOGIC LAND-slide and related information is available from a large number of agencies and institutions in reports on past earthquakes, maps of known or suspected active faults, known and suspected landslides, geologic and soil conditions, etc. This information is available for sale and in numerous reference libraries.

In your search for information, you may begin with this appendix. Major sources are listed, including:

♦ State geologic agencies; all states discussed in this book have organizations—geologic surveys, mining bureaus, etc.—which compile and publish information (their addresses are included). They offer a surprising number of services and constitute an outstanding but often disregarded source of information.

♦ The U.S. Geological Survey: the major source and distributor of earthquake information. The Survey publishes the results of hundreds of geologic studies every year (many are concerned with the earthquake hazard) in the form of reports, maps, atlases and *open-file maps* and *reports* (maps and reports not in final form, subject to revision before final publication). The Survey maintains several Public Inquiries Offices for distribution of its work. Each officer maintains a reference library where the publications may be consulted and provides sales services. Each office is a depository for *open-file reports*.

If you do not find the needed information, check with:

♦ City and county offices: The information is usually in the files of the engineer (or geologist or planner). These files often contain invaluable information on past landslide damage in the area, fault maps, etc. This information is public and is available for your use. Legislation has made it mandatory, at least in California, for city and county offices to compile information on active hazards in their areas.

♦ Local libraries, and university, college, corporate and private libraries.

♦ County and state offices of emergency services.

ALASKA

Selected sources

♦ U.S. Geological Survey, 222 W. 7th Avenue, Anchorage 99513-7546, Tel: 907-271-4307; Alaska Division of Geological and Geophysical Surveys, 3700 Airport Way, Fairbanks 99709-4699, Tel: 907-451-2760.

CALIFORNIA

Selected sources

♦ U.S. Geological Survey, 555 Battery Street, Room 504, San Francisco 94111, Tel: 415-705-1010; 345 Middlefield Road, Menlo Park 94025, Tel: 415-853-8300; 300 North Los Angeles Street, Room 7638, Los Angeles 90012, Tel: 213-894-2850.

- California Division of Mines and Geology, Bay Area Regional Office, 380 Civic Drive, Pleasant Hill 94523-1997, Tel: 415-464-5921; Southern California Regional Office, 107 South Broadway, Room 1065, Los Angeles 90012, Tel: 213-620-3560; Sacramento Publications and Information, 660 Bercut Drive, Sacramento 95814-0131, Tel: 916-445-5716.

- The Southern California Earthquake Preparedness Project (SCEPP), Governor's Office of Emergency Services, 1110 East Green Street, Suite 300, Pasadena 91106, Tel: 818-795-9055.

- Bay Area Regional Earthquake Preparedness Project (BAREPP), Governor's Office of Emergency Services, Metro Center, 101 8th Street, Suite 152, Oakland 94607, Tel: 415-540-2713.

- State Office of Emergency Services, Sacramento, Tel: 916-427-4990 and other local offices of Emergency Service.

- Association of Bay Area Governments, P.O. Box 2050, Oakland, 94604-2050, Tel: 415-464-7900.

NEVADA

Selected Sources

- Nevada Bureau of Mines, 850 Harvard Way, P.O. Box 12000, Reno 89520-0006, Tel: 702-785-6507.

OREGON

Selected Sources

- Oregon State Dept. of Geology and Mineral Industries, 1400 S.W. Avenue, Room 910, Portland 97201, Tel: 503-229-5580.

UTAH

Selected Sources

- U.S. Geological Survey, 717 WBB, University of Utah, Salt Lake City 84112-1183, Tel: 801-581-6553; State of Utah, Department of Natural Resources, Utah Geological and Mineral Survey, 606 Black Hawk Way, Salt Lake City 84108-1280, Tel: 801-581-6831.

WASHINGTON

Selected Sources

- U.S. Geological Survey, W. 920 Riverside Avenue, Room 656, U.S. Court House, Spokane 99201, Tel: 509-353-2641; State of Washington, Division of Geology and Earth Resources, Olympia 98504, Tel: 206-459-6372.

Acknowledgements

I AM INDEBTED TO MY COLLEAGUES— engineers, geologists, architects, other scientists and public officials—who are engaged in a continuing effort to understand and reduce the great risks associated with earthquakes, and who have published their knowledge in the hope of educating everyone about these risks. Many of them gave freely of their time and knowledge to enhance the quality and accuracy of the text and the illustrations.

I am particularly indebted to the following contributors:

My wife, Dr. Kay Philbrick Yanev; my uncle, father and teacher, Dr. Frank Baron, Professor Emeritus of Structural Engineering, University of California, Berkeley.

The staff of EQE Engineering, Inc., California, and particularly Douglas O. Frazier, Dennis E. Kuzak, Stephen Hom, Terry L. Mroczkowski, Matthew W. McCoy, Patrick W. Ellis, Kelly E. Fleming, John Smallwood-Garcia, and Ronald O. Hamburger.

David Strykowski, Contractor; Karl V. Steinbrugge, Professor Emeritus, University of California, Berkeley; Dr. Lloyd S. Cluff, Chairman of the California Seismic Safety Commission and Pacific Gas and Electric Company; the staff of the U.S. Geological Survey; Dr. Allan G. Lindh of the U.S. Geological Survey; Ian Madin of the Oregon Department of Geology and Mineral Industries; Dr. Brian F. Atwater of the U.S. Geological Survey. Gary E. Christenson, Utah Geological and Mineral Survey.

Robert Higginbotham of Berkeley, an architect specializing in residential construction and design, collaborated with me in the first edition illustrations and review of the text.

Fred C. Kintzer, a longtime associate and friend and an engineering geologist, contributed on the appendices regarding California seismology and geology.

W. Rod Smith, President of EIS Incorporated, collaborated with me on the material regarding earthquake insurance.

I am also indebted to Neil P. Smith, James E. Thomas, Dr. Dennis Ostrom and others of the Seismic Qualification Utility Group and Dr. Robert P. Kassawara of the Electric Power Research Institute for their participation in the funding of many earthquake investigations.

INDEX

214

PHOTOGRAPHIC, MAP, AND
ILLUSTRATION CREDITS

ABOUT THE AUTHOR

PETER I. YANEV is co-founder and chairman EQE Engineering Inc. of San Francisco, one of the best known earthquake and structural engineering and risk/safety consulting firms in the world. The company has offices in San Francisco, Costa Mesa, Los Angeles, Sacramento, Boston, the United Kingdom and Germany. The company evaluates thousands of commercial and industrial buildings per year for earthquake resistance, strengthens them and designs new earthquake-resistant buildings. Mr. Yanev has visited and studied the sites of 28 destructive earthquakes around the world since 1971.

Mr. Yanev was raised and resides with his family in the San Francisco Bay Area. He holds degrees in civil and structural engineering from the University of California at Berkeley and the Massachusetts Institute of Technology. He is the author of many technical papers, earthquake investi-

gation reports and articles on earthquake engineering and risk evaluation and reduction. Mr. Yanev writes for the *San Francisco Chronicle* and has appeared frequently on radio and television as a respected commentator on seismic events and their consequences. He is a member of many professional engineering societies.

At the time of the 1989 Loma Prieta earthquake, his sons Andrew, 5, and Alexander, 9, were expert builders with Lego and Duplo blocks. "Immediately after the earthquake, they liked to build poorly designed buildings—like those in which some Californians live—and then shake them apart," says Yanev. "They spent weeks after the earthquake shaking Lego buildings apart. But they also know how to strengthen them, and how to build them right in the first place. It really is not that difficult."